ARTICLES

VOLUME 2

TOM FEXAS

2019

Copyright © by Regina Fexas

All rights reserved.

No part of this book may be reproduced in any form or by any electronic or mechanical means, including information storage and retrieval systems, without written permission from the editor, except for the use of brief quotations in a book review.

Independently Published

Printed in the USA

ISBN: 9781790266470

First Edition

"Hopefully by now you have read the first book in this series entitled "Articles Volume 1" written by renowned naval architect Tom Fexas. In his introduction to Volume 1, Dick Peterson, president of California based Mikelson Yachts, explained in depth why Tom Fexas was recognized as one of the top yacht designers of his generation, and the huge impact he had on the boating industry.

If you did not read the first book, you've really missed a great collection of boating stories. Tom's articles were originally published in Power & Motoryacht Magazine, each month starting with the very first issue back in 1985. PMY, as it quickly became known, was the bible for powerboat owners throughout the 1980's and 1990's. While Jeff Hammond & Bonnie O'Boyle, who co-founded PMY magazine, were big admirers of Tom's skill as a talented yacht designer, they were especially impressed by Tom's ability to find the humor in so many of the things that aggravate boaters around the world. Each month, Tom's column would pick a topic and then put it out there for the subscribers to comment on and boy did the letters to the editor came flying in.

His first article was entitled "Sailing Is Silly" and it set off a firestorm. You talk about a big opening! In the story, Tom compared sailing to standing under an outdoor shower on a cold October day in New England without rain gear while tearing up $100 bills. It was filled with so many anecdotes like, "Why do they have sails when all they do is put-put *around under power at 5 knots all day looking for wind?" Every story Tom wrote was funny, insightful, and in the end it made you think.*

Tom Fexas was one of my closest friends. We travelled all over the world together and wherever we went Tom made new friends for life. He was always fun to hang around with and he made everyone feel special. I think you will get a sense of the man as you read his stories in this second volume."

Michael Joyce, CEO Hargrave Custom Yachts
Fort Lauderdale, Florida

Contents

1987

APRIL - *A Sportfishing Revelation, Part 1*
MAY - *A Sportfishing Revelation, Part 2*
JUNE - *Singapore Fling, Part 1*
JULY - *Singapore Fling, Part 2*
AUGUST - *Rec Rowing*
SEPTEMBER - *The Land of Avocados and Chrome Wheels, Part 1*
OCTOBER - *The Land of Avocados and Chrome Wheels, Part 2*
NOVEMBER – *Marine Terminology*
DECEMBER - *From My Old File Cabinet, Part 1*

1988

JANUARY - *From My Old File Cabinet, Part 2*
FEBRUARY - *Holy Camogli!*
MARCH - *Damn the Torpedoes!*
APRIL - *The Great Contest, Part 1*

MAY – *The Great Contest, Part 2*
JUNE – *The Quest for Mega Speed in Mega Yachts, Part 1*
JULY – *The Quest for Mega Speed in Mega Yachts, Part 2*
AUGUST – *The Quest for Mega Speed in Mega Yachts, Part 3*
SEPTEMBER – *So You Want to be a Yacht Designer, Part 1*
OCTOBER – *So You Want to be a Yacht Designer, Part 2*
NOVEMBER – *So You Want to be a Yacht Designer, Part 3*
DECEMBER – *So You Want to be a Yacht Designer, Part 4*

1989

JANUARY – *Sailing is Sillier than Ever*
FEBRUARY – *The Scarlet Lace Caper of '62*
MARCH – *Italian Holiday, Part 1*
APRIL – *Italian Holiday, Part 2*
MAY – *Mr. Penske, Take Me Home, Part 1*
JUNE – *Mr. Penske, Take Me Home, Part 2*
JULY – *Pondering*
AUGUST – *The Wimpification of Our Boatyards, Part 1*
SEPTEMBER – *Tender Behind, Part 1*

OCTOBER – *Tender Behind, Part 2*
NOVEMBER – *The Wimpification of Our Boatyards, Part 2*
DECEMBER – *Our Prez is a Powerboat Guy, Part 1*

1990

JANUARY – *Our Prez is a Powerboat Guy, Part 2*
FEBRUARY – *The Californication of Florida, Part 1*
MARCH – *The Californication of Florida, Part 2*
APRIL – *The Californication of Florida, Part 3*
MAY – *The Californication of Florida, Part 4*
JUNE – *Two Hamburgers with Fries and a Chocolate Shake to Go, Part 1*
JULY – *Two Hamburgers with Fries and a Chocolate Shake to Go, Part 2*
AUGUST – *Storm Warnings, Part 1*
SEPTEMBER – *Storm Warnings, Part 2*
OCTOBER – *Storm Warnings, Part 3*
NOVEMBER – *Storm Warnings, Part 4*
DECEMBER – *Storm Warnings, Part 5*

1991

JANUARY - *Norway: Land of the Midnight Fun, Part 1*
FEBRUARY – *Norway: Land of the Midnight Fun, Part 2*
MARCH – *You've Been a Very Bad Boy, George*
APRIL - *What is a Yacht?*
MAY – *Rosary Beads and Sausages, Part 1*
JUNE - *Rosary Beads and Sausages, Part 2*
JULY – *The Brazilian Way, Part 1*
AUGUST - *The Brazilian Way, Part 2*
SEPTEMBER – *Inside My Head, Part 1*
OCTOBER – *Deeper Inside My Head, Part 2*
NOVEMBER – *Much Deeper Inside My Head, Part 3*
DECEMBER – *No Article Published*

BONUS ARTICLES

- *Five Favorite Designs – 1984*
- *Engineering a Large Jet Powered Motor Yacht*

A Sportfishing Revelation
Part 1

*E*AST COAST, USA: If one word could be used to describe east coast sportsfishermen and the designers and builders of their boats, that word would be SMUG. Isn't that a great word? SMUG! It sounds exactly like what it is.

The owners and creators of east coast sportsfhishermen have good reason to be smug -- they have what are simply the <u>best</u> <u>sportsfishing</u> <u>boats</u> <u>in</u> <u>the</u> <u>world</u>. Since the end of World War II, east coast sportsfishing boats have evolved from converted family cruisers fitted with bamboo outriggers, one man pipe-podium flyingbridges and fighting chairs mounted on the aft deck <u>behind</u> the cockpit (see Humphrey Bogart's boat in "To Have and Have Not") to highly specialized pocket battlewagons -- fishing machines designed specifically to seek out, raise and catch fish. If Rambo was a boat, he would be a sportsfisherman. A tournament sportsfisherman rigged for battle is truly an awesome sight. They are low and beamy with huge cockpits. They are fitted with the utmost in state-of-the-art electronics, multiple spreader outriggers, triple tier towers, trick fighting chairs and bait preparation areas that look like the bar at the Waldorf. They have huge power for their size to attain great speeds for darting out to the fishing grounds in order to have their lines wet before anyone else.

Cockpits have been so highly refined that they are completely smooth -- devoid of protuberances such as hinges, cleats and fittings that could inadvertently snag a fishing line causing the loss of a record fish (by the way, the ones that are lost are <u>always</u> record fish). Great pains are taken to achieve the "winning edge." Over the years, many unique methods have been tried to attract fish such as: garbage disposal depositing chum directly through the bottom, chrome plated propeller tips, underwater mirrors, underwater strobe lights, and underwater piped <u>music</u> (What kind of music do you play for a fish? Handel's Water Music? Splish Splash?). Sometimes, decoy fish are <u>painted</u> on the boat's bottom. Raising fish has become a mystic art. There are proponents for wooden boats, solid fiberglass boats, cored fiberglass boats, aluminum boats and rubber boats. The advocates for each claim that their material produces just the right harmonic vibration that attracts fish. It is not unusual for an avid fisherman to spend $50,000 for electronics, $20,000 for rods and reels and another $80,000 to equip their vessels with the latest in outriggers, towers, etc., etc. All of this is <u>on</u> <u>top</u> <u>of</u> the cost of the boat. A fully rigged sportsfisherman on the prowl looks kind of like a floating porcupine. It is bristling with antennas, outriggers, gin poles, towers and fishing rods. Hell, the <u>boats</u> <u>themselves</u> look smug. If you really want to catch big fish, this is the kind of machine you need... or do you?

GENOA, ITALY - Leave it to the Italians to innovate. A few years ago they came up with a new type of pasta looking something like a Nautilus shell split in half which was designed – no, styled by a firm called Ital Design to be aesthetically pleasing and to trap sauce in its many crevices and chambers. During the Genoa Boat Show this year, I strolled down to the waterfront to catch some sea air. The weather was warm and the stuffy boat show buildings smelled like a combination of B.O., diesel fuel, bottom paint, fiberglass resin and mortadella. There, along a high stone seawall was the "in the water" portion of the boat show consisting mainly of sailboats. Now you all know how I feel about sailboats (powerboats with tall masts and funny cabins – See Feb 85 article) so I wasn't particularly interested in this part of the show. Then it happened. POW! I was suddenly confronted with a vision that stopped me in my tracks. There, backed into the wharf was, so help me, a SAILBOAT SPORTSFISHERMAN! Yes, a sailboat sportsfisherman complete with a fighting chair on the aft deck, a gin pole, heavy-duty rods and reels in cockpit holders and a neat semi-circular hinged rail that surrounded the fighting chair which was mounted on a small poop deck. I was stunned! There, suspended from the rigging, was a huge mounted Marlin head. I pointed and laughed nervously, trying to retain my east coast fish boat designer smugness. My reactions were as follows: (1) "this is a joke -- a cartoon boat rigged specifically for the boat show by a demented Italian with a twisted sense of humor" (it wasn't); (2) "the fighting chair was deposited on the sailboat's transom after it collided with a real sportsfiherman" (it wasn't); (3) "the Marlin displayed was caught by a real sportsfisherman and simply used on the sailboat for effect" (it wasn't); and (4) "COULD JOHN RYBOVITCH HAVE BEEN WRONG ALL THESE YEARS?" (maybe). Completely dismayed, I stood there in a cold sweat imagining my entire sportsfishing boat design business going down the tubes as people switched from power sportsfisherman to sail sportsfisherman. I could think of only one thing: "If a puff boat can catch fish, do we need all the gizmos, geegaws and gadgets? Have we been going in the wrong direction design wise?" My smugness was fast disappearing. I staggered back to the boat hall uttering to myself: "A sailing sportsfisherman... a sailing sportsfisherman for gosh sakes."

BRIGANTINE, NEW JERSEY, USA - Yacht Designer David Martin deserves to be smug. He is a prolific designer of east coast sportsfishermen, including the Oceans, Egg Harbors and Pacemakers. David Martin may be credited for upping the ante, speed wise, for production sportsfishermen. Only a few years ago 24 knots was fast. Martin's Ocean 55 toped 30. It was akin to Roger Bannister breaking the four minute mile. People thought 30 knots was unattainable in a big production boat until someone did it. Today, production sportsfishermen are pushing through the 35 knot barrier. Well, I'm reading this boating trade magazine one day after returning from the Genoa Boat Show, casually flipping pages, totally bored with what conglomerate was acquiring what company in the boating business. There in the upper right hand corner of one page were profile and arrangement drawings for a little 27' cat boat. Now this isn't the kind of boat that usually catches my eye which is normally drawn to swoopy, droopy, aggressive power boat profiles. But there was something <u>weird</u> about this cat boat. I bolted up from my chair! There, arrayed around the stern in covering board rod holders were four <u>fishing</u> <u>rods</u> and mounted just forward of them were two <u>outriggers</u>! Furthermore, a <u>fighting</u> <u>chair</u> was located in a small fishing cockpit aft of the main cockpit!! The boat was called "Surprise" and it certainly was. After seeing what I saw in Genoa, needless to say, this was a great setback. I cried out "SAY IT ISN'T SO DAVID! Tell me your pen slipped or that a deranged client kidnapped you and <u>forced</u> you to draw it or that you were having a real bad day. <u>Anything</u>, but don't tell me that David Martin -- one of my few <u>heroes</u> in this world - is not turning to <u>puff</u> <u>fisherman</u>!" Another sail sportsfisherman was almost too much to take from one of the world's leading sportsfishing designers.

Sad, dejected and definitely un-smug, I slumped back down in my chair. <u>This</u> would take much thinking and sorting out. Was puff fishing the beginning of a new trend? Has what we've been doing with fishing boats all these years simply been <u>overkill</u>? After turning all this over in my mind for a few years -- like soggy clothes in a dryer, I had my answer. It was so obvious really but, then, most revelations are.

April 1987

A Sportfishing Revelation
Part 2
The Fexas Sportfishing Inverse Relationship Theory

I sat slumped in my chair disillusioned. The discovery of a subculture of puff fishing boats really made me stop and think about the basic principles behind the design of sportfishing boats. I thought about all the places around the world I've been to, and of the sportfishing boats, I'd seen there.

Silly Boats
(So How Come They Work?)

San Diego, California, USA - Southern Californians are a strange lot as evidenced by their "sportfishing boats." Here, some of the strangest sportfishermen of all time are gathered. They just aren't right for sportfishing as we know it.

Cockpit soles are too high off the water. Freeboards aft are too high. Some don't have transom doors. Many boats are fitted with <u>transom platforms</u> (something East Coasters wouldn't be caught dead with). Some of these boats even have fighting chairs mounted on the _foredeck_! Can you imagine? Funny bait bags are often dragged astern in the water. Huge live bait tanks that rival the size of the New York Aquarium are fitted below the cockpit. Others have refrigerated fish boxes the size of a stateroom. Cockpits are commonly loaded with projections: here a fixture for a barbecue grill, there a drink holder (remember this _is_ Southern California). We, the smug ones of the East Coast, could laugh at these rather crude vessels except for one fact: they catch big fish there -- a _lot_ of big fish.

Rio de Janeiro, Brazil - Here, sportfishing boats are even less sophisticated than Southern Californian boats. The boats are slower and much smaller than those in the U.S., cockpits are cluttered, and sophisticated outriggers and high towers are uncommon.

East Coasters could _really_ be smug here except for one thing: When you go sportfishing in Brazil, if you don't hook at least _ten_ large billfish a day (that's one-zero, folks), that day is considered a _dismal failure_! The record for the greatest number of sailfish caught in _one_ day by _one_ boat is -- are you ready smug ones -- 37!

Puerto Azul, Venezuela - There is a none-too-sophisticated charter boat here that guarantees a "grand slam" or you get your money back. The guarantee goes something like this: Fish in this boat for one week and you are guaranteed at least four billfish: a blue marlin, a black marlin, a sailfish and a swordfish, or your money back. Try and get _that_ guarantee in Montauk or Fort Lauderdale, guys!

Gold Coast, Australia - The home of more funny fishing

boats -- many, until recently, big, heavy, slow and old. You guessed it. They catch fish here, too -- big time! Australians will boast that any marlin weighing under a thousand pounds is <u>usually turned loose</u>!

Stuart, Florida, USA (touted, by the way, as the "Sailfish Capital of the World") - Back in my office I am trying to assimilate all this into my little mind. State-of-the-art East Coast boats -- sportfishing sailboats -- funny Californian boats -- primitive Brazilian boats -- crude Australian boats...

The walls of my office in Stuart are littered with plans for sportfishing boats in the design stage or under construction. They are state-of-the-art fishing machines. Could we be wrong? Is what we are doing overkill? Is there a better way?

The Fexas Theory is Born

All of a sudden, the answer was clear and the "Fexas Sportfishing Inverse Relationship Theory" was born. It was so simple really: THE SOPHISTICATION OF A SPORTFISHERMAN VARIES INVERSELY WITH THE NUMBER OF FISH AVAILABLE. Eureka!

Yes, compared to the U.S. West Coast, Australia, Brazil, and many other fishing hotspots around the world, fishing off the East Coast of the United States is -- well, not good. Because of the high population and affluence on the East Coast, we have a situation where we have <u>too many boats</u> hunting for <u>too few fish</u>.

It's the law of the jungle. The most highly tuned, sophisticated sportfishermen catch the fish -- the others are out of luck. Kind of a Darwin's theory of evolution type thing.

Giraffes grew long necks to access leaves high up on trees. Anteaters developed pronounced snouts too seek out ants. And dowdy East Coast cruising boats grew big cockpits, got wider, increased their power and sprouted all kinds of funny antennae, poles, towers, etc... to seek out the elusive big fish.

While all this was going on, of course, man was evolving from a banana eating simian dragging his knuckles on the ground to his present state so he could <u>own</u> a sportfisherman (Sadly, the process is not yet complete and some of us carry heavy callouses on our knuckles, but that is another story.)

In areas where fish are plentiful, a line snagging on a transom door hinge is no big deal. There are plenty more fish out there. On the East Coast, however, this same happening would be a major disaster because that lost fish might be the only hookup for the day -- or the month.

You fellows with the million-and-a-half-dollar fishing machines aren't going to like this much, but the fact is that if fish are plentiful, you can catch them from a <u>bathtub</u>. From a bathtub with a <u>hand line</u>. It's kind of like digging for gold. If the stuff is plentiful you can get at it by scraping the surface with your hands. If it isn't, you need very sophisticated equipment to burrow into the earth.

It's also analogous to a teenager cruising Main Street in his car trying to pick up girls. If there are a lot of girls around, he can get them with a 1947 Plymouth Belvedere in primer with flapping fenders, a leaky muffler, a bad rear end and a cracked windshield. But, when the girls are few and far between, only the guys with Corvettes and Jaguars score.

Yes, it's sad but true folks. THE REASON WHY EAST COAST

FISHING BOATS ARE SUCH HIGHLY TUNES, HIGHLY SOPHISTICATED MACHINES IS -- THERE ARE NO DAMN FISH ON THE EAST COAST!

The Tiger and the Whale

On one hand, it makes no sense at all. On the other hand, it is completely logical. Before you pick up that phone or fire off a nasty letter to yours truly, think about it. In support of this premise I refer you to Boating Magazine's "Ten Best" January issue. One of the "Ten Best" categories was "Ten Best Fishing Holes" and goes on to list Kona, Hawaii; Bay of Islands, New Zealand; Great Barrier Reef, Australia; Nova Scotia; Deep Water Cay, Grand Bahamas; Bahamas East End; Key West, Florida; U.S. Virgin Islands; Grand Cayman Islands; Cabo San Lucas, Mexico and Azores, Portugal.

Please note the only area of the U.S. mentioned is Key West, Florida, which isn't really part of the U.S. East Coast. While the list is deficient in some areas (no mention of South America hotspots like Brazil and Venezuela, for example), it is an indication of conditions existing around the world.

Yes, the reason why East Coast fishing boats are such highly sophisticated, highly tuned, honed machines is that there are no damn fish on the East Coast. When one thinks about it, inverse relationships such as this abound in nature. The adroitness and cunning of a hunter is inversely proportional to the amount of food available.

Take a whale for example. He lazily "hunts" the oceans of the world with his big mouth open sucking in plankton. Plankton is available in abundance, so his hunting skills are dulled and primitive. Whales are the "fat guys drinking beer and watching football in a La-Z-Boy chair" of the sea world. Compare the whale to a tiger in the jungle where survival is tough and competitive. He has been given sharp eyes, acute hearing, stealth, speed, claws and large teeth. He is <u>rigged</u> to survive!

If it will make you East Coast, zillion-dollar sportfishboat owners happier, you can compare the Australian and Brazilian sportfishermen to the lazy, open-mouthed whale. <u>You</u> are the tigers.

And now these countries (and California) with primitive fishing boats are getting into more sophisticated sportfishermen -- not because they're needed but because of affluence -- people can afford them and simply want the best.

If they've been successful in the past with their "funny boats", just think what they can do with a gold-plated, space-age boat! They will be <u>so</u> successful that they will soon overfish their areas, depleting the fish population and thereby making their exotic machines as <u>necessary</u> as they are on the East Coast.

Saving the Marlin

Like the saber tooth tiger, our hunters of the sea could well become extinct if the number and sophistication of sportfishing boats around the world increase and their prey becomes scarce. Someday these magnificent machines could be relegated to "hunting preserve tournaments," where a section of the ocean would be sealed off and the area stocked with a number of thousand-pound marlin, bred in captivity on a marlin farm specifically for sportfishing purposes (just like the famous fighting bulls of Spain). It's already happened ashore where hunting preserves are common.

Not a very happy thought is it? What we all can do to help is to release gamefish after they are bested -- or use our advanced technology to solve this problem.

THAT'S IT! Folks, here's another Fexas "get rich quick in the boat business scheme" that is offered at absolutely no charge. MECHANIZED MARLIN. Yes, robot computerized marlin that would be programmed to strike, jump and tire as the fight progresses. Hey, they did it in the movies Jaws, didn't they?

May 1987

Singapure Fling
Part 1
The Home of Mr. Tan and the Grand Banks

*H*eaven can be found (at a price) at 37,000 feet on a first class seat on a Singapore Airlines 747 bound from L.A. to Singapore. There are 30 seats on first class -- five of which are occupied. The first class cabin is looked after by two very attentive sarong-clad stewardesses and three stewards -- a one-to-one passenger/crew ratio!

Exotic Singapore! Think about Singapore and what comes to mind? Smokey opium dens filled with quadruple-tier bunk racks, snooty English colonialists, dense rain forests filled with exotic animals and shifty-eyed Oriental criminals roaming the streets in black suicide-door Citroen "Traction Avant" cars.

Visions like these are brought about by too many hours spent in scratchy seats at the Bijou absorbing too many B-grade flicks. Here's what I saw in Singapore: a downtown skyline that rivals Houston's; modern shopping malls with stores like Cartier, Yves St. Laurent, Guy Laroche, and

Givenchy; a downtown movie theater called the Lido surrounded by Burger King, Hardees and Baskin-Robbins and a brand new, state-of-the-art airport. Disappointed? Well, don't be. Although Singapore had been westernized, its old world Oriental charm has not been compromised.

Tiny Singapore is about the size of your average U.S. shopping mall parking lot. It is a city/state/country, all at the southern tip of Malaysia presently occupying only a scant 262 square miles. I say "presently" because landfill operations are proceeding at a fast clip, creating new land from the sea (that's where their new airport came from). At its present rate of growth, Singapore should be about the size of the United States by the year 2200!

Singapore may be tiny but she's not small. Until recently she boasted a very robust economy and boasts the largest shipping port in the world, approximately 200 ships per day. The waterfront is an interesting amalgam of pilot boats, steamers, passenger ships, ferries, work boats, junks and a few yachts.

Wine, Politics and Beautiful Women

Yachts! The (supposed) reason for the being of this column. Before this article gets relegated to a magazine like Travel and Leisure or Departures, maybe I'd better say something about yachts. I was invited to Singapore by a client -- Skipper Yachts Ltd. -- to inspect their first two production boats -- a full three years in gestation.

Philip Tan, the driving force behind Skipper Yachts, sat in my office three years ago and told me with a straight face that he intended to build high-tech, world-class sportfishermen in the Orient that, when inspected carefully, would ever betray their Oriental heritage.

"Ha," I snickered to myself. This has never been done in the past and I didn't think it could be done now. Oriental boats just look like <u>Oriental boats</u>! This is not necessarily bad, for there are people who like exotic joiner work, dragon carvings and being surrounded in teak. But three years ago, I didn't really know Philip Tan, a man in his 30s with a vast knowledge of... well, <u>nearly everything</u>.

He is fluent in four languages, has a degree in electrical engineering from a German University and can speak intelligently about such diverse subjects as California strawberries, fast cars, vintage wine, any kind of music from Schumann to shooby doo, beautiful women, world politics and fast boats. Philip Tan shows an easy knowledge of all this and more and, to tell the truth, after spending some time with him, you get the feeling that it's time for you to curl up with a set of the <u>Encyclopedia Britannica</u> for a couple of months. It seems this guy has just about everything.

Anyway, I really didn't think a "generic" world class boat would come from the Orient. I was wrong. Battling severe economic recession and less than ideal facilities, Skipper Yachts has, against all odds, indeed produced a world class vessel. Their 55' sportfisherman weighs a mere 35,000 pounds and with a pair of 700-hp 8-92s she does the measured mile (in Singapore's steamy waters) at 33.4 knots. She carries not one stick of wood in her structure, save for miscellaneous joiner items such as fiddles and door trim. She is cored throughout, including all her joiner work produced from a complicated series of molds.

The result is an interior that rivals the Italian lacquered look. Inspecting her carefully from inside and out this vessel could have been built in Italy, Holland, Australia or Florida.

A Snide Aside about American Stewardesses

The difference between Singapore Airlines and the American carrier which I flew from Florida to California is like day and night. The American planes were ratty. Singapore Airlines' planes were simply immaculate.

The American stewardesses were typical of their breed: faceless mannequins with painted on smiles going through the paces of being stewardesses with a distinct "I really don't have to do this for a living you know" Gloria Steinem libber attitude.

When you enter a first class cabin of Singapore Airlines, the first thing the staff does is memorize your name. Then they call you by name for the rest of the voyage. "Would you like the Wall Street Journal, Mr. Fexas?" "Try the buckwheat seaweed noodles, Mr. Fexas. I think you will like them." "Would you like to be awakened for breakfast, Mr. Fexas?"

My stewardesses, Kim and Lay Nee, make you realize why so many American servicemen stationed in the Orient come back with Oriental wives. Sure, it's their job, but it is also the American stewardesses' job. Why such a difference?

Classic Trawlers

I had a chance to visit American Marine (producers of the

Grand Banks trawler line). My memory of Grand Banks from my last trip to Singapore in 1973 was that of a diminutive carpenter squatting alongside a massive chunk of teak, shaping it with robot-like precision using and adz.

An adz is an axe with its blade turned 90 degrees and a skillful carpenter can cut a rabbet in a keel (using nothing but hand/eye coordination) as if it was done on a computerized milling machine. Today, the carpenter with the adz has been replaced by a guy with a bucket of resin and a roller. Not nearly as romantic (and doesn't smell as nice) but, in the end, it produces better boats.

To their credit American Marine has retained the "wooden feel" of their older trawlers to the extent that if you put a pristinely maintained wooden GB next to an equivalent new model, it would be very difficult to tell the difference between them. Though they may look the same, however, the modern boat is infinitely better than the old one from a maintenance and durability standpoint.

American Marine suffered through some trying economic times but now thrives. At one time Singapore built a substantial number of pleasure boats but, today, only a handful of builders cater to the world yacht market.

Well, I've run out of space and haven't even told you about the Singaporean people, their Big Macs, driving mittens and the boatyard shrine!

Tune in next month for the exciting conclusion.

June 1987

Singapore Fling
Part 2
Culture Shock – in a Nice Way

In the first class cabin of the westbound Singapore Airlines long-range 747, Kim and Lay Nee rolled out a cart laden with Chinese and Western delicacies. Lunch took about two hours and consisted of (in the following order) assorted breads (I chose garlic), sushi, caviar/Russian vodka and satay (spiced marinated meats on a stick).

These appetizers were followed by baked breaded lobster and turkey breast sliced at your seat. Each napkin had a buttonhole sewn into one corner so you could hook it on your shirt. There was luscious pecan cake for desert. I passed on the fruit and cheese course. All this was accompanied by a wonderful selection of wines, champagne and other spirits. Dinner was even better...

The $190,000 BMW

Singapore is inhabited mainly by Chinese, Indians, Malaysians, Arabs and Westerners (mostly Englishmen). The language of Singapore is English. When Singaporeans are with Westerners they speak beautiful, articulate English, but when they speak amongst themselves, they speak with an English/Singaporean dialect in rapid-fire delivery that makes it very difficult for Westerners to understand.

Amongst all exotic peoples are the Englishmen of the island. There are quite a few of them around, so when you bump into one, it is no occident (gee, I <u>am</u> really sorry about that one!). These English colonialist descendants possess and exaggerated British accent which, apparently, has fed on itself within this tiny island and mutated over hundreds of years. I can report that they have now developed their snobbish honk to a new height of complete unintelligibility. I couldn't understand a damn word they said -- they might as well have spoken Chinese!

Singapore, being so tiny, has a problem with cars -- the populace is car crazy. The neat motorways crisscrossing the island invite one to go cruising.

Singapore needed to limit the number of cars brought in and did this very effectively by levying a modest 175% tax on any car imported (think about this the next time you bitch about paying 5% sales tax on your Honda). On top of this, there is a hefty yearly road tax based on engine displacement.

Nevertheless, pristine Porsches, Mercedes, Jaguars and Rolls-Royces cruise the streets. One can even find a few Ferraris and Aston Martins. The lowliest econobox car goes for a cool 20 grand in U.S. dollars! Big BMWs cost $190,000 U.S.! Porsches and Mercedes are about the same.

With prices like these, you'd assume people would take

very good care of their cars and they do. Even in this damp, tropical climate you simply don't see any rust buckets and there is good reason for this. On top of astronomical purchase prices and the early road taxes, the government has decreed that any car over ten years old is subject to a gigantic yearly road tax, thus encouraging owners of cars over ten years old to junk their pampered beauties, which is <u>exactly</u> what they do. All this oppressive auto Nazism simply made me want to come home and <u>buy</u> <u>a</u> <u>car</u> -- like a cheap Ferrari Testarossa at only $120,000 or a bargain basement Porsche at $60,000. So, as soon as I stepped off the plane, I expressed my economic freedom and national pride by placing an order for a new car. I simply couldn't help myself!

Meeting The Best Big Mac

Usually on my trips there is one weird thing that impresses me most. With all the exotica in Singapore, it was the seemingly unimportant things that stuck into my mind, such as signs posted in the taxis saying, "Please refrain from spitting in the back of the cab." And a lady driving a Mercedes with strange white elbow-length mittens.

When asked about the mittens, I was told it came from the colonial days of open-air-motoring, when the fair-skinned English donned these long gloves to protect their hands and arms from sunburn! The fact that this lady was driving an enclosed, air-conditioned car that you can't burn behind glass made no difference -- she was carrying on the colonialist tradition!

The best Big Mac I ever had come close to being the most

memorable thing about my trip. Imagine flying all the way to Singapore to find a Big Mac that looks exactly like the ones they show on TV commercials! The buns are light and fluffy. The burgers patties are plump and juicy. The lettuce is crackling and the whole thing is kind of oozing "special sauce." When you order one at home, it usually looks like an inflatable rubber hamburger with the air let out. The buns are thin and soggy. The beef is skinny and placed of-center on the bun (giving it a distinct port list). The lettuce is limp and the "special sauce" is running down the side on a big glob. Believe it or not, the Big Mac in Singapore was <u>exactly</u> like the ones we've seen on TV all these years. No, it wasn't <u>any</u> of these things that impressed me most about Singapore. What impressed me the most was the <u>shrine</u> at the boatyard.

Honoring an Ancient Profession

There, right on the premises of Skipper Yachts Limited was a bright <u>red shrine</u> erected for the <u>Patron Saint of the Carpenters</u>. THE PATRON SAINT OF THE CARPENTERS!

Don't laugh. This is <u>serious stuff</u> for the people who work here. A medium is hired to scope out the shipyard and locate the shrine in exactly the proper area and orientation. This is done because carpenters are privileged -- their profession is eons old and they are the only trade to have a patron saint. Fiberglass workers, unable to find a fiberglass patron saint, adopted the carpenter's as their own.

The shrine is adorned by intricate ornaments and lighted candles. Daily offerings of bananas and other delicacies are made there and prior to a major event -- like a boat launching -- prayer meetings are conducted here for everything to go well. This is no joke! The devotion to these shrines is impressive. I think American business should take note here. Maybe a few factory shrines are just what a sorry outfit like General Motors needs right now. Maybe this is why the Oriental countries are badly out producing us. Maybe I should become a <u>shrine</u> <u>consultant</u> for Corporate America.

Coffee, Tea or John Madden?

My next stop after Singapore was Brisbane, Australia, and of course I chose Singapore Airlines for this rather short hop. Kim and Lay Nee were replaced by another pair of equally gracious Oriental stewardesses. Service was, again, superb.

After a couple of days in Brisbane, it was time to come home. Since Quantas had the only nonstop from Australia to L.A. I flew them to shorten the traveling time from 18 hours to about 12. It simply wasn't the same. The big, loud, burly Aussie first class flight attendants all looked like John Madden. They did their best, but couldn't hold a candle to Kim and Lay Nee. Besides, they really didn't have the figures for sarongs.

I ordered caviar, a double portion of Sydney rock oysters and a couple of glasses of white wine to ease the pain. Traveling is a bitch.

July 1987

Rec Rowing

Stroke... Stroke... Stroke...

*A*s a designer of power vessels for many years, I have seen all the ads -- some yuppie twit rowing, er... excuse me, <u>sculling</u> down the Charles River in Boston -- excuse me again, <u>Baston</u> -- while he thinks about buying a BMW or Beluga caviar or acquiring a new company. When rowing hits Madison Avenue you know it's "in" but people who do it for <u>fashion</u> won't stay at it for long. You have to love and understand rowing to keep at it.

Rowing is the <u>essence</u> of powerboating. A rowing boat is a pure extension of one's self at sea. It is powered by you -- not by dinosaur fossils or wind puffs which may or may not be available at any specified time. The only purer way of going through the water is swimming. That bubbly (hopefully straight) wake is produced by <u>you</u> and you alone. I have been a recreational rower for 15 years and I am here to say it is a wonderful way to exercise while enjoying nature.

I have owned a few rowing shells -- my latest is 18' long with all the good stuff: sliding seat, outriggers, carbon fiber spooned oars, racing-type oarlocks, stirrups, etc. A real <u>machine</u>. Her hull is black and her interior is tan. I have named her <u>Shoelace</u>.

Learn as You Row
(All Ducks Are Not Alike)

One can learn a lot about boats and hydrodynamics from rowing. You can <u>feel</u> your boat slow when traversing shallow areas as she sucks down. You can <u>feel</u> wind and wave resistance and observe their effects on speed (and your arms). One can also learn a lot about nature from rowing.

My daily row takes me down a canal in the back of my house into the wide St. Lucie River which I usually cross (depending on wind direction). A typical "row" takes about 45 minutes. When you are finished you feel <u>good</u>. On these daily treks, I can't help but observe my surroundings.

I am able to keep tabs on the duck population in the canal and learn about them. Muscovys are much smarter and considerably friendlier than Mallards. They're also quieter -- Muscovys make no sound while Mallards have an obnoxious honk. I've observed that white ducklings have a dismal survival rate compared to dark or mottled ducklings, though I'm not sure why.

I have learned also about blue herons. I have always thought herons caught fish by grabbing them with their beak. No so. A heron <u>spears</u> its prey then carefully manipulates it so it can swallow it whole, head first, in the direction of least resistance. Then there are some <u>other</u> forms of nature to be seen.

When I row down my canal, I have to pass the house of a loud-mouthed wise guy. Every time I go by, he runs out of his patio yelling "stroke... stroke... stroke..." this had been going on for years now. Ah, but revenge is sweet. One day I was rowing in the evening, leaving at dusk and returning in the dark. As I passed loudmouth's house, I glanced into his screened patio only to see him, shall we say, "in the throes of passion" with a young lady. As I quietly slid by, I hollered: "STOKE...STROKE...STROKE..." Ruined his whole week.

The Hazards of Rowing

Once you clear land and get into the open river you are alone with nature. Look at the water... observe the ducks... watch the leaping fish... see the playful porpoises... look at the speedboat about to run you down while the driver is ogling his girlfriend who is falling out of her bikini as the boat slams along (It is for this reason -- being noticed -- more than patriotism, that I fly an oversized ensign on a flagstaff at the stern of my little craft.)

It is well documented that rowing is an excellent all-around exercise since it uses most of the body muscles -- legs, stomach, upper body, arms (and mouth -- I tend to sing a lot when rowing).

There was a time when I used to jog but after developing ankle problems, being run off the road by countless cars, and being chased by mean dogs (I had to run with a big "ugly club" stuck in the back of my pants for protection) I decided there must be a better way. Besides, only my legs and lungs were being exercised.

Now when rowing, I only need to worry about stray alligators in the canal or being assaulted by renegade fish

(One day an impolite mullet leapt out of the water and hit me on the shoulder before falling into the bottom of the boat.)

Rocky VI
(Nice Guys, Finish First)

What I always liked most about rowing was that it was pure -- just you, nature and the boat. No transistors, engines, bells and whistles -- no nothing. But a couple of weeks ago, I was on a trip to California and had a chance to work out at an exercise spa in one of the hotels I stayed at. There, in an air-conditioned room, was an interesting looking rowing machine. Of course, I had to try it.

There was a sliding seat mounted on a track in conventional fashion but forward of the seat was what could best be described as a dashboard complete with video screen, touch-pad number entry, speakers, switches, dials, etc. It looked for all the world like the dashboard of a Buick Riviera.

In the center of the "dashboard" was a handlebar attached to a cable that led through and opening to some kind of variable friction pulley mechanism behind it. You select the number of strokes per minute desired, the degree of difficulty and the total time you wished to exercise. Punch the numbers into the keypad, press "enter" and you're off.

There, appearing on the screen , was an electronic picture showing two rowing shells at an electronic starting line on a neatly laid out video water course complete with red video floats dividing the two lanes. There were video markers every ten meters.

In the corner of the screen was a starting gun with the

words "Ready, Get Set, Go." The gun fired and a loud pop emanated from the speakers.

The little guy in the lower boat in the screen started rowing furiously. He was my pace boat. My <u>competition</u>. My boat, in the upper part of the screen, had little oars that were synchronized to my "strokes" on the handlebar.

The 20-minute race proceeded with me off to a slow start, fascinated and distracted by the wonderful graphics on the screen. Pretty soon a sign flashed and a voice yelled, "YOU ARE TWO BOAT LENGHTS BEHIND...PICK UP THE PACE."

"Yes sir, yes sir," I shouted as I furiously started pulling on the "oars" to make up for lost time.

Little electronic shrubbery and skylines slid by as the boats proceeded. There were little electronic ducks on the course. "This is really something wonderful," I thought as my screen constantly read out elapsed time, time to go, and my strokes per minute. I was repeatedly reprimanded over the loud speaker to "Keep your back straight" and "Use your legs!"

"YOU ARE ONE BOAT LENGTH BEHIND," blared the dashboard. I was catching up but my opponent was a truly wily one. I pulled little harder and faster. Pretty soon the voice announced that I was three boat lengths ahead. "Gotcha you little electronic bugger," I cried.

There were about three minutes to go and I thought I would make the finish exciting so I slacked off, letting the pace boat pass me.

With one minute to go, I was two boat lengths behind and I put on a big, dramatic push to finish as my strokes increased to 38 per minute. The positions of the boats were accurately represented on the screen, so I could see myself gaining and when we crossed the finish line, I was about a quarter of a boat length ahead!

"You won, you won," announced the speaker.

WHAT AN EXCITING RACE! Accolades flashed on the screen and electronic cheering blared out of the loudspeaker. The crowd loved me. This was <u>great</u>!

Uncle Leo Puts It in a Nutshell

Now I am having trouble going back to my plain old rowing shell on plain old water in the plain old waterway with plain old ducks. How am I going to row if I don't know how much time I have left or how many strokes per minute I am doing? Who is going to remind me to keep my back straight and use my legs? What do I do about <u>heat</u> and what if it <u>rains</u>?

This kind of thinking reminded me of my dear crazy Uncle Leo, the family clown. Many years ago, we were visiting Florida taking in the sites on the west coast. On the list of things to do was to visit Silver Springs -- magnificent crystal clear water springs with interesting wildlife and underwater plants that one viewed through glass-bottomed boats. This place was a true tribute to Mother's Nature beauty and creativity.

The other place on the list was an establishment called "Weeki-Wachee." This was an oversized swimming pool with glass sides. Spectators sat in darkened grandstands below pool level, leering at skimpily clad maidens performing underwater acrobatics. Anyway, someone asked my uncle if he'd rather go to Silver Springs or Weeki-Wachee. The answer was immediate! "What good is Silver Springs? They don't have a <u>show</u>."

That's a good example of Mother Nature overshadowed by pure showmanship and glitz!

Yupscale Rowing
(Air Conditioning, Maybe?)

Now, I'm making plans to install a dashboard on my rowing shell complete with video screen, touch pads and loudspeakers. Then, I thought one of those automatic, built-in bars might be nice, fitted somewhere in the dashboard along with, of course, TV and stereo. Then I could enclose the cockpit in a bubble to protect me if it rains and maybe install a small generator and an air conditioning/heating system...

August 1987

The Land of Avocados and Chrome Wheels
Part 1

I am always looking for excuses to go to California. I <u>belong</u> in California. My <u>boats</u> belong in California. My <u>cars</u> belong in California. My mentality and lifestyle screams West Coast. Nevertheless, here I am hopelessly rooted in the east, without much I can do about it.

Everything you've heard about California is true -- well, <u>almost</u> everything. It might as well be said here at the outset that the Beach Boys have lied to us all these years. Think about California and what do you envision: teeny weeny yellow polka dot bikinis frolicking in the ocean, sun-bronzed bodies surfing the curls...

Well, it's not so. The fact is the Pacific water is damn <u>cold</u> even in the summer and very few native Californians venture into the water unless they are wearing wetsuits or the water is contained in their backyard swimming pools. Let's face it, seals ain't exactly tropical animals and these furry little whiskered critters proliferate off the West Coast.

Gearhead Heaven

What the Beach Boys didn't lie to us about was the West Coast car culture. Most people here are just plain car crazy and the craziness intensifies the farther into Southern California you venture, probably culminating at its chrome-plated, candy-appled best in a little town called Newport Beach.

Newport Beach! Gearhead heaven! Where the Pacific Coast Highway winds through Newport, there are miles of exotic-car lots stacked one after another. They need to erect a huge Christmas tree overt this area, for it's truly adult toyland. There is even a store that sells nothing but sheepskin car seat covers.

Exotic cars that would make any enthusiast cry are lined up wheel-to-wheel like so many battered Corvettes on used car lot in South Bronx. There are dealers for Jaguar, Ferrari, Porsche, Rolls-Royce, Mercedes, Corvette and Lamborghini. There are exotic used car dealers peddling the likes of beautifully restored XKE's, or Lamborghini Miuras, or Maserati Mexicos. One place sells Porsches and Donzis side by side. But, hey, this is Southern California and a stock, standard, out-of-the-showroom Jaguar, Ferrari, or Porsche just won't do.

If you are <u>really</u> into cars, you'll need a yuppie low rider. What's a yuppie low rider? Well, it's a tricked-out, customized, exotic car. Yes, to really be in with the in crowd, you will need a Ruf Porsche or a Lister Jaguar or a Greenwood

Corvette or a Koenig Ferrari. These outfits take your standard, off-the-shelf exotic car and customize it. Take for example the slant-nosed Ruf Porsche. Here Mr. Ruf will take a standard $58,000 Porsche and massage it to the tune of $135,000!

<u>Nobody</u> except supermarket bag boys drives a plain old brand new Mercedes. Stock Mercedes are for peasants. In California you need a tricked out AMG Mercedes with fat, low, gumball tires, lowered suspension, hopped up engine, aerobody modifications, gold-plated hardware, and chrome-plated wheels.

And you don't just take stock Mercedes wheels and have them chrome-plated. No, sir. These are imported, German custom wheels -- deep-dished spokers so bright you could <u>shave</u> in them, with bold gold Mercedes stars mounted on center. These things run about $400 each (without the tires). Even the damn wheel balance weights are beautifully chrome-plated. I would say there are more custom wheels in Southern California than anywhere else in the world. I wonder where all the discarded standard wheels go?

Happy Berth Days

And the boats -- boats that East Coasters have never seen or heard of. Boats with names like Marlineers, Harko, Elliott and Stephens. California is a boat aficionado's delight, opening up a whole new horizon of heretofore undiscovered boats. It's almost like visiting another country. Hell, California <u>is</u> another country!

People who own boats in California <u>have</u> to be true

enthusiasts to put up with the problems involved in boat ownership. The principal problem is owning a boat in California is that there is <u>no damn place to cruise to</u>! Harbors are packed with crowded marinas or mooring areas offering no transient space -- and there is no place to anchor in most of them.

As far as I can see, California weekend cruising mostly involves cruises to nowhere -- going out in the ocean, turning around and coming back -- or simply sitting in the cockpit at your slip drinking. There really <u>is</u> no place to go. I remembered one "California Cruise" where we cast off the docklines in the marina and rafted up with another boat in the marina <u>turning basin</u> with engines running, backing and filling (and drinking).

It is not uncommon for used boats to sell <u>with their slips</u>. The purchase of a new boat involves the traumatic experience of finding a place to put the thing. I know a guy in Newport who purchased a large yacht and couldn't find a slip for her. In desperation, he <u>bought a marina</u> in downtown Newport! This is a true story folks.

It is not uncommon for people to pay a million dollars for a little narrow railroad-car house fronting a place like Balboa Bay -- just for the boat slip. The house stays <u>unoccupied</u>! Aside from the fact there is no place to go with your boat and there is no place to keep your boat, there is one final hassle to boat ownership. There is no place to <u>service</u> your boat unless you are willing to pay exorbitant rates at one of the manicured, designer boatyards with rates like $55 or $60 per hour. But despite all this, Californians <u>are</u> boat enthusiast and purchase boats in great number.

Of Sprouts and Wholesome Vessels

It seems the preponderance of new boats is from the Orient. Very few Hatterases and Bertrams -- the Cadillacs and Lincolns of the East Coast -- are found out there. Why do Californians go for Oriental boats? Some say it's because Californians are, well...er...thrifty. Some say it's due to their appreciation of "wholesome" vessels. I really don't know what the reason is, but I <u>do</u> know that Hatteras has only one dealer on the whole California coast, while a similar area in the east might have a dozen.

Contrary to what we have heard about Californians (that they are trendsetters and prefer far out, avant-garde things), they seem to truly like and appreciate basic, wholesome boats. My theory is that Californians are really into basics: exercise, avocados, sprouts, meditation, whale watching, etc., etc., and this possibly carries into their boat buying habits. I know one 42' cruiser -- that Californians go bonkers over, while the same models dies a slow death on the East Coast.

Californians might go for conservative boats, but they sure don't restrain themselves with paint schemes. Multicolor paint jobs and wild striping is common. A California harbor on Sunday looks like a box of melted Crayolas. There was one boat in Newport Harbor that really had me puzzled. It was <u>white</u> when traveling south and <u>black</u> when going north! For a good while, I thought I'd had one too many avocados. Every time I glanced at the boat, it <u>changed</u> <u>color</u>! Then I happened to look at it bow on and realized that one hullside was white and the other black! Only in California!

Well people, that's about all for this month. In the next issue (which by the way is the very exciting "Scuppers of the World" collector's issue), I will tell you about California boat shows, West Coast people, the fitness craze and the whale watching. Don't miss it.

September 1987

The Land of Avocados and Chrome Wheels Part 2

I have been to enough California boat shows to have some strong impressions about the way things work out there. California boat shows have a completely different feeling about them from East Coast shows. Friendly faces are everywhere inviting you to board their boats. There is very little of the haughty "no commoners allowed aboard" attitude of the East Coast sellers. An easy give-and-take exists between salesmen and potential buyers, as opposed to East Coast snobbish or hard-sell tactics. Since the boat-buying community is smaller in California, everybody seems to know everybody else and a refreshing, relaxed atmosphere prevails.

Yes, the shows definitely have a different atmosphere on the West Coast -- probably because they are smaller than East Coast shows. The Newport show, for example, is, size wise, where the Fort Lauderdale show was ten years ago. It's presently held at the extreme north end of Balboa Bay at the

Lido Marina which supports a complex of great stores and restaurants overlooking the boats.

The place has a wonderful village aura about it, but the law of "creeping floatism" and is in effect every year the show and the boats get "bigger and better" and the floating docks are pushed out into the bay farther and farther. In a few years, you'll be able to walk on water across Balboa from the west to the east side. I'm not complaining, mind you -- this is good for business. Small, quaint shows are, however, really a nice change.

Smog – Skin's Best Friend?

And California people! People are <u>different</u> out there. First of all, <u>nobody</u> is married (everyone <u>has been</u> married at least once in the past, but presently no one <u>is</u> married). And they look healthier -- even guys with zits and pot bellies look better in California than their counterparts back east.

People dress differently in California. Adult men dress like retired beach boys. Women tend to show a lot of skin. I've never really seen this "California look" duplicated anywhere else. An East Coaster could steal the clothes off a Californian's back, don them and <u>still</u> not look like a Californian. Men's hair is cut differently there too. Everyone seems to have a kind of tousled, Pacific-breeze-in-the-hair look.

It is a general rule that everyone in California is older than he appears. I met a lady who appeared to be a couple of years out of college who was a <u>grandmother</u>, for gosh sakes. Keep up the good work, Vicki! Then there was Karen (with the strange and wonderful leather "catch me, jump me" pants with zippers that go <u>all</u> <u>around</u> from front to back) who looked 25, but turned out to have a 21-year old son in the Air Force! Either California women have kids when they are four years old or they <u>age</u> very well.

I have a theory concerning why people look so young there. It's the SMOG AND THE AVOCADOS! The smog, you see, filters out skin-damaging sun rays and the avocados provide healthy vitamins and minerals. What else could explain this?

California people -- I love them all, but certain individuals stand out in my mind. There's Christy, the actress, model and magic-fingered masseuse (who I always assumed was around 24, but I'm sure is more like 55). Then there is Julie the actress, model and ex-Rams cheerleader -- a lovely lady who doesn't cuss and has a perpetual cheery outlook on life.

And what about Bob with the gorgeous $5,000 pearlescent-white paint job on his Corvette that looks like the inside of an oyster shell? Or Lee and his lovely wife Mary Ellen who threw a dynamite California BBQ party -- with a selection of vegetables that looked like the produce stand at Grand Union. And how about Ron, boat captain extraordinaire and toastmaster who, by his own description after a tough night on the town "cleans up pretty good after a shower."

Then there's Dick Peterson and Pat Sullivan, the beach boy yacht brokers out of Mikelson Yachts in San Diego -- they run a successful, laid-back, cool business that seems to cater to successful, laid-back, cool clients. Dick, in his early 30s, could sell steering wheels to camel drivers. His sales technique is unique. At boat shows, when someone comes aboard one of his boats, he overwhelms his potential buyers with. "Gee, isn't this a great boat! Don't you love it! Golly, gee whiz, this is a wonderful boat." This goes on for about ten minutes. His enthusiasm is so sincere and contagious, people buy a <u>lot</u> of boats.

Of Whales and Joggers

Californians really <u>are</u> into fitness. It's all around you. Joggers pound the pavement morning, noon and late into the night. On Saturday morning, the bikers come out. Not the leather-jacketed, skull-and-cross-boned, voom-voom bikers, but the <u>pedal</u> bikers. And these aren't fat guys riding balloon-tired Schwinns. No, these are "boy racers" wearing streamlined helmets and body suits on $1,500 Maserati bicycles. Saturday morning in Newport Beach looks like the Tour of France.

Whale watching is very big here, too. Yacht broker Dave Jackson told me a story concerning this. He was driving south from San Francisco along the Pacific Coastal Highway and was attracted by a crowd of people standing on a promontory. All had binoculars and were excitedly pointing toward the ocean.

Sensing some sort of major disaster was taking place, Dave stopped and walked up to the agitated crowd. When he asked what was going on, a guy informed him (without taking his eyes away from his binoculars) that he was whale watching. Dave asked this guy how long he'd been there and how many whales he has seen. "Five hours and four whales," the fellow answered brusquely.

Jackson stood there for three minutes and saw <u>ten</u> whales. The problem was the people on the point had <u>tunnel vision</u> -- they were only viewing the small area bounded by their binoculars, while Jackson -- without benefit of binoculars -- saw the whole panorama.

After Dave sighted his tenth whale, the people with the binoculars were getting teed off, upset that his interloper saw more in three minutes than they had in <u>hours</u>. It turned out that the ocean was full of huge, gray mammals -- the place was teeming with them.

Always one to throw a barb when he can, Jackson noted these guys were devout conservationists -- members of Greenpeace, the Sierra club and the like. So he casually asked, "Gee, if there are so many out there, why don't people <u>fish</u> for them?" He then beat a hasty retreat -- crass East Coasters are all alike.

The Color Plum

The colors of California are plum and avocado. It seems <u>everything</u> in California is plum and avocado. I'll bet the <u>state flag</u> is plum and avocado.

There is a great resort in Newport called The Newporter that is done entirely in plum and avocado. I am talking the buildings, the rooms, the menus, the hotel cars, the uniforms, the umbrellas, the pavement, the restaurant, the drink, the food – even the <u>grass</u>!

Yes, I <u>do</u> belong on the West Coast and I am continually scheming up ways to get out there. Here is my latest plan: PERPETUAL YOUTH IN A CAN.

I am going to start a California company that packages avocados in a sealed can of compressed L.A. smog -- the sooty brown stuff -- and distribute it worldwide, so everyone can look like Vicki and Karen.

It will have a California laid-back name. Something like "Tommy's Avocado Man." I'll make a fortune and be able to cultivate the retired beach boy look myself.

October 1987

Marine Terminology
Do Landlubbers Understand What We Are Saying?

Marine Terminology is a can of worms. For example a "ceiling" is the liner on the "sides" of the hull. What you think would be the "ceiling" of a cabin is called the "overhead." Confusing, isn't it?

What difference does it <u>really</u> make if you call the pointy end of a boat the "bow" or the "front?"

What difference does it make if you say "I am turning to port" or "I am turning left?"

I've observed that people with the most boating experience use the fewest marine terms. Just like you'll seldom find an experienced yachtsman wearing one of those cheap captain's hats you buy in the marine store, complete with scrambled eggs on the visor and "Captain" emblazoned in rhinestones, you'll not likely find an experienced individual throwing marine jargon about it.

In any field, it's the insecure <u>neophytes</u> who learn the terminology and use it to show their compatriots that they are knowledgeable. The guys already in the field don't worry about this and usually call things what they damn well please, knowing that it is <u>results</u> that count. After you've rammed the dock, it doesn't really matter if you say, "Gee, I stove in the stem on the bollard" or "Gee, I crashed the front end on that dock thing" does it?

Using marine terminology can even be <u>dangerous</u> since it is fraught with double meanings. Did you ever think how a landlubber might interpret your nautical jargon? Here is a list of marine terms as they might be defined by a landlubber.

- Carvel Planking – The skin of a hull made up of soft ice cream.
- Dinghy – A dark, dirty place.
- Ballast – One who participates in ballet dancing.
- Camber – A type of French cheese.
- Halyard – A grassy area around a house owned by Hal.
- Strut – A peculiar way of walking employed by women to attract men.
- Rudder – A name for people having ruddy complexions.
- Fairbody – A physique that is not particularly exceptional, but is not poor either.
- Prop – What you use your arm for to support your chin at the bar.
- Port – What you drink at the bar.
- Starboard – A listless movie actor.
- Bow – What you do after performing an outstanding docking maneuver.
- Stern – The way you feel after bashing a piling.
- Folkboat – Boat anchored off the three-mile limit for the purpose of prostitution (think about it).
- Scupper – The meal after lunch.

- Slip – The next-to-last article of clothing you remove from a woman's body.
- Berth – Sometimes the result of removing the last article of clothing.
- Freeboard – A cruise on a vessel that you don't pay for.
- Chainplate – A method of securing dinnerware to the table when at sea.
- Stemhead – The guy with a long neck and a small head.
- Kelp – What you yell for when you're in trouble.
- Dockline – Direct telephone access to a physician.
- Flying Bridge – A type of card game played on an aircraft.
- Seacock – A nautical rooster.
- Bulkhead – A person with a very large cranium.
- Fuel Tanks – Giving thanks for having fuel available.
- Berth Board – A condition that afflicts women who've had too many children.
- Windward – A section of a hospital for people with chronic gas problems.
- Windlass – A condition resulting from successful treatment in a windward.
- Chine – What the sun does.
- Oar – A woman of ill repute.
- Oar Lock – A security device that women of ill repute have on their doors.
- Cabin Sole – A pet fish kept in the cabin.
- Thwart – A bump on the skin thought by some to be caused by toads.
- Skeg – What beer comes in.

- Ketch – A game of ball.
- Sloop – One who dribbles food when he eats.
- Metacenter – A place where singles gather to meet other singles.
- Polyester – Frank Ester's sister.
- Rudder Stock – Shares in a rubber company.
- Scantling – The newborn of a scant.

Of Course There Are Great Restaurants in Stuart!

I am sure I've only scratched the surface here folks. I know you can do better, so send those cards and letters. The person with the best nautical definition shall win the grand prize: I'll spring for dinner at a world-class restaurant of the winner's choice (so long as it is in Stuart, Florida). The winner will be determined by the staff and your not-so-humble writer.

Oh yes -- with the above definitions in mind, think twice the next time you're at a fancy restaurant or your church social telling sea stories. Think how <u>this</u> will sound to a blue-haired grandmother type: "I went out on the folkboat, inspected her fairbody, then checked her strut. Since I didn't want anyone else to use them, I put the oars in my cabin."

November 1987

From My Old File Cabinet Part 1

*I*n the top drawer of the file cabinet in my office there's a big file labeled "Articles Ideas." Since I started writing in February 1985, I've been scribbling down ideas and the file has grown to the size of a typical Senate subcommittee transcript.

Most of the ideas that could be developed into full articles already have been and the rest are just languishing there. Some of it is pretty good stuff, so this month -- because I couldn't think of anything better to write -- I thought I'd clean out the file and present to you a conglomeration of ideas, thoughts, sayings and other trivia, most of which relates to boats and boating.

On Macho Boats

While on a rare vacation in Treasure Cay, I docked next to a smartly rigged 55' Hatteras. The boat was called -- would you believe it? -- Beastmaster -- BEASTMASTER!

The name says it all, doesn't it? A more macho name isn't to be found anywhere. There on the transom was air-brushed a leaping marlin, straddled by an angler wearing a Stetson hat who was riding the fish like bucking bronco. Homeport of Dallas, Texas. Figures.

BEASTMASTER! Roll that one over your tongue a few times, folks. It evokes thoughts of medieval knights in Grade C dragon movies. If the owner were named Beowulf, I wouldn't be surprised. The Beastmaster crew looked the part -- all big, burly linebacker types. I could just picture their fast and furious life partying, smoking, partying, fighting, partying and barfing. BEASTMASTER -- what a great name!

I so happens that Mike Joyce, a yacht broker friend, was one of the group at Treasure Cay. Now Mike and I are the antithesis of the Beastmaster type of person. We don't smoke, don't really drink and are definitely not into nightlife and partying. Feeling intimidated by the awesome Beastmaster, we set out planning our own sportfisherman to do the tournament circuits. We decided our boat would be called WHIMPMASTER.

In place of the fighting chair in the cockpit, we would install a highchair with one of those fold-down trays in front of it in order that milk and cookies could be served while trolling for fish. Life aboard Whimpmaster would be a little different. Shirley Temples and Pink Ladies would be served in the cockpit at precisely 6:00 p.m., after which a nourishing dinner would arrive (the cook making sure that we ate all our vegetables). After dinner, video tapes would be available in the saloon, with movies like Mary Poppins or The Sound of Music, after which the crew would be put to bed no later than 9 p.m. Watch for Whimpmaster on the tournament next year.

On Men's Names

Experience has shown me that you should never trust a grown man who calls himself Bobby, Joey, Jimmy, Frankie, Billy or the like. Even less trustworthy are guys with two first names, the first of which is one of the above, for example: Bobby Joe, Jimmy Lee, Billy Bob, etc.

More on Boat Names

I received a lot of letters from people as a result of this column. I'm still getting letters concerning the transom-pollution/transom-sewage pieces I did about boat names.

A while back, a boat owner wrote me a snotty letter saying he is into horses and was highly indignant about my column. He claimed that this was a free country and people can name their boats damn well anything they please and the guys like me shouldn't be writing articles about guys like him who own boats with horrible names and what was bad taste to one person may not be bad taste to another.

Well folks, I'll let you judge this one for yourselves. His boat's name was HORSE SHIP. Wonderful.

On Trends in Megayachts

Nowadays, everyone is trying to out megayacht everyone else and it's really getting hard to come up with new features that no one else has. Well, potential megayachts owners, here are some suggestions to one-up your neighbor on the megayacht next to you: How about a barn and exercise track for a couple of thoroughbred horses? How about a dog kennel and an aviary? Or an exotic garden (an exact replica of the Hanging Gardens of Babylon would be nice)? Why not a huge transom platform covered in deep sand so you can carry around your own beach? Some palm trees could be planted in one corner with a hotdog stand in the other. Some sand fleas, driftwood and discarded beer bottles would complete the scene.

How about a petting zoo for kids? Or a catapult for fixed-wing aircraft -- everyone has helicopters these days. Torpedo tubes could be installed in the bow for getting rid of those pesky sailboats that always get in the way.

You know those foolish "Baby on Board" signs you see in the back windows of yuppie cars? These signs proclaim to the world that the car owners are capable of producing little yuppies (yuppettes?). How about signs that can be hung on the transoms of megayachts, proclaiming to the world important things about the vessel?

Let's face it, a lot of the big-buck installed on megayachts is never seen by the public. What's the use of spending all that money on stuff that nobody can see, right? Well, my idea is to have signs that say things like "MTUs on Board" or "Rolls-Royces on Board" or "Kamewa Water Jets on Board" or "Seven Jacuzzis on Board."

Megayachts usually have their tenders stowed on the afterdeck. A recent trend here is not simply name the tender, but to paint on the tender's topsides "Tender to Yacht Stubbed Toe." Now anybody can look at the damn yacht with the tender mounted securely in its cradle on the deck and glean that it's the tender to the yacht Stubbed Toe without having it spelled out. I got to thinking about why people do this. The only thing I could come up with is that when high-roller megayachts owners are riding around in their 18' tenders, there's no way people can know they also own a big, beautiful yacht. Well, I think this is a wonderful idea, but I suggest that it be expanded.

Why not paint "Anchor to Yacht <u>Stubbed</u> <u>Toe</u>" on the anchor or "Davit to the Yacht <u>Stubbed</u> <u>Toe</u>" on the davit. Hell, why not label <u>everything</u> on the boat so it looks like a floating marine billboard?

On Yuppies

We all know there are certain products associated with yuppies – Häagen-Dazs and BMW come to mind. I've often wondered what the ultimate yuppie powerboat would be, but haven't been able to come up with anything. Any of you out there have any thoughts? What's the marine equivalent of a BMW?

Well, that clears out about half of the file. Next time, we'll talk about Robin Leach, sinning, shapes of boats, exhaust pipes and more.

December 1987

From My Old File Cabinet Part 2

There's ol' Robin Leach on the tube again wrapping up his latest "Loif Stoiles of the Rich and Faimous" with his screaming, obnoxious, English-nasal whine whishing us "Champaigne Wishes and Caviar Dreiams." Robin looks a little ragged around the edges from too many nights of trying to keep up with the "beautiful people." His wrinkled shirt is stained with dribbles of champagne and there are traces of dried caviar around the corners of his mouth. Behind him sits a magnificent 170' megayacht which he claims was built of "solid 24-carat gold at the cost of BILLIONS by elves in the black forest for a Bavarian magnate whose name shall remain anonymous."

Well, I have some problems with Robin Leach. First of all, can you really trust a guy who calls himself "Robin?" And why is he screaming all the time? Mr. Leach is <u>so</u> obnoxious that, on the show, they need an announcer with a low-key, beautifully modulated voice named David Perry to spell Robin, since nobody can take him for a full hour (it's doubtful

Robin's shrill voice could last for a full hour anyhow).

Why do the rich and famous put up with this fellow trying to butt into their wonderful, beautiful lives like a pesty, pudgy mosquito? Hell, if I were rich and famous, I'd boot him out of my beautiful world in a minute.

Robin Leach -- the English Howard Cosell. Why would anyone watch this show? What really bothers me is that I <u>do</u> catch the show now and then and, secretly, enjoy it. One time they even featured one of <u>my</u> boats with Robin's voiceover describing the magnificent multi-million dollar yacht in Lyford Cay, Nassau, Bahamas. The "magnificent yacht" happened to be a 48' cruiser but that's neither here nor there. I'm sure that you're a really nice guy, Robin but just tone it down a few octaves, would you please?

Thoughts on Sinning

I am, admittedly, from humble boat beginnings. I grew up in the late '40s and '50s -- boats without generators fitted with alcohol stoves and iceboxes (with real blocks of ice in them) and manual water pumps at sinks and big old plunger bilge pumps and puny 6v electrical systems. "Air conditioning" was via Mother Nature's breeze no matter how warm it was. Our sole means of navigation was a small binnacle compass, charts and a good pair of binoculars. Bathing meant saltwater soap at the beach or freshwater sponge baths.

It first really hit while cruising Joan and Dough Kerr's good yacht <u>The</u> <u>Lady</u> <u>Morrison</u> <u>VI</u> -- a brand new 83' Cheoy Lee. She placidly swung on the hook at Great Sail Cay in the

Bahamas. The sun was bright, the water was clear and we were all swimming, snorkeling, diving, etc... off the boat. The sun was scorching.

I came out of the water, had a warm fresh water shower in the cockpit, toweled off and stepped into the darkened, plush, air conditioning saloon. BAM! That's when it hit me.

Here we were anchored on an isolated spit of land in the Bahamas away from civilization. One minute I was among the raw elements -- water, sun, fresh air, wind -- then I opened a door and... I was entering the Twilight Zone! I found myself in a plush, Park Avenue living room! Over there is a big screen TV with video. Here is a wet bar with a cabinet fitted for crystal goblets. My first thought was, "Forgive me, for I have sinned!"

After the boats I was used to cruising on, the huge, beautiful sea foam green carpeted room just plain sinful! And this was only the beginning of the sinning. Yes, taking two or three hot showers a day at sea was sinful. Having access to Häagen-Dazs Chocolate Chip ice cream anytime aboard a boat is sinful. Hot dog roasts on the flying bridge grill were sinful. Three-course lamb dinners served in the dining saloon with all the fixings was sinful.

Those of you who got into boating after generators, showers and the like were the norm will never realize that you are sinning and I truly feel sorry for all of you. At least I, realizing my sins, can repent by retrieving an anchor manually or abstaining from showers aboard or sleeping with the portholes open. At least I know better. For the rest of you, there's little hope. When your boating days come to an end you can all expect to pay for your sins by being banished to a place where you will have to <u>bag</u> <u>sails</u> for the rest of your existence.

REPENT SINNERS AND SHUT DOWN YOUR GENERATORS!

On the Shape of Boats

Did you ever wonder why all the hot dog speedboats are needle-nose? So they'll slide past one another during head-on collisions in the Intracoastal Waterway.

Great Expectations – Blasted

Experience in life has shown me that things don't always work out the way you think they will. I've been down the pike far enough to realize that, most times, things work about completely different than you've planned.

This has led me to postulate the Fexas Reverse Expectancy Theorem or "FRET" which states that if you go into a situation with an "Oh Boy, this is going to be great" attitude, things usually turn out to be a dismal failure. On the other hand, things you dread doing usually turn out to be terrific.

I Told You So

A couple of years ago in this column, I proposed my great idea for the ideal sportfisherman. This was a dissertation proposing completely round sportfishing boats to prevent fishing lines from snagging on sharp corners.

Most of you thought this was a joke, but apparently some people took it seriously. Now I see that a company called Water Ventures is marketing what they call a "Tobbie Boat."

You guessed it friends, it's a completely round fiberglass hull surrounded by big BF Goodrich inner tube. It's outboard-powered and available in six designer colors and comes with matching Bimini top and a built-in beverage cooler. The vessel, approximately six feet in diameter goes for $2,795 (add $100 for transparent bottom).

Ode to and Exhaust Pipe
Oh little pipes in the stern
Expelling gasses engines burn,
No one pays you much ado
Except possibly to say "poo"!

Exhaust pipes are an often ignored but important part of a vessel's character and I will write more about this in the future.

Well, the idea file is now nearly empty -- a mere shadow of its former bloated magnificence. The stuff that's left will form the nucleus for future articles on topics like "No Wake" signs and the Brazilian boatbuilding industry and a marine "what's in and out" column. Then there's this follow-up piece on the now infamous "Sailing is Silly" article which is sure to draw some hate mail. I haven't gotten any hate mail for months and I miss it.

January 1988

Holy Camogli!

Two years ago I wrote an article on the Genoa Boat Show which started "if Genoa was a person, it would be a bum lying in the gutter badly needing a shower and a shave." Having just returned from the 1987 Genoa Boat Show, that sentence can now be rewritten as follows: "if Genoa was a person, it would be a bum living in a rehabilitation center with only a mild case of B.O. and stubbly whiskers." Genoa is cleaning up its act. In anticipation of the Christopher Columbus celebration which will take place in 1992 (Chris was born in Genoa), Genoa was visibly cleaner and neater than it was just a year ago during the '86 boat show.

This year's Genoa Boat Show was like most other Genoa Boat Shows -- a trip into never-never marine land. Genoa is the one boat show in the world where many new ideas seem to be introduced for nothing more than shock value. Sometimes one thinks the attitude is "try something new... anything... even if it is wrong!" Genoa is the California of the boat show circuit -- a place where fads and trends are born. This year, your humble writer saw quite a few new trends in the making most of which we probably will never see in the United States. More on this later.

Traditionally, when you attended the Genoa boat show, you usually stayed in a seedy hotel in downtown Genoa. Genoa doesn't have any decent hotels and won't have one until 1992 when a brand new, first class hotel will be opened for the Chris Columbus celebration. This year, we decided to do something different... go native... stay in a small fishing village south of Genoa... take the train to work just like the locals. We stayed in the small seaside village of Camogli, situated to the west of Portofino. Population: 6700. Camogli, dating back to the 10th century, has an ancient tradition in navigation of sailing vessels which reached its peak in the second half of the 19th century only to decline after the spread of steam navigation. Camogli, a town populated with people who are <u>never late</u> for an appointment with very well developed <u>calf muscles</u> and <u>big bags</u> under their eyes! Let me explain. Camogli is built in a wall of rock fronting the Mediterranean. The city must have been conceived by a member of an ant colony -- it's built on <u>four different levels</u> starting with sea level, each separated by about 60 feet. As it expanded, there was no place to go but up into the rock wall which is exactly what they did. The original village is at sea level. The hotel and a bunch of shops are on the second level followed by the railroad station and more shops on the third level and, finally, a residential area on the top level. The only way to get from level to level is to climb steep steps. You can just imagine a housewife living on level four doing her weekly shopping with the grocer on level one, the baker on level two and the butcher on level three. The multilevel town explains the calf muscles but what about bags under their eyes and never being late for an appointment? Well, it's like this. Although Camogli is a sleepy little fishing village, you really don't get much sleep there. First there is the church. Of course, every little Italian village had its own church prominently located in the center of the town. This one has a humongous bell which sounded off every fifteen minutes around the clock. Sure it is quaint to hear church bells in a seaside town but consider this: it is nearly 11:00 at night and you are dog tired from climbing in and out of too many funny Italian boats and eating too many funny Genoa salami sandwiches and talking to too many funny people. You collapse into your bed ready for a good night's sleep. The shutter doors leading out to your spacious patio overlooking the Mediterranean are wide open and a beautiful sea breeze wafts through your room. You are just drifting off when... BONG, BONG, BONG, BONG... is it morning already? No, it is 11:00 PM and you must wait through eleven painfully slow "bongs" before you can go to sleep. That over with, you finally fall sound asleep. BONG, BONG, BONG... now it is 11:15 as the bell peals eleven times plus one for the quarter hour. At 11:30 it is eleven bongs plus two and at 11:45 it is eleven bongs plus three which leads to midnight and twelve great BONGS. Excedrin Headache #23. The whole scene repeats every fifteen minutes until 1:00 when the gong mercifully bongs only once. Then at 7:00 in the morning the bells goes berserk ripping off bongs for about two straight minutes (time to go to work? time to go to church? time to go back to sleep?). On top of the obnoxious bongs, there is the very efficient train system. Trains zip through Camogli all night blasting their whistles and slowing for no one. Since the town is small and intimate, you feel like you are sleeping on a bench at the station, as a couple of trains blast through every hour. Then there are the fishermen. As with many quaint fishing village, the beach is lined with Mediterranean type double-ended fish boats which go out at night to bag the catch of the day. But technology has overtaken the fisherman. Upon close inspection, about 80% of the "quaint, old fashioned" fishing boats are actually fabricated of fiberglass! Most of them are fitted with generators. I'm not talking about Onans or Westerbekes nestled in sound boxes with waterlift mufflers rendering the machines whisper silent. These are little two cycle Japanese screamer engines running open mufflers. They are used to power heliarc lights which apparently attract fish and help the fisherman work at night. The fleet of fishing boats working just offshore makes it sound like you are sleeping in the middle of a damn motorcross race. Yes, if you stay in Camogli you can forget about restful sleep. In the otherwise silent, quaint little village, all these sounds stand out like a burp in a pew.

Of the 6700 inhabitants of Camogli, 6000 of them must be cats. Camogli has a tremendous cat population and they all congregate on the town's many precipitous stairways partying, fighting, sleeping and generally catting around. Although the cats are wild they are, unlike wild cats of other cities, extremely friendly and appear to be well fed.

As I mentioned earlier, the Genoa Boat Show is a

trendsetter and every year there is always at least one exhibit that blows me away. Last year it was the sailing sportsfisherman. This year there were two. The first was a real shocker. With all the large, high priced motor yachts at the show (I'd say there were at least ten boats over 70' displayed ashore and a 110'er in the water) the star of the show was in my humble opinion, a power boat that was, are you ready for this folks, <u>14'9"</u> <u>long</u>! You read it right... 14'9" long. It is the spectacular DYNAMIC TRICK produced by a company called Eurovinil. The DYNAMIC TRICK is a fairly prosaic inflatable tender with a twist (or "dynamic trick" if you will). You see, this inflatable tender <u>flies</u>. I don't mean it flies as in going through the water at a high rate of speed. I mean it <u>flies</u>. Let me quote the brochure. "The Dynamic Trick is an ultralight airplane, two-man motorized hang glider adaptable for use in air, sea or land according to the kind of accessories fitted. Trick is simply a miracle of imagination and technology, a multi-purpose machine which greatly increases the chances of amusement whatever the environment. The base for takeoff is a standard EV 37 Dynamic boat equipped with Polaric wings and a Rotax 2-stroke engine. Setting up time is just 10 minutes and the space needed for takeoff and landing is only 30 to 50 meters. Cruising speed in the air is around 60 to 70 km/h. No sailing or flying licenses are required and it only takes a few hours to get to know how to handle it, as it uses a system that is common to most ultralight airplanes the world over. Having savored the elation of flight, you can quickly return to the sea and dismantle the wings to transform the DYNAMIC TRICK into a powerful air-propelled boat that carries up to four people at a speed of 60 km/h." WOW! A flying boat for the common man. Imagine impressing your friends at the yacht club gala arriving in formal dress by air in your very own airboat tender! Or flying to shore for groceries or taking your very own aerial shots of your boat underway or scoping out treacherous waters ahead. The possibilities are limitless! If the Italians can do this, how far away are we from a <u>flying 85' motor yacht</u>?

Guess what folks? I'm out of space again so this will have to be another two parter. Next month in the March issue (which, incidentally, is the very exciting Bilge System issue) I'll clue you on exotic engines, fads, returning rental cars in Genoa and a startling new trend in yacht finishing which you won't believe.

February 1988

Damn The Torpedoes!

It's gloating time again folks. Regular readers of this column know how I love to gloat when my predictions come true. About two and a half years ago, I wrote a column entitled "Yacht Fakery" in which I undertook describing what I thought would be the ultimate macho boat. To quote in part: "the hull would be painted flat back all over -- bottom, topsides, deck and cockpit. A barbed ram would be affixed to the bow (sort of like the one on the "NAUTILUS" in Jules Verne 20,000,000 Leagues Under the Sea)..." But really guys... I WAS ONLY JOKING!!! You Italians didn't have to take me seriously.

There, at the end of the main hall of the Genoa Boat Show was a big, fast, menacing Baglietto about 86 feet long. She was roughly finished and so ominous looking that a couple of these babies in the Persian Gulf would send the Ayatollah back to his tent. Has the Age of the Paramilitary Motor Yacht arrived? Will we, in the future, cruise about in motor yachts that look like well-used gun boats or floating agricultural implements? When you think about it, it's really the next logical step. Year after year as the finishes of motor yachts improve to the point that they are floating polished gemstones with flawless exteriors that look like fine lacquered furniture, there is no room for improvement. Time to readjust your sights -- time to shake people up and try something new. Once you've reached perfection, there's nowhere to go but <u>down</u> and, since the Italians decided they couldn't improve on some of the beautiful finishes they were producing, they decided to go the other way and produce a truly rough, unfinished, industrial grade motor yacht -- the marine equivalent of fatigues. The vessel was aluminum and the hull was completely unfaired. Hull plating was allowed to appear "as welded" and it was "washboard city" with rough welds and wavy rails flaunted. The paint was so flat it looked like ultra-suede. A big, blunt <u>battering ram</u> was welded to the bow. The vessel was "finished" (I use that word loosely) in khaki and silver. Although she had a name on her side, <u>numbers</u> would have been more appropriate. I carefully studied her lines. There... up in the flyingbridge... something strange but I couldn't put my finger on it. After further scrutiny, I realized that the flyingbridge was <u>asymmetrical</u>! Intentionally asymmetrical! The mast was also off center and... what is that funny box aft of the flyingbridge? I couldn't figure it out until I went aboard. I couldn't believe it. There, aft of the bridge and accessible to it via a door was, half sunken into the level below, a little, dark room with a seat in it. Everything inside was black and there was one porthole on the starboard side fitted with blackout curtains. Close the door and you are in a <u>cave</u>. This was the <u>navigation room</u> of the boat and arrayed around the blackness were state-of-the-art navigation electronics. It wasn't hard to see that the room would also make an excellent <u>Combat Information Center</u>. The next logical step is, of course, fitting cannons and missile launchers fore and aft -- recreational cannons and missile launchers of course. A couple of recreational torpedo tubes would be nice too. Powered by Kamewa waterjets and a pair of 2600 HP MTU's, speeds of over 50 knots are quoted. All in all, the boat looked like a trade school project for tenth graders.

Now laugh if you will but, if you <u>are</u> laughing you are missing the whole point here. It isn't that Baglietto can't build fair, glossy, highly finished boats. Hell, just outside in the water Baglietto had a beautiful, smooth, rounded 115'er named "ADLER" with a magnificent paint job on her. This shipyard is indeed a capable one. The point is that they <u>didn't want to build a fair, beautiful boat</u>. They <u>wanted</u> it to look like this! A salesman told me that owners actually like this look because it saves weight in fairing putty therefore making the boat faster. The fact is, however, that fairing putty in a well-built yacht is but a minute fraction of her total weight. Besides, aluminum yachts have, in the past, been built that are <u>so</u> fair that they need no fairing compound (and cruised around with unfinished topsides to advertise the fact). No, there is no practical reason for this in a yacht -- some people just plain like the rough look. I was informed that nine or ten of these vessels had been built thus far and they expect to build more. Reinforcing this trend was Riva who has always been known for flawless fiberglass gel coating, perfect stainless steel and magnificent woodwork. But, alas, outside on a cradle sat a 60' "Black Corsaro" it's flawless, normally shiny, ebony gelcoat roughed up by what looked like 200 grit sand paper producing a very flat, black finish. It is one thing to build a boat from scratch to look rough but another thing entirely when you take a finely finished craft and <u>downgrade it</u> all in the name of high fashion! So, trendsetters, if you truly want to be "in with the in marine crowd" be the first in your marina to take a <u>belt</u> <u>sander</u> to your beautifully awlgripped topsides. Then apply a ball peen hammer to your stainless steel rubrails. Give the cleats and ventilators a few shots while you're at it. And your bowrails… bend a couple of pronounced "wows" in them. A couple of shattered windows would be nice and, for the finishing touch, how about a couple of well placed, deep gouges in your teak toerail?

Other trends noted: a resurgence of beautifully finished all wood interiors as opposed to the "lacquered look" so prominent in Italian boats past. Waterjet propulsion is making big strides and, unbelievably, exhaust blisters are back in vogue. I've written about them before but, for those who might have missed it, exhaust blisters are back in vogue. I've written about them before but, for those who might have missed, exhaust blisters are huge fiberglass or aluminum cowlings fitted over exhaust pipes which lead from the engines out through the side of the hull and aft to the transom. These cowlings are typically 12" or 14" square and about 15' long grafted to the sides of the boat just above the waterline. Docking a boat with blisters protruding 12" from the hull proper had got to be a hassle but, unbelievably, Italian exhaust blisters are never fitted with rub rails or rubbing strips. It is the "look" you see. Transom of large motor yachts appear like the business end of an Atlas booster rocket. To make matters worse, these things slap terribly when the vessel rolls even moderately.

All sorts of exotic engines are finding their way into the marine field. Porsche is making inroads with their nifty V8 928 four-valve engine, as is Lamborghini with their screaming, beautiful 12-cylinder machines, CRM displayed an absolutely stunning 18-cylinder 1.850-hp diesel engine that weighed only 3.861 pounds with an aluminum block and three banks of six cylinders each.

I walked around this engine totally astounded by its beauty. The entire unit was finished in black crackle-finish paint and all the hardware was polished aluminum or chrome-plated. Sixteen chrome fuel lines flowed around the block like linguini around a sausage.

Now, I'm sure this is a great marine engine. Its power-to-weight ratio is astounding and the exhaust cry must be awesome. Still, one terrible thought kept popping into my head: "This engine would make a wonderful coffee table."

What else did I see? I noted that bow rails fitted with a huge hoop forward (high enough for a man to walk under) are the norm here, but I couldn't figure out why because they served no discernable purpose. Upon talking to a prominent European designer, it was explained to me that these hoops are of absolutely no practical purpose. They were carried over from the days when SSB antennas were run from the mast forward -- they served to elevate the antennas forward so one could walk under them.

I noted the very beginning of a trend to murals or frescos

appearing on cabin or hullside. Oh, yes -- strange English boat names are "in." There was a large motoryacht displayed on the main floor named <u>Darling</u> <u>Boys</u>. Probably one of those boats fitted with a "his-and-his" head.

How to Return a Rental Car

One of the high points of this trip was my valiant attempt at returning a rental car in Genoa (rented well to the south of Genoa in another city). In <u>downtown</u> Genoa. On a <u>Friday</u> morning. During <u>rush</u> <u>hour</u>. In the <u>rain</u>!

With only the most basic instructions on how to find the drop-off office (I was told only which exit to take off the Autostrada), we used the "hunt and peck" method to find it. I'll never forget the name of the road: Via Montevideo. The road map to downtown Genoa looked like a damn streptococci convention and didn't cover the area we were looking for, anyway.

My game plan was to stop at every gas station we passed and asked instructions on the theory that each one would get us closer to our ultimate destination. Employing rudimentary Italian, Portuguese and many gestures, we had a fine tour of the city.

After a couple of hours of aimlessly driving around, I started getting giddy, laughing uncontrollably and saying "We're never going to find this place. They're going to find our bones along the side of the road!" I suspect that the major portion of Genoa's bum population are former American Yuppies who, after trying to return a rental car in Genoa, eventually ran out of gas, missed their planes, ran out of money and lost their jobs. I was one of the lucky ones.

The 1987 Genoa Boat Show will be remembered fondly. The boats and equipment were fantastic. The show was well organized. Our stay in Camogli was almost dreamlike (except next year I'll bring ear plugs -- see last month's column and you'll know why). The food was outstanding and Italy, in general, was delightful. I look forward to Genoa 1988 with bated garlic breath!

March 1988

The Great Contest
Part 1
Preliminaries

Dear Editor:

Realizing you have probably made an agreement with Mr. Fexas that is unbreakable, I thought I'd do my part in helping you fill space by entering his contest. (It gives the appearance that someone read his article.) The $100.00 prize is attractive, but dinner in Stuart, Florida is not on my list of "Things Most Wanted to Do." I have attended dinner functions with Mr. Fexas in the past and <u>every</u> <u>time</u> the fries were greasy and the burgers were cold. A better prize would be to have Tom come out to the "Reality" of dinners with sunshine and avocados -- on our account.

Enclosed is a list of definitions that are sure to win.
Sincerely,
Captain Ron Bowers and Crew
Motoryacht "Reality"
San Diego, California

This is about representative of the way this contest went.

And this guy is a friend of mine. For those of you who just tuned in, my November column entitled "Marine Terminology" put forth the proposition that marine jargon can actually be dangerous since it is fraught with double meanings. It asked the question "Did you ever think how a land lubber might interpret your nautical jargon?" At the end of this piece, I issued forth a challenge. In that article, I was hard pressed to come up with my 41 definitions in the five minutes I allot per month to write this masterpiece. I thought you readers could come up with a lot more, so I proposed a contest and ended prophetically with "come on you people with the twisted, demented minds, here is your chance to chine!"

After my "Transom Pollution" Part 1 and 2 articles on boat names, you people deluged me with perverted, rotten, foolish and disgusting boat names. This lead me to suspect that many boatsmen had a definite raunchy bent. Now I'm certain of it. You people are bent. The 26 entries included an unbelievable 303 twisted marine definitions, all vying for the grand prize of $100.00 and dinner with me at the Blue Moon Dinner in glamorous Stuart, Florida.

Trouble is, half of the people submitted stuff that can't be printed in a family publication and half of the remaining half simply didn't understand what was going on. Many of them didn't even suspect anything was going on. Let me explain.

The point of all this foolishness was how some nautical jargon would be interpreted by land lubbers. Simple, no? Quoting from the list of gems included in my article were such definitions as:

- Ballast - Ones who partakes in ballet dancing
- Carvel Planking - The skin of a hull made up of soft ice cream
- Camber - A type of French cheese
- Scantling - The newborn of a scant

You get the idea... well, some of you didn't. Here are some clinkers that left me muttering and wondering:

- Pointy End - Normally the front of the boat (?)
- Head - Commonly referred to as a bathroom, nicknamed "Head" due to the damage one usually acquires to theirs while using it (Head definitions were plentiful but this was not one of the better ones folks)
- Running Lights - Multicolored lights that rarely work due to saltwater corrosion (??)
- Bottom Job - Usually costing two times what you figured with you doing all the work. Includes replacing and repairing everything you never see all year (???)
- Spring Line - A spring on a line so that it expands (????)
- Bimini - Top of mountain on an island off Florida (?????)

I don't understand. I really don't. I mean it was so simple. One of these entries ended with a definition that perfectly describes these people who missed the point:

- Captain Know-It-All - An individual found around most boating areas offering a virtual compendium of worthless knowledge and unsolicited opinions

Many of you got the point but didn't use much imagination. Some dullsville examples:

- Genoa - Goes well on an Italian hero
- Runabout - What your friends let your kids do all weekend while on a cruise
- Hatch - What eggs do
- Bootstripe - Stripe found on one's foot apparel
- Heave - What one does over the side in rough seas
- Broach - A large ornamental pin worn on the neck or bosom of a dress
- Pacemaker - Keeps the captain's heart beating
- Shaft - A black detective
- Painter - The guy with the brush and paint bucket
- Sportfish - A fish that likes baseball, football and various other sports
- Radar - A character on <u>MASH</u>
- Gimbals - Macy's Competition

Snore. Snore. Come on guys and gals. You can do better than this. This stuff is <u>drivel</u>!

As I said, some of the best definitions are unprintable, but many of them had to with words like LAY LINE, CLAWING OFF, SNATCH BLOCK, LIE TO, STUFFING BOX, SEA COCK, LIMBER HOLE, SEXTANT, BOOM CROTCH and the like. Use your imagination. Actually, some of these definitions were quite good. In fact, had this been Penthouse Magazine, the winner would have been Michele Roberts from Port Aransas, Texas for her definition of "CLEAT." Unfortunately no one but Michele and I will ever see this definition, but, I assure you, it <u>is</u> terrific.

Of the 26 entries, five were considered finalist material but one of these guys advertised himself as a "professional writer," wanted to retain the right to use the material in the future and required me to "communicate in writing if you select these for publication." Well, I simply don't have time to communicate in writing during the five minutes that my writer's creative juices are flowing. Hell, <u>three</u> of those minutes are already used up, so I'd better get moving. Chucking out the professional writer's entry leaves four finalists, but, unfortunately, I'm <u>out</u> <u>of</u> <u>space</u>! WHAT SUSPENSE! You'll now have to wait until the May issue (which, incidentally, is the Gala Spring Seagoing Gardening issue featuring such articles as "Flowerboxes for your Flyingbridge," "Cultivating a Lawn on Your Main Deck" and "Growing Veggies in your Holding Tank the Natural Way") to learn who the winner is. Don't miss it.

April 1988

The Great Contest Part 2

And the Winner is

As I said last month, just before I was so rudely interrupted by lack of space, we were down to four finalists in our great Marine Terminology Contest. The winner was determined simply by who, in my near-humble opinion, had the greatest number of outstanding printable definitions. Before we get to the winners, however, some of the folks who didn't make the finals had some great definitions that deserve recognition.

Mr. and Mrs. Larry Childs of Ronkonkoma, New York submitted "EXCESSIVE WAKE - A flamboyant funeral." Not bad. Mike Pearson of Massapequa, New York had a few good ones. How about "LIFE RAFT - George's brother," "SHEERLINE - A run in the first mate's stocking," "SKEG - A real ugly first mate" and, one I especially like "TRANSOM - Made by Pontiac - a sharp looking car used in <u>Smokey & The Bandit</u>." Michele O'Neal of Minneapolis submitted "LONGITUDE - A generous attitude." Al Conrad, MD of Washington, D.C. had "CHOCK - What you get if someone throws the switch while you hold the wire" and Paul Jackson of Auburn, New York sent us "BEACON - What you eat with eggs." Mr. D. Simpson of Dauphin Island, Alabama submitted three goodies: "FANTAIL - Sally Rand's behind, TRUE NORTH - They call him Ollie, TRIANGULATION - Ménage à trois." And how about the disgusting but clever "HEAVE TO - When a pair of crew members vomit at the same time" from Mr. M. Smith of Beach Haven, New Jersey. We even got a number of entries from <u>sailboat people</u> who to a man (or woman) made it a point to tell us that "The magazine was passed on from some "stinkpot" friends" or "I found your magazine in one of the stalls at the Yacht Club head" or "A friend gets the magazine and accidentally left it aboard my sailboat." Right guys! You're the same people who discover the "National Enquirer" magically appearing in their food bags without buying it. One of these ragbagger entries was from Katie and Andrew Smith from Boynton Beach, Florida: "LUFF - The reason people in Russia get married."

Well, I bet the suspense is killing you! Of the four finalists, one of them, Ron Bowers, who I quoted at the opening of part one is, as I said, a friend, albeit a disgusting one, who had to be eliminated because of conflict of interest or some such thing. Nevertheless, he came up with twelve definitions some of which were printable and I have listed for your enjoyment:

- Waterline - Seagoing African animal (think about it)
- Engine Governor - Political overseer of aquatic locomotion
- AC/DC Panel - Gay arbitrators
- Cockpit - Male bulldog

- Foredeck – That part of the deck trimmed for religious purposes

Nice going Ron and I'm glad to see you're back on the streets after the flashing indictment.

That leaves three finalists. Third runner up was Mr. George Lamb of Long Beach, New York who seemingly effortlessly zipped off four terrific definitions on a sheet of yellow paper. Noteworthy is the fact that he didn't need 30 entries to get four good ones, each one was a gem. His definitions were:

- Rooster Tail – Easy chickens
- Spring Line – Easter fashions
- Deadrise – Halloween magic
- Danforth Anchor – Brother of singer Paul (I love it!)

Second runner up was Captain Sid Martin from none other than Stuart, Florida. Mr. Martin completely overwhelmed us with a total of 56 definitions, 10 of which were excellent. (Actually, fourteen were excellent but four were unprintable). Here we go:

- Hammock – A pig running amok
- Heave Short – When you throw up down the front of your shirt
- Between Decks – When they open a new deck at a card game
- Breast Hooks – Snaps on a woman's bra
- Topping Lift – The high part of breast hooks
- Binnacle – A small barnacle
- Pintle – A small pint
- Cistern – Your sister's backside
- Stevedore – A girl who loves Steve

- Clove Hitch – The knot that holds the cloves in a Christmas ham

As for the winner, the grand prize is reluctantly awarded to a mystery entrant who chose to remain anonymous going by the name of Mr. "G. B. Yards" of Guilford, Connecticut (a P.S. at the end of his letter indicates that this stands of "Guilford Boat Yards." Cute). I say "reluctantly awarded" because I suspect from some of the words he defined that he's really a ragwagon man but I won't hold that against him too much. Mr. "Yards" had twelve outstanding definitions out of a total of 25 submitted. Here are the winners:

- Clew – What you don't have as to why your engine quits
- Coamings – What clogs up a drain in the shower
- Broad on the Bow – The most effective distress signal
- Abreast – What you see much of on the other guys boat
- Whisker Pole – A survey by Harris on beards
- Capsize – A measure of ego of an owner of a new performance boat
- Cavitation Plate – Dental plate used to prevent tooth decay
- Sister Frames – When a young girl convinces her parents that her sibling is to blame
- Reef Cringle – The little known brother of a famous holiday saint
- Bedding Compound – A prescription for a sleeping pill
- Bright Work – A term paper with a good grade
- Deviation – An act performed by deviates

Congratulations Mr. "Yards." You get the $100.00 prize on

me next time you are in Stuart. Considering that you are probably a sailboat guy, I know you won't mind a chepo, dinner at a place like ROACH HAVEN (since that's what you are accustomed to I'm sure). Just kidding. OH yes... in order to claim the prize, you'll have to "come clean" and divulge your name. Why are you afraid to tell us your name? Are you a bottom painter at Guilford Boat Yard who stole away from the job to surreptitiously enter our contest? Do you own the yard and don't want to appear foolish to your employees and customers? Are you really Billy Joel (he lives around there) and don't want to upset Christie? Are you "on the lamb"? Does it possibly have anything to do with "DEVIATION"?

May 1988

The Quest for Mega Speed in Mega Yachts
Part 1

I get calls quite often from people in the boating press asking me for my predictions concerning megayacht megatrends. Frequently during interviews the question arises "What will be the megayacht of the future?"

To be totally honest with you, when being interviewed by one of the big time boating magazines, I'm expected to be totally professional and give yacht designer type answers. So I put on my yacht designer's hat and prepare to answer questions in yacht designer techno-talk. My voice drops a few octaves and I assume my "William F. Buckley posture," leaning way back in my chair with a heavy list to starboard teetering on the brink of disaster. By the way, I suspect that part of Mr. Buckley's popularity stems from people watching Firing Line in anticipation of the big moment when Mr. Buckley's CG exceeds the boundaries of his chair legs and he, very slowly at first, starts keeling over without missing a polysyllabic word on his way down to the floor. What a great T.V. moment that would be!

Anyway, like I said, during official interviews I wear my yacht designer's hat. In this column however, I can sport my writer's hat, and I am lucky enough to have the freedom to say things I wouldn't or couldn't say in an interview (for your information, a power yacht designer's hat is a beanie with a four bladed prop on it. A sailboat designer's hat is fitted with a full rigged mast, boom and sails and clears the wearer's sinuses every time he jibes. A writer's hat is modeled after the tip of a pencil -- sort of like a dunce cap). I've already written some about trends in megayachts in past articles. When viewed strictly from a hedonistic (excuse me I forgot I'm wearing my writer's hat now and don't have to use William F. Buckley-type words) point of view, the megayacht has about maxed out. Modern yachts are being festooned with everything from laser lit Technicolor waterfalls to handrails that glow in the dark. Stuff like onyx, whale scrotum covered barstools, gold fixtures, inside and outside whirlpool tubs, barbeques, lobster tanks, soda fountains, hair dressing salons, automobiles, mini-subs, jet skis, hobie cats, carpathian, burl, computer controlled ambient lighting, sculpture, double satcoms, crystal, original artwork, audio visual systems and mink sculptured carpeting is being done to mega death. Mega styling runs the gamut from the good, the bad and the ugly. Many yachts would look at home rendezvousing with the Starship Enterprise orbiting the planet Vulcan! No, when it comes to sybaritic (sorry -- there's another one of those words again) accoutrements (I can't stop!) and styling, it's very difficult to come up with something new. But there is one feature of large yachts that will always be new. SPEED!! Big speed! Blow the sunglasses off your head speed. Overtaking Cigarrete speed. Straighten your hair speed. Blow your bikini top off speed. Speed that, only a few years ago, boats in the 40' range could attain. Speed will never be dated or overused. The quest for ever higher speeds in large yachts is the big story today and will be the big story of the future. Just a few years ago, a fast large yacht (for the record let's call a "large yacht" anything over 100' though I'm sure this will upset some people with 150'ers) did 20 knots max. Twenty knots in any kind of boat is respectable speed. Twenty knots (23 mph) on the water is pretty darn fast. These days many large, fast yachts slow cruise at 20 knots and top 30 knots.

Large, fast yachts have always been around but they were extremely rare, built for the odd sheikh or king there. Palmer Johnson was one of the pioneers of mega speed. They built the King of Spain's 100' "FORTUNA," which, powered with two diesels totaling 2900 HP and a single gas turbine putting out another 4500 HP (total 7400 HP), did an astounding <u>50 knots</u> in <u>1979</u> and to this day is one of if not <u>the</u> fastest megas in the world. Then there's "SHERGAR" at 153' powered by an unbelievable 16,990 HP which attains 45 knots. While these two vessels stand out as high water marks in mega speed, it's safe to predict that yachts, such as these, will become more common in the future.

It's now time for me to don my yacht designer's hat to put forth some technical mega info. Please try to stay awake. The speed/power curve for a fast yacht looks something like Bob Hope's nose in profile. It starts out rather flat but gets ever steeper as speed is increased until it is nearly vertical. True, higher speeds can always be attained by stuffing in more horsepower, however, the fact is that, above 30 knots, the large mono hull is fighting a losing battle.

The Scandinavians have already been this route. The coast of Norway looks like a paramecium under a microscope. It's loaded with harbors, waterways and fjords. Waterways are the main transportation link between towns and cities and are serviced by high speed ferries. They developed their mono hulls up to around 30 knots but their customers were demanding still more speed so Norwegian designers went to the catamaran configuration and thereafter to surface effect vessels for still higher speeds (100 foot, 100 passenger 42 knot ferries are common there). The logical assumption would be that, in the near future, large motor yachts would go the catamaran or surface effect configuration. Logic, however, does not always work with yachtsmen. Whether these parking lot shaped cats as SES craft will ever be accepted as true yachts remain a big question. Yachts have always been graceful and pointy at one end. Additionally, I wonder about the sea keeping capability of these ultra wide craft in the open sea. There's simply too much flat impact area under the deck forward and when these vessels have to slow down for really big seas, they could be in trouble. There are hydrofoils, of course. But I doubt these will ever be integrated into the large yacht field with fixed foil drafts of maybe 15' or with retracted foils that when stowed make a vessel appear as a giant, deranged, waterlogged praying mantis. Other high speed large vessel oddities include surface piercers which, in effect, are huge platforms with two pontoon hulls per side stacked atop one another looking like two mating catamarans (maybe that's where hobie cats come from?). The sea-keeping abilities of these vessels in the open sea is, in my opinion, also questionable. Lindsey Lord, who literally wrote the book on high speed mono hull design, has developed a very promising concept which, in effect, combines the lift capabilities of a planning hull with the low resistance characteristics of a submerged hull.

Are you mega bored with all this technical stuff yet? The fact is, I needed to explain the state of the art in high speed hulls in order that what will follow (when I again wear my writer's hat) will make some sense.

The quest for mega speed. How far can it go? What's the next bold step? Next Month, in the very exciting Spring Freeing Port Flap issue, I will suggest two outrageous mega directions for the large, fast yacht. Stay tuned. You won't believe it!

June 1988

The Quest for Mega Speed in Mega Yachts Part 2

*L*ightweight mono hulls, catamarans, surface effect vessels, surface piercing vessels, hydra foils. These are "state-of-the-art" 1988 high speed mega craft. Where do we go from here? Well, I propose that we do it ... that we <u>really</u> do it. Let's quit fooling around with innovations such as round windows instead of rectangular windows or nonfunctional tail fins. Let's bypass the next logical steps and make a great leap forward. Strangely enough, what I will propose now -- with tongue only lightly planted in cheek -- comes from technology that's been available since the early 1900's.

Picture this. A sleek, finned 120'er, rests at anchor in a sun drenched blue Mediterranean lagoon. The scene looks like an old Bridgette Bardot movie. The owner's party is lounging on deck, playing cards and taking in the sun. Others are snorkeling around the vessel. Music wafts from the on deck loud speakers and the tinkle of ice on crystal carries about the lagoon. It's late Sunday afternoon and the shadows are growing long. The owner glances at his watch. 3:30 p.m. He needs to be in New York (which is six hours ahead) at 5:30 p.m. Sunday evening for an important meeting. He gives the captain the "high sign" and the crew immediately starts scurrying about stowing gear and getting the guests aboard. The shrill whine of hydraulic motors is heard and, unbelievably, the sleek hull proceeds to <u>deploy</u> <u>wings</u> like a butterfly just out of the cocoon! The high pitched hydraulic whine continues until the wings lock in their service position. More hydraulic sounds are heard and massive flaps emerge from the leading and trailing edges of the wings. Then a whine much higher and more powerful than the first is heard as the port then the middle and finally the starboard jet engines are lit off. The sleepy little Mediterranean lagoon now sounds like the main runway at JFK! The anchor is retrieved and the owner's party waves good-bye to the other yachts anchored in the lagoon as they taxi to open water. The shriek of the jets increase and the hull lifts off at 100 knots in a glorious blast of spray, kero fumes and heat waves. Once up, they do a tight 180 and buzz their companions below before setting course for New York City, three thousand miles and six hours away.

Or, how about this? One of the yachts left behind in the lagoon is a sleek 115' vessel with an extremely low profile. The teardrop shaped hull glistens in the late afternoon sun but the day is drawing to a close and it's time to leave. The crew makes ready for sea, the anchor is stowed and the vessel slowly and silently makes her way out into open water. It's extremely rough outside with the wind blowing 35 knots and seas six to nine feet. The captain is unconcerned. Once out, he gives the command to open the vents and flood all tanks. The sleek vessel <u>disappears</u> <u>below</u> <u>the</u> <u>surface</u> <u>of</u> <u>the</u> <u>sea</u> and heads home at her underwater cruising speed of a very efficient 60 knots. The owner's party adjourns to the extreme bow where the "Nemo Cabin" with clear lexan hull panels all around is located. Hull resistance is lessened by artificial porpoise skin applied to the shell and introduction of a lubricant in the bow area to lessen skin friction. The atomic reactor, which is the size of your average garbage pail, produces silent, effortless power to the high speed turbines.

Well, there you go laughing again. They laughed at Leonardo's helicopter too. In fact, Pan Am had what amounted to flying yachts (their famous Clipper Flying Boats) <u>53 years ago</u> and submarines have been around since the <u>Civil War</u>! The two scenarios presented above may be entirely possible for the well-heeled private individual.

An impossible dream you say. Well, despite American Industry bashing which is so popular nowadays, I have great faith in the capabilities of the American Industrial Machine when it comes to responding to new challenges or developing new technology. Most of the "GEE" technology that wows us these days in such fields as plastics, computers and communications originated in the USA as spinoffs from massive government funded NASA-type programs such as the moon landing, the space shuttle and the Jupiter flybys. While these milestones themselves are astounding, the means of <u>achieving</u> these achievements is less than astounding. Given government backing, <u>anything</u> can be accomplished simply by throwing massive doses of taxpayer's money at it. It's private industry that really impresses me, companies that go out and spend their own little money to develop new products. Companies that have the foresight and guts to put their profits into bold new ideas. What impresses the hell out of me are the less prominent but no less spectacular accomplishments of private industry.

Next month, we shall explore, in detail, an example of American ingenuity in the private manufacturing sector and explore the reasons why flying boats and subyachts could become the wave of the future. One may say that flying boats and submarines will be too expensive to be privately owned. To this, I can only reply that the modern mega yacht of 1988 is nearly as complicated as a big, modern plane or sub. Secondly, all it takes is bushels of dollars (which seems to be no problem nowadays and a uranium permit - should the sub route be taken). Hell, there must be a <u>dozen</u> <u>guys</u> that I personally know who have the modern equivalent of more money than Pan Am had in 1935. Some of these guys have more money than Pan Am has <u>now</u>!

July 1988

The Quest for Mega Speed in Mega Yachts
Part 3

Since the turn of the century private industry had produced numerous astounding achievements that could fill a complete book on the subject. This month, I'll pick one recent development that highlights the capability of American private industry.

I'm happy to report that the U.S. has become the preeminent leader in Raisin Square technology. That's right, I said <u>Raisin Square technology</u>. The Russians presently have spacecraft and nuclear submarines and supersonic planes (just as we do) but I'll bet <u>anything</u> they don't have Raisin Squares. In fact, if I were the Russian Government, I'd be far more fearful of Raisin Square technology than of the latest military developments because Raisin Squares have the power to appeal directly to the people who can relate to Raisin Squares in their bowls at breakfast time far easier than missiles. I'll bet there's a major KGB effort going on right now to steal the secrets of Raisin Squares. Wars have been started over lesser things (would it be called the Great Raisin Square War?).

After seeing Kellogg's "Raisin in the Middle" commercials on T.V., I was, I admit, skeptical. I thought to myself "How could any company --- even a big, sophisticated one like Kellogg's, possibly develop the technology to place raisins in the centers of billions of cereal squares?" It was mind boggling. Even though I've never really liked raisins, I went out and bought a bunch of boxes of the stuff strictly in the name of research. I scientifically took a number of random samples from each box and carefully dissected each one. Sure enough -- there embedded in the center of each cereal square was ... a raisin! What was really impressive was that none of the raisins were near the surface or placed off center. Each little raisin was embedded in the exact <u>geometric</u> <u>center</u> of each cereal square, and every one was absolutely perfect. <u>This</u> is the kind of thing that truly amazes me about private American industry. This is American technology at it's very best. Congratulations Kellogg's.

My point is that if Kellogg's can precisely place raisins in the exact center of billions of cereal squares then absolutely <u>nothing</u> is impossible -- even flying or submersible yachts.

When you look back at Pan Am's famous Clipper flying boats, one realizes that modern versions would make excellent mega yachts -- even considering today's standards. These Pan Am Clippers, designed and built by Boeing, were 109' long and, although the beam was a little tight by today's standards, there was space in her two carpeted levels for 74 passengers in five compartments and a crew of six.

Additionally, she could sleep 40 in individual berths. There was a dining saloon for fifteen people, rivaling the best restaurants of the day. There was even a honeymoon suite aft. Separate dressing rooms for men and women were fitted -- each with its own toilet. The cabins were fitted out like the yachts of their day with beautiful paneling and lovely "art deco" fittings and hardware. Her gross weight was only 82,500 pounds and her range was about 4,200 miles at a cruising speed of approximately 150 m.p.h. You say 109' is a bit small? Then may I suggest a trip to Long Beach, California for a visit to Howard Hughes' unbelievable "H-4 Hercules" better known as the "Spruce Goose." In fact, it was my visit there last year that gave me the idea for this piece. Here is a flying boat. The "Goose" is 218 feet in length with a 25 foot beam. The hull is 30 feet high which would nicely accommodate three full decks.

Today, only small "recreational submarines" exist but the technology is certainly available to produce a "megasubyacht." Even if uranium could not be obtained for reactors, modern day deep cycle batteries and high efficiency electric motors could power these subyachts for long periods of time when submerged. Think of traveling submerged at 60 or 70 knots with virtually vibrationless, silent power in a craft without motion, even though 20 foot waves rage above. Of course, there are other advantages to a megasubyacht: Submerged, one could sneak out of marinas without paying the bill. One could make mock torpedo runs at his friend's helpless surface yachts. Presently in the Mediterranean there is a trend towards paramilitary motor yachts.

Well, here's the <u>ultimate</u>! Imagine yourself standing in the <u>conning</u> <u>tower</u>, binoculars dangling around your neck, cigarette dropping out of your mouth with a full scruffy beard. You are surrounded by a little collapsible windshield. You are Otto Kretschmer (the Ace German WWII U Boat Commander). At your side is your beautiful blonde secretary. That Errol Flynn look in your eyes and you pace from port to starboard in your best John Wayne walk as you scan the horizon for "Bogies." Although there are six showers and plenty water aboard, you haven't bathed in four days so you can really play (and smell!) the part. Suddenly, on the horizon you spy a private jet. Good God! That's <u>your</u> jet and that's <u>your</u> <u>wife</u> out looking for you! Calmly, you give the "dive" order as you slide down the hatch. You pass under the plane undetected. So come on high rollers, let's quit fooling around. Let's do it. Let's <u>really</u> do it! Let's be the first one in your stock exchange to own a megaflyingyacht or megasubyacht. The technology is available. Hell, I used to work for Electric Boat Company (the world's foremost sub designers/builders in Groton, Connecticut) and have access to the finest submarine designers in the world so I figure I'm in on the ground floor. And for those of you who want to fly, I'm willing to set up an avionics division to accommodate you. All it really takes is bucks, imagination ... and Raisin Squares.

August 1988

So You Want to be a Yacht Designer? Part 1

Dear Mr. Fexas,

My name is David Martin. I am 12 years old and in the seventh grade. I was given an English assignment to write to somebody famous, and I chose you. I'm glad this assignment has been given to me because I have been waiting to write to you for a long time.

I have been boating since I was two years old and I love it. It is practically all I do in the summer, and in the winter, I dream about it and read about it.

We have a 31' Jersey, live on the water and close to marinas. I go to the marinas often, throughout the whole year, to look at boats and keep up with the latest designs.

I would like to be a Naval Architect when I grow up. I admire what you have done in your career and hope I can do the same. I hope you can answer the following questions and write back to me with the answers:

1. What classes did you take in high school and in college?

2. Where did you get your training? Did you go to college or a "special" school?

3. Did you start as a Naval Architect, or did you work your way up?

4. Is there a need for Naval Architects? Do you think there would be a call for this when I am old enough?

5. What classes do you have to be "strong" in to be a successful Naval Architect? I am very good in math, does that help?

6. If you had it to do over again, would you still want to be a Naval Architect, or would you pick another career?

7. About how long would it take to design a 40' Sportfisherman?

8. What do you think the best college, or schooling, is in the field of naval Architecture?

Any advice, in addition to the above questions, would be very much appreciated by myself, as well as my parents.

Thank you very much for your time. I know you must be very busy designing boats and writing articles. I enjoy reading your articles each month and look forward to them. I hope to hear from you in the near future.

Sincerely,

David Martin

Surprise, David Martin! I bet you thought I'd <u>never</u> answer your letter. Actually I've been saving it for this article. I hope you don't mind if I answer your questions in public because I think your letter and the answers to it will be of great interest to others your age thinking of entering the yacht design field and cut down on the number of inquiries I receive on the subject.

Green Hair – The Wave of the Future?

I get letters like this from kids (and grown-ups in unsatisfying jobs) all the time. David Martin's neatly typed letter was better thought out and presented than most (which usually come in a plain brown wrapper on lined yellow paper) but that doesn't really matter much. We hear a lot these days about how kids have changed and, for the most part, I'm sure that's true.

"What's this world coming to?"
"There's no hope for future generations!"
"I never did that when <u>I</u> was a kid!"

These are kid clichés of today. Drugs, stick your finger into 440 volt AC socket hairdos and preteen sex didn't exist in <u>my</u> little 12 year old world. What we <u>did</u> was try to smoke "punks" (cigar shaped swamp plant pods). These were really rank and turned me away from smoking for life. We also sported "DA" hairdos and wore shirts with "Mr. B" long collars. Pegged pants were hot too. "Sex" was dancing close at a sock hop. But take heart, there <u>are</u> exceptions today. Here we have young David Martin living in Michigan who, "goes to the marinas often, <u>throughout</u> <u>the</u> <u>whole</u> <u>year</u>, to look at boats and to keep up with the latest designs." Here's a kid (I'll bet anything David Martin doesn't have a punk hairdo) who braves Michigan's cold, windy winters to check out boats in bubbler storage at icy marinas. I love it! Maybe there's hope after all!

Real Guys Are Named Earl

Right now, I have working in my office, a young fellow of 21 who is refreshingly different from most of the clods out there. Here's a guy who came in early and left late. He's always well dressed, extremely polite and thoroughly professional. Hell, this kid is more professional than <u>I</u> am! Even his <u>name</u> is refreshing. Amongst all the trendy Boyds, Martins, Kevins and Jonathans so prevalent today, his name stands out. It's <u>Earl</u>. No fooling around. No affectations. EARL!

My point is, good kids are around. You just have to dig a little deeper to find them. You know, now that I think about it, my office is <u>full</u> of real names: Nick, Russ, Wyatt, Jim, Stuart, and Dick. Now that I think some <u>more</u> about it, I can't think of any trendy names in the boat business at all! At least not in the <u>power</u> boat business! All the people I deal with are named Dave, Mike, Lynn, Frank, Diane, Walter and the like. The only guys in the business with trendy, funny names design <u>sailboats</u>! You remember sailboats, don't you?

Well, young David, I'd like to answer your questions. I really would. My longwinded introduction, however, will necessitate a two or three "parter" once again. Next month in very exciting "Marine Bidet" issue, I promise to get right to your questions. All I can say now is you're off to a good start. At least your name isn't "Boyd."

September 1988

So You Want to be a Yacht Designer? Part 2

I can't stall any longer, kid. I've been mulling over your questions for a couple of months now. I hope these answers will be helpful. Your first and second questions asked what classes I took in high school, if I went to college and where I got my training. This is a long story which will be partially told in this month's piece. (Most of you, I'm sure, couldn't care less about my high school/college days but this is for the "David Martins" out there. I suggest the rest of you turn directly to articles that might interest you.)

Silas Marner?

In high school, young David, I took the regular old stuff. You know, Silas Marner, cutting up frogs and trying to figure out just what the hell "X" is. I finished high school with a solid B average without working too hard. Since there was never any doubt what I wanted to do with my life, I really didn't feel that college was important. No college offered a "Boat Degree" and I felt the best place to learn "Boats" was in slimy bilges. When I was growing up, I really wasn't much interested in anything but boats, in facts, my whole life revolved around the boating season in the Northeast. Since I was a little kid, I hung around boat yards the way yuppies kids today hang around shopping malls. A visit to Minneford Yacht Yard in City Island for me was like a visit to Bloomies for my sister. Besides, there where these two guys working in our boat yard in Whitestone, New York. I'll never forget them. Mickey and Sonny. To me, their life was idyllic. In the fifties when I was twelve or thirteen, they were probably in their late teens or early twenties. By day they worked in the boat yard moving and repairing boats. By night they tooled around in their slick cars chasing women and partying. I remember one day one of them came to work telling me he was badly hung over from an all night party and spent most of the day hanging over the seawall heaving. I thought that was great! What was the point of going to college if this is what I really wanted to do (working at a boat yard but not necessarily heaving)? I had it all figured. I would go to work in a boat yard, get a '54 Mercury Convertible (all black, lowered all around with skirts, glasspacks, foxtails and little purple dots in the taillights), spend days learning every possible thing about boats and nights tooling around with my bimbo blonde girlfriend (at the time I didn't have a blonde bimbo girlfriend but I figured they came with the car). Teenage heaven! I suspect in every kid's life there are a Mickey and Sonny leading them astray.

College Days

My parents, however, had other ideas. My dad, you see, came to this country via Ellis Island in the early 1900's. My mom was born in the United States of immigrant parents and they both attended college the hard way while working full time jobs. Do you think <u>their</u> kid was not going to attend college? There was a little hassle, but not much. Back then, kids usually did what they were told.

Time to choose a college, but what college? I knew that universities teaching Naval Architecture taught <u>Ship</u> naval Architecture. While the principals are the same, it's a whole different field from Yacht Design. Ships were cold and drab and always tried to run you down in the river. I was accepted at a number of good schools including the prestigious Rhode Island School of Design (for Industrial Design), the University of Michigan (Naval Architecture) and the New York Maritime College (Marine Engineering). I figure an Engineering background was the way to go, so I chose the New York State Maritime College at Fort Schuyler going for a degree of "Bachelor of Marine Engineering." My dreams of a car would have to wait three years until I was a senior, however, the blonde bimbo materialized when I was a freshman! One out of two ain't bad and, besides, I talked my dad into buying a slick '57 Plymouth Convertible (which I converted for my use on the weekends by installing bubble skirts).

Everyone said the first semester of college is the toughest. Besides, this was a <u>military</u> college. My high school advisors didn't give me much of a chance being the kind of mocking, laid back, unmilitary guy that I am. It turned out, that the first semester was a breeze! During indoctrination I got some advice from a guy in my class whose brother went to the same school. The advice was, essentially, "consider all this military stuff a <u>game</u>. Simply play the game, never taking it too seriously and you'll do okay." This advice, it turned out, was invaluable both in school and, generally, in <u>life</u>. I ended the semester on the <u>Dean's</u> <u>List</u> with a 3.5 (B+) average (!) and no demerits. I was cool. This college stuff was a snap. Then things started going downhill fast. While New York State Maritime was an excellent school, whose graduates were highly thought of in the industry, for me it had some tremendous disadvantages, namely:

1) It's location on Long Island Sound
2) The library

My decline in college isn't a pretty story, kid. It happened, however, for a good reason. Looking back, I see that if it <u>hadn't</u> happened, I'd probably be working at some interesting job like tube scale analysis or studying high nutrition fish diets for gland seals (inside Marine Engineer's joke). See you next month, kid.

October 1988

So You Want to be a Yacht Designer? Part 3

When things don't go right for a guy in school, he tends to heap the blame on everything but the real reason for his problems. The teacher is a turkey; The sun was in my eyes; My underwear was too tight. In my case, however, I knew <u>exactly</u> what to attribute my declining grades to. It was the damned <u>peninsula</u> and the <u>library</u> -- no doubt about it.

See, the New York State Maritime College is built around an old fort located on a peninsula jutting out into Long Island Sound -- one of the prime pleasure boating areas of the world. Dotting the shores around the fort were places like City Island, Bayside Harbor and Manhasset Bay. The setting was picturesque and, needless to say to a certified boat nut, downright distracting. The main channel went around the peninsula and, I must admit, I spent a lot of time up on the roof of the fort. From my vantage point it was easy to study wake patterns of different hulls. Huckins, Colonial, Chris Craft, Matthews, Wheeler, Richardson. New and old, they were all there. Imagine trying to concentrate in stuff like Mohr's Circle and Adiabatic Compression with this constant parade of boats swirling around the peninsula. I was like a little kid being told to eat his asparagus while a carousel of candy revolved around him. Yes, the peninsula was definitely worth at least a half point on this cadet's average.

My real downfall in college, however, was the discovery of the "Caves" in the library during the latter part of my freshman year. I figure this cost my average at least a point. This particular library was built inside the old, massive, stone, pentagon shaped, fortress. There were no windows, only <u>gun</u> <u>slits</u> (I'm serious!) and the walls were about four feet thick. One small, dark, dreary room of the library had floor-to-ceiling stacks of books hidden amongst which were four little desks and chairs each located next to a gun slit (for easy defense of the forth while studying, I suppose). We called this place "The Caves." The Caves! What a great place to work (or sleep, or hide). I became known as "Caveman." At first, I went there legitimately to find a quiet place to study. But after I wandered around the library a bit, I discovered, to my great excitement, complete, hardbound, back issues of Motor Boating and Yachting magazines from the turn of the century to date! Around 1350 magazines lay there to be devoured. To a boat guy like me, this was akin to archeologists discovering the Dead Sea scrolls. At the time I was trying to fathom stuff like Fluid Mechanics,

Thermodynamics, Differential Equations and Strength of Materials. How could any of these drab subjects compare with studying drawings of a 65' John Wells designed high speed Consolidated commuter boat or a graceful 41' Elco Cruisette? Things got worse. I discovered Lindsey Lord's book "Naval Architecture of Planing Hulls," which I quickly confiscated to prevent some dishonest guy from stealing.

You ask, "Where did I get my training?" Well, a good part of it came from "hands on" experience with my dad's boats and complete immersion in back issues of Yachting and Motor Boating magazines. There was a wealth of information in those magazines: technical articles, prolific new design sections (sometimes a dozen new designs per issue) and "how to" articles. Simultaneously, I started studying Lindsey Lord's book -- the Koran of high-speed yacht design. <u>Here</u> was a book that I could really relate to. After this, Thermodynamics and Fluid Mechanics didn't interest me too much except when I could relate them to boat designs. My grades suffered, but I never failed a course and I <u>did</u> get through college finishing in a proud but undistinguished ranking in my class. Why proud? Well, my class started with around 90 guys. By the time we were First Classmen (seniors), we were down to about 20. Just <u>being there</u> was an accomplishment. I was a survivor! After graduation, I took a job as Third Engineer on the passenger ship "SS INDEPENDENCE" and immediately signed on with the Westlawn School of Yacht Design. Did I need to attend college? Looking back now, the answer is a definite "yes." While most of the stuff you learn in college is immediately relegated to the dumpster of your mind, there's one thing you learn that stays with you. College teaches you <u>how to think</u>.

Before answering your third question concerning "whether I started out as a Naval Architect or worked my way up," let's get our terms straight. Technically, a "Naval Architect" is one who has a degree in Naval Architecture. A Yacht Designer may or may not be a Naval Architect. The answer to your question is I started out as a "Marine Engineer" <u>and</u> worked my way up. Assuming one has the proper background, if one wants to become a Yacht Designer he has two ways to go: hang out a shingle and start "cold turkey" or go to work for an established office. I chose the "cold turkey" route but, unless one has a wealthy family to support him during the lean years, he must take on other work or the "cold turkey" may become cold Spam. I supported myself with a "straight" job for <u>ten years</u> while I developed the business doing marine survey work and taking on any odd design jobs (believe me, many <u>were</u> odd). Listen carefully, young David. Ten years of tapping on punkey hulls with a mallet. Ten years of aft deck enclosure and flyingbridge designs. Ten years of guys with cigars promising designs that never happened. You have to be stubborn and never give up (cigar smoke notwithstanding).

In answer to your forth question concerning the "need" for "Naval Architects" and if I think there will be a call for them in the future, there is an important fact you must realize. Nobody <u>needs</u> a pleasure boat. People may want pleasure boats, people may <u>like</u> pleasure boats, but absolutely no one <u>needs</u> a pleasure boat (save for dope runners, I guess but, then, this would come under the "commercial" definition wouldn't it?) So, unless you're involved in the commercial or naval design field, a Yacht Designer is, essentially, a person who doesn't feel "needed." A Yacht Designer's business is directly tied to the state of the economy. Simply put, when times are good, people order boats and, conversely, when times are tough, people turn to buying things they <u>need</u> like Cornflakes and Spam. You ask if there will be a call for designers when you are old enough. Well, you're twelve years old now. In ten or fifteen years, I figure the American pleasure boat industry will have gone the way of the auto industry. Sixty years ago there were hundreds of American automobile companies -- now, sadly, there are really only three. Merger mania is now rampant in the boat business. There will be a great demand for designers in these huge conglomerates but, unfortunately, they will have to play the old corporate game. You know, three piece suit and wing tips, duplicate memos in triplicate, power lunches and all the rotten, back stabbing politics involved in a large corporation. To succeed, you must become a corporate dip. Unfortunately, Yacht Designers are usually nonconformists, otherwise they'd go into a real profession like rooting around molars or animal husbandry (why isn't there "animal wifery" in this liberated age?) and, I'll bet, most would-be Yacht Designers will have a difficult time playing silly corporate games. I've been there. Fortunately, there will always be a market for custom boats -- especially large custom boats. Imagine spending $3,000,000.00 for a production 100'er only to find five identical vessels berthed around you and the only way you can tell your floating palace from the others is to read the transom. Consequently, there will always be small design offices where young architects can find employment, wear topsiders to work and save the wing tips for weddings and bar mitzvahs.

Well, kid, I'll finish your questions next month. In the meantime, study hard and, whatever you do, STAY OUT OF LIBRARIES!

November 1988

So You Want to be a Yacht Designer? Part 4

(And Hopefully the Last)

*P*art four! When I first got David Martin's letter I thought it was a good basis for a little piece about Yacht Design since I get letters all the time from kids inquiring about the business... But four parts! I guess there's more to this business than I thought. On to David's questions.

You asked if I had to do it over again would I still want to be a Yacht Designer or pick another career? Well, right now, I have a couple of days left before leaving for Italy to attend the Genoa Boat Show. In addition to finishing this masterpiece, I need to complete: an arrangement for a 100'er; a preliminary arrangement for a 140'er; a set of hull lines for an 82'er and check a good number of plans that are stocked up like cordwood in my office. Besides, all this, I'm in the midst of an on going detailed weight calculation for a 78'er that is almost completed. So, young David, right now isn't really a

great time to ask this question and, in fact, I have a list of vocations that look <u>real</u> good to me at this point:
1) Professional Gigolô
2) Unprofessional Gigolô
3) Cotton Stuffer in an Aspirin Bottling Plant
4) Maine Coon Cat Breeder
5) Piano Player in a Bordello

To tell you the truth, I think next time around I'll be a <u>Yacht</u> <u>Broker</u>. These guys have it made. Mostly what these guys do, is drive around in Aston Martin Lagondas with their Gucci topsiders, blue blazers and khaki slacks while talking into their cellular phones. Occasionally, they leave their cars for fancy lunches and dinners or to ride around on luxurious yachts. They fly around the world a lot (first class-Concorde if possible), meeting clients and they make more money selling a given boat that the designer got to design it. So, here I am in the midst of my weight calculations trying to figure out stuff like just how much a half full kitty litter box weights. Yeah, Yacht Brokers have it made. (Before you guys in the business sit down and rip off poison pen letters to me describing how Yacht Designers have it made... This is only a joke okay?) Question: How do you identify a Yacht Broker? Answer: He's the guy with one muscular arm and one anemic arm. The muscular arm is the one that carries the eighteen pound gold Rolex. (Okay, okay, I'd love to have a gold Rolex myself). Fact is, young David, I think I have the best job in the world: conjuring diabolically complicated fiberglass and aluminum puzzles for yacht builders to solve.

In answer to your question number seven, "How long

would it take to design a 40' Sportfisherman?" I must tell you that you've hit a sore spot here. I'm sure most clients would answer, "Way too long." It is a given rule in the Yacht Design World that no client in the RECORDED HISTORY OF MANKIND has ever appreciated how long it takes a Yacht Designer to complete a given piece of work. "YOU SPENT <u>THIS</u> MANY HOURS ON THAT LITTLE DRAWING?" You've got to learn to live with it kid. An Engine/Driveline Installation Drawing, for example, looks deceivingly simple when it's completed but, in fact, requires hours of calculation, research and telephone calls (engine manufacturers hardly ever specify centers of gravities of their engines), in addition to the time drawing the little devil. The fact is, it will take between 500 and 750 hours to properly produce all necessary drawings, calculations and specifications for a modern, high tech, 40' Sportfisherman. WARNING: It's very difficult to make money designing small boats although this is the way most designers must start in the business. The fact is, it takes as long (sometimes longer) to design a 30'er as it does a 50'er. The same number of drawings have to be drawn, the same calculations have to be calculated and the same specifications have to be specked. The designs we've taken a bath on have, invariably, been the 30' and 36'ers.

Finally, to your last question. "What do you think the best college, or schooling, is in the field of Naval Architecture?" Well, you're in it right now kid... in that marina that you go to "throughout the whole year" walking up and down the docks, studying boats and running your family's 31' Jersey.

That's the best way to learn -- that's how I learned. These days, however, in addition to being "dock smart" a college degree in Engineering or Naval Architecture would be most helpful since boats are getting ever more complicated and highly engineered. Besides, as I mentioned before, college teaches one how to think and you'll be doing a lot of that if you become a designer. One of the best schools is Stevens Institute of Technology in Hoboken, New Joisey. (Hoboken? I know it is hard to believe there's anything good in Hoboken, but it is true). There's also, amongst others, Webb, MIT, The University of Michigan and, of course, my alma mater The New York State Marine College at Fort Schuyler. Then, after you finish college (or before) you will need to take a Yacht Design course. Here, there are only two ways to go -- the Westlawn School of Yacht Design (which has a correspondence course founded in 1930) or The Yacht Design Institute which is a residency program. An Engineering or Naval Architecture Degree isn't enough -- you'll need training in small craft design also.

This reminds me of an ad that Westlawn is currently running in all the magazines. Please don't get me wrong -- I like Westlawn... I'm a graduate of Westlawn... I'm on the Board of Directors of Westlawn... but I really think the agency that put the ad together missed the point. Most of you have seen it I'm sure. It's a full page black and white spread leading off with big headlines stating "For love... Or Money." (I think it's important, David Martin, that the question you didn't ask are as important as the ones you did. One of the questions you didn't ask is one that almost everyone else does: "Can you get rich designing yachts?" Guys who go into Yacht Designing to get rich will never be successful. I suggest that Westlawn's headline should read "For Love ... THEN Money".) Anyway, here we see these three guys in the foreground with a largish (40 plus foot) sailboat in the background (That's a laugh -- nobody will ever make any money designing sailboats and, in fact, these days we're seeing a great scramble of ragwagon designers jumping on the power boat bandwagon but that's grist for another article sometime.) Well, here we have these three guys and it's obvious at a glance who they are. They are really caricatures of what people perceive them to be. The one on the left is a salty, gritty looking older guy wearing a watch cap and coveralls and sporting a scrawny beard. He's obviously the jaundiced, seen-it-all, Master Boat Builder. The middle aged guy on the right is wearing a suit and tie and sports and $80.00 Dan Rather haircut. He looks like he just stepped off his corporate jet. Of course, he's the Client. (In fact, this guy really looks like a model trying to look like a guy who just stepped off his corporate jet.) The young guy in the middle is wearing pleated pants, a preppy striped business shirt and a tie. Clutched in his hands is a blueprint partially unrolled. He's kind of a flaky, yokely looking guy who is grimacing while the client is forcefully pointing to the blueprint. This guy, of course, is the Yacht Designer. Looking at the picture, I can imagine they're going saying something like this:

Client to Architect: "You made the damn boat 20' too short."

Architect Thinking to Himself: "I shulda been a Yacht

Broker."

Builder Thinking to Himself: "What damn jerks these guys are."

Thanks for the letter young David. Not only did they provide me the basis for four months of articles but they also will allow me to send reprints of the stories to kids sending me similar letters. Go to it kid. Work hard and, when you're done, call me. You're the kind of guy I'd love to hire.

December 1988

Sailing is Sillier than Ever

It's September 7, 1988. I'm firmly planted in "Ol' Gray," my trusty leather sofa in front of the tube. I'm there to watch the latest America's Cup race. I know what you're thinking. Yes, it's embarrassing to admit that I watch sailboat races but, really folks, I wasn't watching this one for the race -- everyone knew it would be tortoise and hare affair. In past cup races, one might have watched to catch the subtleties of sail changes, or the psychology of tacking duels. This year, however, the only reason I watched the races was to see if any of my boats were in the spectator fleet! I'm serious! Mikelson Yachts in San Diego sells a lot of my boats and I just wanted to see how many showed up for the fiasco in Diego. With the outcome of the race predetermined, America's Cup 27 could be nothing else but a crashing bore. Required couch potato equipment for watching this race: a large bottle of No-Doz, a fresh battery in the remote control and a stack of magazines. When it was over, due to the one-sidedness of the competition and the seedy treatment of the challengers by

Conner and his team, I wasn't real proud to be an American. So Dennis Conner, Sail America and the San Diego Yacht Club, won the America's Cup again. Well big deal and who really cares? Yes, Dennie beat the Kiwi's and the Chicago Bears can beat the Duluth Muskrats and the U.S. can beat Granada and a Ferrari can beat a V.W. bug. Like I said, who cares.

Those of you who tuned in to see the races on T.V. were treated to numerous close-ups of a chubby guy sitting on a cushion on the windward hull of this Catamaran, tiller in one hand, diet Pepsi in the other. It was, of course, our hero, Dennie. I wondered why Dennie was the only one allowed the privilege of a seat cushion. All the rest of his crew had to sit on hard, cold, carbon fibre decks. I also wondered, when he tacked, if he had someone <u>carry</u> his cushion to the opposite hull for him. He reminded me of that famous comic strip character "The Little King." And why does he put that white stuff on his lips all the time? He looks like a kid after a losing battle with a melting vanilla ice cream cone. Somebody give that guy a napkin for God's sake!

Anyone who isn't completely dead from the neck up knows that a 6,000 pound, 60' Catamaran could trounce a 133' Monohull. Once Sail America made the decision to compete in a cat, they went through this huge production: assembling teams of designers, experimenting with exotic materials, having Burt Rutan design a wing sail, retaining and training Dennie and his crew and, finally, building a couple of 60' boats. To call this "overkill" would be "underkill." Hell, a couple of kids -- <u>girl</u> <u>type</u> <u>kids</u> -- in a stock, out of the box <u>Hobie</u> <u>Cat</u> would have been faster than KZ-1 and would have saved Sail America big bucks and much trouble (plus, the kids would have handled the press conferences better than Dennie and his crew). The fact is that KZ-1 was a very fast monohull but a mono is no competition for a cat and everyone knew it. What people didn't know, however, was that Dennie Conner would be such a bore. Truth is, the press conferences after the races offered more competition than what we saw at sea. Here we were treated to the sight of Dennie, surrounded by his beefy bodyguards/crew bravely telling Bruce Far (designer of the KZ-1 Challenger) "Get off the stage you little (bleep). You're a loser." Can you imagine? The America's Cup has finally come to this courtesy of Dennie Conner. One wonders why this man is so pompous. After all, he's the only American in the recorded history of the United States to ever lose the America's Cup. Yes, in the two races and the prerace hype, Dennis was certainly a menace. Not only a menace to the cup races themselves but to the concept of good sportsmanship. He not only beat the Kiwis but he rubbed their noses in it. Well, Dennie, maybe it's time your nose got a little dirty too.

   Call me unpatriotic, but, I've come up with this nefarious, sure fire, scheme by which a challenging country can easily defeat Dennis the Menace and make him look foolish to boot. LISTEN UP YACHT CLUBS OF THE WORLD. What you need to do is challenge the San Diego Yacht Club to race in powerboats. Yes, powerboats. Not any old powerboats, mind you, but big, hairy offshore 50' superboats the likes of "Jesse James" and "Popeyes." One hundred forty mile per hour powerboats. Let's face it. Sailboat racing as a spectator sport is about as exciting as watching a bridge rust. What America's Cup really needs is some excitement: unmuffled exhausts, bright colors, wave jumping at 100 m.p.h..

But, you say, "this is impossible -- the America's Cup is for sailboats only." Well, if one interprets the revered America's Cup Deed of Gift the way Sail America and the San Diego Yacht Club did, it could indeed become a powerboat race. Just as the Deed of Gift didn't specifically state that Catamarans couldn't compete, it <u>also</u> doesn't specifically state that powerboats can't compete. I've got the ol' deed in front of me and it says right here that competition will be "with a yacht or vessel propelled by sails only ...." Well, you sputter, "that obviously eliminates powerboats." Wrong, spinnaker breath. Here's the way it would work: the foreign syndicate offering the challenge would simply form an engine manufacturing company called "SAILS MARINE ENGINES." They would then proceed to develop a marine engine, four of which would power their challenging vessel. WITH A RIG LIKE THIS, NO ONE IN THE WORLD COULD SAY THAT THEIR VESSEL WAS NOT "PROPELLED BY SAILS." The boat would, of course, have a small mast about 12" high to comply with the fifth paragraph of the Deed requiring a mast. Brilliant, no? Don't you love it? It's foolproof! Of course, the SDYC will go to court to challenge the challenge and, certainly, the court will make a similar silly ruling as they did when they allowed the Catamaran to sail against the Monohull.

Imagine then, a helmeted Dennie suited up at the wheel of an Offshore Ocean Racer <u>in completely alien surroundings</u>

(looking something like Mike Dukakis in that tank). While Dennie may know everything about stuff like spinnakers and luffing and weather helm, I'll bet he doesn't know <u>nothing</u> about trim planes or spray rails or surface props. He'd be a sure loser. Then, pompous, Dennie can go back to doing what he does best -- making drapes. By the way, Dennis, I need this set of balloon curtains for my bedroom.....

January 1989

The Scarlet Lace Caper of '62

I can picture it clearly. A night watchman is making his rounds amongst the mothballed Navy and Merchant ships lying in the Hudson River. As he climbs from ship to ship, his flashlight continually scans for something amiss. There on deck of an ex-Navy transport ship, he sees a flash of red in his beam. Stopping to investigate, he leans down and picks up a scrap of <u>red</u> <u>lace</u>. Momentarily he dwells on the fact that this is a strange place to find a piece of lace but this is quickly forgotten and he continues on his rounds. Little did he know that this shred of cloth was all that remained of one of the boldest peacetime undercover operations of all time -- an operation so secret only five people on this earth ever knew about it ... until now.

Surely the statute of limitations on this type of thing has run out by now and I can tell the full story. While I'm sure this expose could be sold to 60 Minutes, I am making the supreme sacrifice of presenting it exclusively for the first time here for a mere fraction of what I could get from 60

Minutes. Sorry Mike, Harry, Ed and Diane.

As some of you may know, my college alma mater is the New York State Maritime College at Fort Schuyler, New York. It's a military college and one of the best in the world for marine engineering and marine science. The way the school worked is that one attended classes from September through June, then at the end of the school year, took a three month cruise to Europe on the school's training ship. The purpose of the cruise was to give cadets "hands on" experience (I must say we got a lot of "hands on" experience especially during liberties ashore in ports like Nice, Oslo and Copenhagen.) Normally one would make his last cruise at the end of his second class (or Junior) year, thereafter becoming a first classman (Senior) and graduating in June. In my class however, there were five of us who, for one reason or another, missed a cruise and therefore had to make it up <u>after</u> our senior year was completed. What this meant was that, for the five of us, as soon as the ship returned to her dock at Fort Schuyler, we were graduated. We all therefore treated this last cruise as somewhat of a long, fully paid lark. As long as one didn't screw up too badly graduation was assured.

I remember that cruise of '62 with great affection. I believe we visited Italy, France, Holland and Spain that year. I <u>know</u> we visited Holland, for it was in Rotterdam that one of our band of five (it wasn't me -- honest) obtained a coveted trophy. This treasure happened to be a woman's unmentionable. Well, to elaborate a bit, it was an undergarment from one of the local Rotterdam young ladies. Oh hell, why don't I just come out and say it. It was a pair of

<u>red</u> <u>lace</u> <u>panties</u> obtained from a bimbo in the infamous Canal Street area! Okay? Bikini style as I remember. The conditions concerning exactly how and why this cadet obtained the garment was never really clear and doesn't really matter. The fact is it was now late August and the ship was steaming home and this guy had in his possession a pair of red lace bimbo's panties (from Rotterdam).

Let me set the scene. Here we have mom and dad's prized sons returning from a three month European training cruise. For those on their first cruise it was, probably, the first time they'd ever been away from home. Their departure was a sad experience and their arrival would be one of intense joy. For us grizzled veterans of three cruises, it was the end of an era. We had made it through three cruises, four years of military tyranny and difficult higher education. Upon setting foot ashore we would become graduated, degreed, licensed free civilians going off into the world to real jobs.

The ship had anchored off Riker's Island in Long Island Sound the afternoon before arrival (which was a Sunday) and, like every other year, after the anchor was set, our ship was surrounded by boats -- <u>American</u> boats full of <u>American</u> people and, most importantly, <u>American</u> girls. It was the first time we'd seen Americans in three months! That night our little band of five held a party for the ship's officers for which we broke out our best (illegal) hidden rations. We made some nice hors d'oeuvres, set up a bar and played music on our homemade gimbal mounted turntable secretly located in a locker. Like I said, we really didn't care and it was too late for anybody to do anything about it. It was that night over our "Bay Rum Surprises" (tastes awful, smells great) that our band of five conspired to pull off the greatest cadet coup of all times. Before we became civilians the next morning, we wanted a great, final, unforgettable gesture of thumbing our noses at the military establishment. So we put together a nefarious plan.

Here was this guy with a pair of red lace bimbo's panties (from Rotterdam) and he really didn't know what to do with them. Tomorrow, he would meet <u>his girl</u> on the dock..... <u>the love of his life</u> ... the girl who was soon to become his <u>wife</u>. How could he explain his souvenir from Rotterdam? Yet, his trophy was too precious to merely throw in the garbage or over the side. It deserved something better. We knew as soon as the ship rounded the peninsula the next morning, we would be greeted by a dock full of sweethearts, mothers, fathers, brothers, sisters, wives, grandmothers, grandfathers, uncles, aunts and nieces. Some brought their pets. This was a big event for the families: the homecoming of their precious sons after a long, tough summer overseas. Us cadets would be lined up around the decks at parade rest in our smart uniforms. What a magnificent, proud moment for the families. Their loved ones were home at last.

Our nefarious plan went like this. When a ship is underway, she carries her colors on the mast yardarm. As soon as a ship is docked or anchored, however, the crew "shifts colors" meaning that the ensign comes down from the yardarm while, simultaneously, another goes up on the flagstaff at the stern -- the proper place to display colors while in port. The next morning we were underway bound for the dock, a short 20 minutes away. As soon as the anchor was slipped and the ensign was run up the yardarm, one of us stealthily climbed atop the superstructure below and adjacent to the yardarm halyards and carefully hid the aforementioned red lace bimbo's panties (from Rotterdam) atop a big ventilator. They were affixed at the waist by thin, invisible, threads to the part of the halyard that would run <u>up</u> when the colors came down.

The plan was flawless and the night before we excitedly pictured the whole thing. The ship approaches the dock, the cadets are at parade rest in their spotless uniforms, the dock is jammed with the cadets' proud loved ones eagerly waiting to see their sons. The tension is unbearable. The ship docks. The colors are shifted and as the ensign comes down, up goes a pair of red lace bimbo's panties (from Rotterdam) rippling proudly in the stiff breeze! Simultaneously, we had prepared on a bed sheet a big sign that would be unfurled as the panties went up saying "Out of the Zoo n '62." What a scene! <u>Take</u> <u>that</u>, <u>establishment</u>!

The great morning finally arrived but, sadly, it turned out to be a bomb. The "zoo" sign went down all right but the panties never went up. Upon investigation after the fact, it was found that heavy dew from the night before weighed down the red lace bimbo's panties (from Rotterdam) such that the threads broke as the colors were being shifted and the panties remained atop the vent to be forgotten forever (or at least until I remembered them 26 years later).

We all come close to moments of true greatness. Many times fate or some small unplanned incident intrudes to ruin the best laid plans. We didn't count on the red lace bimbo's panties (from Rotterdam) getting soaked with morning dew. Call it bad engineering. Had the scheme worked it would have been logged in the annals of the great Fort Schuyler legends taking its place atop the list including: the cadet who got his girlfriend pregnant atop the fort, the green shirted madman who streaked around the ship yelling obscenities (it was one of us but we had the officers convinced that a green shirted madman was on the ship), the guys who raided King's Point (that trade school across the river) and stole their huge bell, the cadet riot on Newport field, the day the Captain tore part of a Sicilian dock away when he forgot to release the stern lines and, finally, the famous ravaging of Spanish society girls at a Barcelona tea party in '59.

But the fact is that it <u>didn't</u> work and, therefore, the scheme must be relegated to the "what might have been" file. It was one of the major disappointments of my life. Now the five of us must go through life wondering what might have been had the red lace bimbo's panties (from Rotterdam) deployed as per plan. What makes things worse is the knowledge that we literally came <u>within</u> <u>a</u> <u>thread</u> of greatness.

February 1989

Italian Holiday
Part 1

*I*ntroductory Note: You are a part of marine publishing history. This is a benchmark article -- it is probably the first ever to appear in a boating magazine that has nothing whatsoever to do with boats -- a true milestone in the marine literary field. "What is this," you say, "Travel and Leisure" magazine?" In reply, may I state as I have before that I really don't care since these articles are basically written for my own amusement. This is a two part article, the second part of which does deal somewhat with boats. It just so happened that the article had to be divided at a point where boats were not mentioned in part one. Sorry. If you want to read about boats, I suggest you turn to the articles elsewhere in this book including the one on converting bikini tops to fender holders. As far as I'm concerned, since this trip ultimately was for the purpose of attending the Genoa Boat Show, this is an article about boats.

It was a side trip planned before the Genoa Show the purpose of which was to explore in Milano -- supposedly the style center of the world -- then shoot north to Lago Maggiore to experience Italy's fabled northern lake region. During our trip, my wife Regina and I encountered many strange and wonderful things. The strange part started at J.F.K. airport the night of departure...

As we walked down the tunnel entering the T.W.A. boarding lounge, we were aware of great commotion ahead of us. There about 50' down the tunnel was a big guy also walking towards the lounge, I mean a big guy -- his silhouette obscured the light at the end of this particular tunnel. We could see people coming the other way staring up at him with slack jaws and terror in their eyes while shrinking back into the dark recesses of the passageway to let him pass. It looked like a scene from a King Kong movie. We walked a little faster. As we got closer, although we were still only viewing the back of this hulk, I knew immediately who he was. Though I'm no wrestling fan, it was obvious that it was <u>Andre</u> <u>the</u> <u>Giant</u>! Andre the Giant -- one of the most famous professional wrestlers in the world. The moniker is an accurate one: Andre is over 7' tall, weighing in at something above 500 pounds. After we got to the lounge area, Andre disappeared -- probably into one of the V.I.P. (Very Imposing People) lounges.

After we boarded, took off and settled down for the crossing, I realized Andre was seated in the front of our plane. I wondered where giants sat on a 747 (in the middle occupying two seats so the plane could fly without a list). I wondered if they charged Andre for extra weight. I wondered if they charged him for two seats. Unfortunately, these questions will probably never be answered. My main wonder, however, was "why is Andre the Giant going to Milano?" I started thinking that, possibly, there was a man of culture under that huge, tough visage. Yeah, that's it, this hard guy image was all P.R. Andre was going to take in the cathedrals and the museums of Milano and maybe have some Italian silk suits tailored for him. This thought was dashed as soon as we got into town. Everywhere you went, there was Andre meanly staring at you from a big poster with huge letters reading "Wrestling!" So much for giant culture and so much for the image of Milano as a bastion of culture and refinement. Call me uncultured, call me unrefined but, in my humble opinion, Milano was disappointing -- just another big, drab, industrial city. On the Fexas fun-o-meter scale of one to ten, Milano rates a four. The fact is, we couldn't wait to get out of Milano. The city's one redeeming feature (though no fault of its own) was its ability to keep one amused because prices are truly laughable.

The jokes started with the taxi ride from the airport to downtown Milan ($75.00 plus tip). The hotel was supposedly a five star. It's funny, but hotel stars in Milano must be burnt out, dormant stars -- they're certainly not quasars. I rated the hotel no more than a two and a half in spite of the fact that Mark Gastineau and Brigitte what's her name stayed there and a magnificent red Ferrari Testarossa was parked out front (average room about $375.00 a night).

A walk through town confirmed our greatest fears. We had lunch for two, consisting of little more than bread and water ($20.00). Afterwards, we stopped at a pastry place and foolishly bought one chocolate truffle and a small piece of almond crisp ($13.00). We took a five minute taxi ride back to the hotel ($10.00 plus tip). That night we had an average dinner ($200.00). The next day we went back into town to experience more wonders. In a shoe store was a pair of Topsiders made in the United States ($220.00). In a bakery we saw a small chocolate cake about six inches in diameter ($25.00). On Designer Row, we saw a black wool going-to-work dress ($1400.00). There were many fancy stores, some of which with entire fascias of beautiful varnished teak and polished brass trim looking like the superstructure of an old Trumpy (be prepared to pay a brightwork surcharge on whatever you buy there). Another lunch ($25.00) and another cab ride back to the hotel ($10.00 plus tip) and another mediocre dinner ($220.00) and we were really ready the next morning (Sunday) to bail out of Milano. We're just not big city people, I guess.

At Hertz, I couldn't get the car I reserved (I *never* get the car I reserve.) All they had was a cheap Opel which was unwashed with a badly stained driver's seat, a rear view mirror that kept falling off, a buzzy engine, a fuzzy carpet and an empty gas tank ($70.00 per day). Our major amusement on the trip North was endless speculation about just how the driver's seat got stained. Use your imagination. With the tank empty and all the service stations closed on Sunday, we were forced to go to one of the few automated gas stations in the city. I don't understand. I really don't. Above the automated pumps was a large sign saying you can absolutely have no more than 40,000 liras worth of gasoline (about $30.00). Now $30.00 only half fills the tank of your average European econobox, so we thought we'd have to find another station to fill up. But wait a minute. Cars were lined up to use these pumps and, with a flash of brilliant deductive reasoning, I realized that the machine didn't know if it was me or the guy behind me getting the next 40,000 liras worth of gas. In a few seconds the machine <u>recycles</u> itself and you can have another 40,000 ... and another 40,000 ... and another 40,000 -- in fact as much as you want. I really don't understand.

Next month, I promise I will talk a bit about boats -- mutant lake boats to be specific. Oh yes -- please don't send me letters saying I'm anti-Italian. Fact is, I <u>love</u> Italy, her people, her great food, her cars, her boats and the Italian way of life. It's not Italy's fault that things are expensive because the dollar is lower than <u>whale</u> <u>poop</u>!

March 1989

Italian Holiday
Part 2
The Vongole Incident

Last month, you were treated to a piece about Milano that had absolutely nothing whatsoever to do with boats. This month, as promised, part of the article will address boats as we look at the mutant lake boats of Lake Maggiore. Next month the entire piece will concern boating (more or less).

Unlike Milano, the hotel on Lake Maggiore (one of Italy's magnificent lakes in her Northern Alps region) was a quasar five star. Des Iles Borromees was at least a hundred years old and was restored to exquisite turn-of-the-century condition. Our room faced the lake, the hotel restaurant was outstanding and the tab for room and meals was quite a bit less than Milano. (Travel tips: 1) When traveling Italy, look for the little restaurants with crummy looking handwritten menus displayed outside. These little mom-and-pop places usually have outstanding food at reasonable prices. 2) For outstanding lunches hit the local delis in town, buying an assortment of Italian breads, salamis, mortadella, veal, a bottle of vino, some mineral water and a couple of gigantic bosc pears. Everything will cost about $15.00 for two people and it will truly make you redefine the term "pig out."

(Here comes the boat part folks. Pay attention -- it's not that long.) Lago Maggiore is served by a large fleet of water taxis between 30' and 35' long with V-drive engines in the extreme stern. They are very clean, well-kept, craft and run people from points on the shore or to one of the islands in the middle of the lake. There are no docks around the lake -- only makeshift platforms cantilevered out from the bank. The bottom is rocky and rolls up from the lakebed. The first time we docked, I couldn't believe what was happening. Our skipper headed for the platform at a good clip. We were only a few feet from shore when I realized that he must have lost control of the boat or the engine controls jammed because he didn't slow down. As we prepared for the impact and ducked for cover, the boat hit the rocks. It's enough to make a boat lover cringe. What happened was nothing! <u>Nothing</u>! The boat slid smoothly up on the rocks coming to a stop with the companionway exactly aligned with the platform. <u>These guys had it wired</u>! The captain cut the engine, opened the door in the forward part of the cabin and let the passengers out. Business as usual on Lago Maggiore. WARNING THIS STUNT WAS PERFORMED BY PROFESSIONALS. DO NOT TRY THIS WITH YOUR BERTRAM AT THE YACHT CLUB. The boats -- of fiberglass or wood -- have evolved (or mutated) to take this kind of abuse with beefed up stems and cut away forefoots. Since there is no tide on the lake, the boats are left this way overnight. They don't even need docklines. To undock, it's simply full astern and the boat slides back down into the water.

Our five days in Lago Maggiore ended too quickly but it was time to drive to the coast in order to be at the Genoa boat show Saturday morning. Our plan was to stay over in Camogli Thursday night, take Friday to explore the coast by car, return the car in the major port of La Spezia at the southern end of the Ligurian coast and be back in Camogli Friday night. It was on this last day before the boat show that one of the highlights of the trip occurred.

We left Camogli in the early morning in our little white Opal with the badly stained driver's seat and rearview mirror that kept falling off. The first town we visited was the beautiful city of Rapallo. Rapallo has one of the largest marinas I've ever seen chock full of Italian zoomo, go-fast boats. The great number of "big speedboats" from 50' to 70' surprised me. Day boating is very popular there. Continuing south, we encountered Portofino, Chiavari and stopped at Sestri Levanti for lunch. We picked a beautiful restaurant with big picture windows overlooking the Mediterranean and the small port. Because of what would follow, I'll never forget what my wife Regina and I had for lunch: <u>Spaghetti</u> <u>Vongole</u> (spaghetti in garlic and oil with a generous portion of tiny clams mixed in). It was complemented by delicious bread and butter and a few glasses of local white vino. Great lunch! We continued south and, for the final leg, decided to go inland through the mountains to La Spezia. Italian mountain driving! Here I was stuck with this abysmal Opel Italian rent-a-bomb instead of the performance car I asked for. Where was my Corvette with the gumball tires when I needed it? The road in the mountains was switchback city -- blind curves, smaller mountains between larger mountains, narrow tunnels, no traffic and no "Radar Nazis" hidden behind every billboard. <u>Driver's paradise</u>! Since we were going south, the edge of the road was mostly sheer drop offs with no protective guard rail to keep things interesting. So here I am in the crummy Opel and I figure what the hell, I'll drive the car at its limit however meager it may be. So I'm upshifting, downshifting, heel and toeing, clipping apexes and, generally, having a blast doing my best Fangio imitation. Even with a rotten car, it was great. My sweet wife strapped in next to me withstood the torture without a word until, about fifteen minutes into the ride she remarked "I don't feel well." Regina was becoming a bit green as the spaghetti vongole careened around in her stomach. The precipitous cliffs just outside her window didn't help. We continued on. I few minutes later I heard "I <u>really</u> don't feel well. You'll have to stop the car." Luckily I found a spot with a wide shoulder, pulled off the road and turned off the car. The lovely Regina stepped out and proceeded to lose part of her spaghetti vongole. The trip continued. Soon, I heard "You need to stop the car again" but this time there was absolutely no place to stop with sheer granite to the left and 500'dropoffs to the right. As we continued at a slower pace, I told Regina that, if an emergency came up, to put her head out the window and not worry about it which is exactly what she did. This made her feel much better and I forged on. Now we were coming down out of the mountains encountering small villages. The first one was a typical sleepy mountain village with a few stone and masonry houses along the road, a Carabiniere station, some small stores, the requisite church and groups of people who always seem to be in the streets. As we drove through at a greatly reduced pace, I started noticing people pointing to our car. When we came to a stoplight, people turned away as they walked by. What the hell was going on? The next town was a little bigger and closer to the road. We got the same reaction there. Now we were coming down the steep hills into La Spezia. Not knowing exactly where the rental drop off was, we ended up lost-driving through an area of street vendors. Both sides of the road were filled with stalls selling all kinds of things: food, clothes, hardware but mostly food. The streets were jammed with people. As we drove through, little kids looked at the car with wide eyes, pointed and ran away waving their arms and screaming. Dogs retreated with tails between their legs. Grownups gestured, became a bit green and turned away with their hands over their mouths. When we reached a quiet spot, I stopped and investigated. The entire passenger door of our little white Opel was adorned with spaghetti vongole! It almost looked fresh. The run through the mountains had dried it somewhat but its origin was unmistakable. We continued through town trying to keep the passenger side of the car hidden against walls, shrubbery, etcetera. "We really can't return the car like this" Regina said and I agreed thinking of a great spaghetti vongole penalty atop the already steep rental costs. We would have to get rid of it, but how?

We devised a scheme. We found a gas station, pulled in and hid the passenger side against a whitewashed wall. While Regina got out and diverted the attendant by asking instructions and adjusting her skirt, I grabbed a sponge and bucket that was lying around and quickly washed the door. Hertz never knew a thing.

That evening we hopped a train for Camogli and the next morning attended the fantastic Genoa Boat Show which was better than ever. Although it wasn't funny at that time, Regina and I laugh about the Spaghetti Vongole incident frequently now. I only wish I had taken pictures. She's even added it to our menu at home. Next year, we plan to make a similar excursion but with a better car... and a big bucket.

April 1989

Mr. Penske, Take me Home
Part 1
An Open Letter to Roger Penske

Dear Mr. Penske:

Although we've never met, we have corresponded a while back about boats. I feel I know you. I've been following your career from the time when you were racing Corvettes in the sixties through your car dealerships, D.D.A. distributor, truck fleet and, of course, at Indianapolis every May. I've always admired your cool demeanor and organizational skills. Now that you have acquired Detroit Diesel Allison (now called Detroit Diesel Corporation), we have to talk.

This letter is prompted by your new company's announcement concerning computerizing our trusty, reliable friendly Detroit Diesels. I am not an engineering conservative and, in fact, if Mike Dukakis were an engineer, I'd probably be on his side. We've always prided ourselves on advanced engineering in our designs. We designed the first large, fully composite production fiberglass boat in 1980 and since then have graduated to vinyl esters, unidirectionals, carbon fibres, etc., etc.. We consider our designs "the highest of tech". Of course, when we look to fit engines in our hulls, we look for the same: high power to weight ratio, compact size, ease of maintenance, reliability, etc.. We are responsible for hundreds of Detroit Diesel installations in our designs all over the world. Also, we have a great number of new designs on the boards designed to take Detroit Diesel power, so I was very interested to read about your plans to <u>electronically control</u> combustion in the 92 series engines. In short, the old familiar, reliable mechanical fuel injection pump and push/pull, hydraulic or air controls will be replaced by electronic injectors at each cylinder and "fly by wire" controls run entirely by that nemesis of the average man -- the dreaded black box.

Over two years ago when the magazine was just a skinny rag, I wrote an article titled "A Plea For Low Tech." In it, I bemoaned the fact that black boxes are creeping into our marine engine rooms. An excerpt: "Look what's happening! Marine engine manufacturers are introducing <u>fuel injection</u> to their gasoline engines and breakerless ignitions and computerized engine controls. The latest fuel injection systems are of the "port injection" type, where a computer sends a command to a little solenoid valve at each cylinder telling it when to open and close. This type of system can't be far behind on diesel engines either. Scary! Some larger yachts are already controlled by "fly-by-wire" systems, where steering and engine controls are cycled purely through electrical impulses via wires. Scarier! In a hydraulic system, you can look at lines and cylinders to detect a malfunction, but you can't "see" an electrical leak. You can't look at a printed circuit board and see if there's a problem. You can't "see" what's going on inside those funny little diodes and chips. One can't stop progress Mr. Penske and, I know, whether we like it or not, we are in the black box age. (Creeping black boxism first showed up in our T.V.'s, then in our computers, then in our cars and now they are invading our engine rooms like a modern day Black Plague!) This stuff really looks terrific in a four color spread in a magazine but, believe me, it won't look so great on a wet and stormy Sunday afternoon when the same poor slob who admired the ad is all "asses and elbows" in the engine compartment trying to get the engine running so he can get home Sunday night and be on the job Monday morning to pay for the boat.

Although I'm an engineering liberal, when it comes to marine engines, I am ultra conservative. Let me tell you a little story based on personal experience. Our first acquaintance with electronic engine management systems was one of our large yachts. On startup and sea trials, where an engine manufacturer would normally supply one mechanic, we always had at least two. One was your typical diesel mechanic type. A burley bloke who had grease on his arms and a gruff manner. The other guy was from the moon. His job was to attend the computers that managed the engines. This guy looked like the robot on "Lost In Space." He had harnesses strapped all over him with funny looking meters and test equipment in every pocket. He was surrounded by an aura of mystery and superiority and never lifted a wrench or got his hands dirty. He was the "computer nerd" technician whose sole job was to attend to the black boxes. As I remember it, sea trials were progressing nicely but the port engine was hunting badly at idle. It so happened that the computer nerd was away for a few days and when he returned, he strapped on his gear, went down to the engine room and after what was no more than a few minutes, returned with the engine now idling smoothly. "What did you do?" he was queried. I must say his answer set me back. In fact it stunned me. The answer was a nonchalant "Oh, just readdressed the chip. ("READDRESSED THE CHIP? WHAT THE HELL DOES THAT MEAN? Do you go down the engine room, bow and say to the black box "NICE TO SEE YOU AGAIN MR. CHIP?") I've always considered myself a more than adequate marine mechanic, most times able to get myself out of nearly any mechanical fix imposed on me, but what the hell do I do if I have to "readdress a chip?" Well, I'll tell you what "readdressing a chip" means. It means that on any extended voyage it is almost mandatory that a computer nerd accompany you. In fact, these computer guys are making regular trips across the Atlantic on the various electronically controlled megayachts doing crossings these days.

I'm sorry, Mr. Penske, but I've run out of space and will have to continue this letter next month. Please consider this introductory material. Next month I'll get to my point. In the meantime, I've resigned myself to the fact that I'll have to become an antennae head computer nerd myself if I'm to be able to repair modern machinery. To that end, I've already sprung to action and taken the first step: got a pair of horned rim glasses, then I broke them in two places and taped them

ARTICLES

together with a big globs of masking tape ...

May 1989

Mr. Penske, Take me Home Part 2

Mr. Penske, let me put this on a basis near and dear to your heart -- the automotive field. Among the cars I own are three Corvettes. The stark contrast in engines between the oldest one -- a '57 with mechanical fuel injection versus the newest one -- Chevy's latest high tech, electronically controlled gewgaw laden missile is truly, like night and day.

The long and the short of it is with some fairly simple tools I can maintain, repair and even rebuild my '57 in my little shop at home. The fuel injection system is strictly mechanical and by reading the manual, one can easily understand how it works and what each component does and, by deduction, how to repair each item if it goes wrong. The ignition system is conventional old style: coil/condenser/distributor with rotor. The utilitarian, easy to access, uncrowded engine space is a sight to behold. The installation is stark and clean with a minimum of wiring and piping running about the space. It's a real pleasure to work on this engine. The fact is that the engine installation in my '57 Corvette can be directly compared to the typical marine engine installation of today -- straightforward and clean. The new Corvette is a different story altogether. The "tuned port fuel injection" system and the ignition system are controlled by the <u>Black</u> <u>Plague</u> -- mysterious black boxes which, it seems, have gained a foothold in the engine room of this car and multiplied prolifically. I'd no sooner try to troubleshoot this engine than I would my Hewlett Packard computer (based on my experience, even Chevy has a problem maintaining this beauty). The new Corvette's engine room is <u>packed</u> <u>full</u> of gear. It looks like Chevy put in all the necessary equipment, then sent the car to a <u>crusher</u> to squeeze the body and frame around the machinery! If you want to do anything more complicated than changing a plug, better call Mr. Goodnerd. Both engines utilize the <u>same</u> <u>block</u>! It's important to note, that while the new car obviously has better aerodynamics, more sophisticated suspension and far better tires, the old car is about a <u>second</u> <u>quicker</u> to sixty and produces wonderful free revving, flowing power in a nice, predictable band. Your foot on the accelerator is directly connected to a flap that meters the amount of charge entering the engine. Engine revs are directly proportional to accelerator position and it <u>feels</u> <u>good</u>! You know the feeling I'm sure. In the new car, the fast pedal is connected to the "tuned ports" via a jungle of servos, sensors, chips, diodes, wires, capacitors, etcetera. The engine never really idles very smoothly hunting anywhere from 580 to 790 rpm (the chip probably needs to be re-addressed -- see, I'm learning). Pressing on the accelerator gives one a kind of detached, remote controlled feeling of power. Is this what we're destined for in the marine field? I fear, the difference between my '57 and new Corvette is exactly what we'll be seeing in marine engine rooms in the future as power accessories, sensors, servos and black boxes are added. If my '57 dies on the street I, with my little tool box in the trunk, can pop the hood and, with a screwdriver, wrench, coat hanger and tape (and sometimes a big hammer), get the car running again to get home. When the new Corvette gives up, it's time to call for the hook. In short, the "take home mode" in the '57 is my box of tools. In the new Vette, it's the soles of my shoes. This is the crux of my letter, Mr. Penske: <u>getting one home</u>.

I know we can't stop progress and I know your electronic fuel injection system has been used successfully in trucks for many years and I know that, for example, on an 8-92 the system represents about 25 additional horsepower for which I am thankful. But I also know that getting stranded on the road is a little different than getting stranded at sea. If we can't have an engine that the average guy can troubleshoot and repair with wrenches and screwdrivers (and a big hammer) and if we are to live with the Black Plague, consider giving us a backup, <u>emergency</u> "get home" mode designed into the system. It doesn't matter if, in this "get home mode," the engine runs rough or blows black smoke or doesn't attain optimal fuel efficiency. The important thing is that it <u>will</u> <u>run</u> and get one to the dock.

While you're at it, consider a backup on the electronic engine controls too. Let's face it, electrical stuff on boats was never any great shakes. From the time the first light bulb was hooked up to a primitive battery at sea, man has been fighting the dreaded green electrical crud. I'm talking simple electrical stuff here like a positive and negative wire connected to a six volt lightbulb. Electrical connections in a harsh, saltwater marine environment slowly turn to caca. The difference is that, back then, if you lost a light it was no big deal but, nowadays, with electrical systems controlling engine throttle, clutch and, maybe, steering, it's another matter entirely. Most of these systems are presently installed on large yachts. These vessels usually carry a <u>trained engineer</u> who can diagnose and fix simple problems and who, more importantly, constantly <u>maintains</u> his vessel's systems. Things are a little different when these same systems are installed on Uncle Frank's 50' Condo Craft, whose engine room looks like the <u>LaBraya tar</u> pits.

I'm sure you and your engineers have already addressed these problems and probably have solutions to them now (or will have by the time the engines are available). In any case, I'm glad to see a guy like you has taken over a major marine engine firm. With your experience with things mechanical and your management skills, only good things will result. The fact is, if there wasn't someone like you heading up a company like Detroit Diesel Corporation, I could never write a letter like this. Writing a letter to some faceless corporate head is a little different than writing a letter to the man I used to watch race Corvettes in the sixties and the guy I now see on the tube every Memorial Day. Keep up the good work Mr. Penske but, with your new engines, please find a way to TAKE ME HOME!

Sincerely,
Tom Fexas

June 1989

Pondering

It is 9:10 a.m., La Guardia Airport, New York. My Delta flight 494Y scheduled to leave for West Palm Beach at 8:10 a.m. is still on the ground. The problem is a rather simple one -- the communications system between the cockpit and the stewardess station at the aft end of the plane is inoperable. Regulations require that the plane can't fly until this link is restored. The apologetic pilot comes on the P.A. and announces that, unfortunately, this system is "computer controlled" thereby making the fix much more complicated than it would have been had an old fashioned communication system been installed. This glitch was discovered about a half hour before scheduled roll back and six of Delta's finest technicians have been feverishly scurrying around for an hour and a half with no results. Figuring I deserved it (having bad mouthed computers in this column for the past two months) I sat back and pondered. When computers go down one has a lot of time to ponder. Here we have a mega million dollar aircraft a Lockheed L1011 to be exact -- dead on the ground because one of its computers crapped out. The technicians with gear strapped all over them as (computer technicians are wont to do) are working hard to find the problem. One guy in the back, Joe, is yelling to the guy in the cockpit "HEY FRANK, CAN YOU HEAR ME NOW?" Frank replies in the negative. Now if Frank and Joe can communicate by hollering back and forth I wondered, why do we need electronic communication at all?

Computers have been developed to a stage where they are super reliable. The fact is, however, that no matter how reliable they may be they can and do fail. Just think: how many times have you been stymied by the phrase "Sorry, the computer is down." This has happened to all of us at airports, hotels, banks, credit card companies, etc. When this occurs, your little world is thrown into an uproar since you can't get your air reservations or your hotel room or your bank balance or your credit card approved. When the computer goes down on your boat, it can ruin your entire weekend... or worse. But, at least you will have time to ponder...

I've got a real Dan Rather for you: we are in the midst of a great plot by an elite group of individuals to take over the world! The Commies have tried to control the world and have failed miserably (they can't control their own countries much less the world). This elite group, however, has nearly succeeded in a very short period of time.

Who are these people? Perhaps a Spector-like organization as in the James Bond movies? Aliens from outer space? The Mafia? No, it's really much less complicated than that. It's NERDS. Computer nerds to be exact and their absolute control of this planet is the ultimate REVENGE OF THE NERDS.

Yeah, that foolish movie wasn't too far astray.

You know when you were a kid in high school, there were always these skinny guys in your class with squeaky voices, glasses and pimples? These were the "90 pound weaklings" that got sand kicked in their faces on the beach. These were the guys who buttoned the top button of their shirts and struck out with girls and carried big black lunch boxes to school. These were the guys who stayed home studying while the rest of us were out driving fast cars and chasing bad women. Well, these guys grew up with a great resentment towards the rest of the world and a vengeance to get even. These are the guys that, when they grew up, became <u>computer</u> technicians.

And, now, the world is nearly theirs. What Hitler with his great war machine couldn't do in eight years and what the commies and all their propaganda and expansionist policies couldn't do in forty years, these guys have done with a keyboard and a video screen in ten years. Now it's 9:40 a.m. and the plane is yet to get rolling. I'm thinking that we should have treated these guys better back in high school.

Pretty soon, you know, we won't be able to <u>go to the can</u> unless a computer is up. Think I'm joking? Let me introduce you to a little gizmo called the Washlet, a technological wonder manufactured by Toto from our friends in Japan. This is an object that completely goes against the mechanics credo which states "if it ain't broke don't fix it." Now there's hardly anything in the world more reliable than a toilet. You flip the lever, opening a valve which allows water to flow by gravity through the bowl. A marvel of simplicity. What this little Japanese whizzer is, see, is a fully computerized toilet/bidet controlled by a handheld wireless remote control unit just like the one for your T.V. set. Press the remote and the toilet flushes. You can even do it from across the room. But that's only the beginning. Press another button and you will hear the sound of a servomotor extending a wand from the bowl. This oscillating wand emits a stream of warm water which automatically rinses your better end. Press another button and you get dried with a blast of warm air. The seat is electrically warmed and included is a built in deodorizer (computer controlled of course).

I'm not joking here! Never ones to let good things remain static, Toto is further improving this wonderful invention. They are developing a toilet that, in addition to the previously described features, automatically analyzes urine, announces blood pressure and heartbeat rate! THIS IS ON THE LEVEL FOLKS. Believe me, even I couldn't dream up something like this.

The problem is we are being over-computerized. Initially computers took over functions that were becoming impossible to accomplish manually like file keeping, airlines reservations, etc. Now with all these reductive functions used up, the nerds are searching for ever more fertile territory. Do you know your station wagon will soon have computer controlled steering, suspension, engine combustion, breaking traction control and even muffling. Yes, muffling. There's this little computer, see, that analyzes the noise made by the engine and produces "anti-noise" 180 degrees out from the engine noise thus nullifying the initial sound. I said it before, and I'll say it again. PRETTY SOON YOU WON'T BE ABLE TO

TOW YOUR DAMN CAR AWAY UNLESS A COMPUTER IS UP.

Things are clearly getting out of hand. 10:10 a.m. Delta's technicians continue screaming back and forth but they still haven't closed the door. I resume pondering... What can we do to fight this terrible scourge? Some brave Americans are fighting back already with something called "retrotech" or "yestertech": bringing back yesterday's technology. Most of our enginerooms are "yestertech" -- much the same as they have been for 50 years but it can't remain so for long. Though I have never been a big fan of the Chrysler Corporation, they should be congratulated for a car now making the rounds that will, hopefully, go into production soon. It's called the Viper and it's a throwback to the Ford Cobra of the sixties. Remember the Ford Cobra? Not much more than a chassis and body with a huge engine. It was designed to do three things and three things only: accelerate, stop and maneuver. (What more does a car really need to do?) The Viper is much the same though wrapped in a voluptuously aerodynamic body. They say it may not even have roll down windows and certainly won't be ladened with the computered gadgets that even today's cheapest cars sport. Powered by a huge V-10 engine, this car is designed for fun at the usable low end of the scale -- not 200 m.p.h. It will be straightforward and simple a true breath of fresh air in today's over complicated automotive world.

I want one.

The point is that, if we don't fight back, the nerds will soon take over the pleasure boating industry and have control of our weekends as well as our weekdays. There are some things that nothing but a computer can do. However, there are other things that the nerds should leave alone... like my toilet and boat. It's now 11:10 a.m. -- we are three hours late and still on the ground. Frank and Joe continue to communicate the old fashioned way via soundwaves in the air (hollering). By now you would think they'd have come up with a practical fix. Hasn't Delta heard of two tin cans and a wire?

July 1989

The Wimpification of Our Boatyards Part 1

As we speak, a national treasure is being destroyed before our yes. A great part of this country's maritime heritage -- old dirty boatyards are being cast aside for that which is trendy.

Take, for example, The Ramp in San Francisco -- this was one of California's grittiest, saltiest boatyards catering to working vessels of gnarly local fisherman and knowledgeable pleasure boatmen. I've been there. This was a <u>real</u> boatyard, a <u>waterman's</u> boatyard. What happened to it is almost too horrible to relay here. A perfectly good working boatyard has been turned into a ... a ... DAMNED YUPPIE BOATYARD/CAFE! Imagine! A <u>boatyard/cafe</u>! Yes friends, The Ramp (a strong, simple name that came from the steep concrete launch ramp at the yard) has been bought out. It's now The San Francisco Boatyard. Yes friends, the day of the yuppie boatyard has arrived and yuppies will be descending on boatyards the way a horde of cockroaches would attack a scrap of moldy food left under the sink.

We all know that Californians are trendsetters and what happens here spreads to the rest of the country and, thereafter, the world. Yes, the yuppie cockroaches are coming to a boatyard near you (if they're not already there). This is a truly nefarious development for boatsmen who have known and loved boatyards all their lives and flags the end of boatyards as we know them and the beginning of the yupyard. To quote an article in the <u>Western Boatman</u> (February '89) about the transformation of The Ramp: "Every Sunday, for example, hordes of young San Franciscans swarm into the cafe's outdoor patio for eggs benedict and clarinet marmalade. Boat owners in the adjacent yard are adjunct listeners to the jazz concerts that are staged amid the clattering plates and chattering customers." <u>EGGS BENEDICT? CLARINET MARMALADE? JAZZ CONCERTS? CLATTERING PLATES? CHATTERING CUSTOMERS? IN A BOATYARD?</u>

Old boatyards! I love them with a passion. Old boatyards have a friendly feeling to them that's difficult to describe. There's something about the bottom paint-spattered dirt (<u>real</u> boatyards are never paved), the old sheds and the rickety docks that make one <u>feel good</u>. There are a few left in every boating town, but they're disappearing fast. Connecticut has a good number left as does Long Island, New York. The Lakes region has some good ones and there are a very few left in Florida. South Jersey probably has some of the best old yards in the country. These great yards are fast being replaced by wimpy places called "Boating Centers" with Butler buildings and dry stack storage and, yes, <u>cafes</u>.

Yuppies. God I hate them and all they stand for. "Yuppie," initially referred to young urban professionals -- in other words, young people with bucks. It was originally a <u>complimentary</u> term. Six or seven years ago, one could be proud to be a yuppie. Now, yuppieism has turned into a fanatic cult -- a cult with its own uniforms, language and rituals. Worse are yuppie imposters who can't really qualify as yups but do their best to act like them. The original yuppies shun all the foolishness and are doing their own thing now. Today "yuppie" is an extremely derogatory term, one which I would think twice about applying to my worst enemy. Yuppies today are phony, pompous, back stabbers to whom "getting ahead" is paramount. They accumulate things just to have <u>things</u> -- not because they like them. Yuppies drive, no <u>wear</u> BMW's and Mercedes not because they appreciate their features but because they are part of the dress code. A car is like a pair of loafers or a jacket -- simply an accessory with a three pointed star or kidney grilles for the express purpose of impressing other yups. They don't care, nor are they aware of, the car's great heritage or their handling and brakes. What's important is <u>image</u>.

Yuppies are: investment bankers, stock analysts, doctors and, yes, worst of all, <u>lawyers</u>. With Topsiders and fake bomber jackets and imported sweaters and $85.00 haircuts and gold Rolexes and $300.00 sunglasses (with unnecessary straps around their necks). You can almost see "Calvin Klein" written all over their damn underpants. You know, when I was in the Merchant Marines I, too, wore underwear with a name on it. It was <u>my</u> name stenciled on the waistband. In those days, nobody would even dream of wearing underwear with another guy's name on it -- especially a guy like Calvin Klein! What's this world coming to?

To me, boatyards were always a kind of refuge from the world -- a not quite respectable place where one could go and become part of an underground fraternity that people on the outside didn't understand. They were places where, without feeling like a criminal, you could spit and do other bad things I can't even mention here. They were places to which you wouldn't take your mother. They were places where guys could get together, scratch, belch, say rotten things, laugh and drink beer while they worked. A boatyard was a place where you could take a pee in the woodpile. No more. How could you with hundreds of sunglassed yuppo eyes staring at your every move. Besides, these yupyards have spotless his and hers bathrooms now. What these yuppies and yuppie imposters do, see, is descend on the cafe/boatyards on the weekends, stuff eggs benedict and quiche (we all know what kind of people eat quiche) into their manicured faces and watch guys working on boats. Did you get that folks? They watch guys working on boats. Nearly everyone seats facing the boatyard like it's a damn stage show. I can just hear one of these phonies in his affected singsong voice say to his wife "Oh look dear -- there's a man actually painting a bottom! I often wondered how bottoms got painted." BOATYARDS HAVE BECOME A YUPPIE SPECTATOR SPORT. What's his world coming to? Maybe it's a commie plot. Boatyard soda machines which once dispensed bad stuff like high octane sodas -- tough drinks that rotted your teeth on contact -- will now dispense Perrier and Evian. Boatyard marine stores are changing too. Now they sell stuff like drain plugs and bronze wool in <u>designer packages</u>. Anything liquid you buy like turpentine and thinner now has a foolish safety cap on it. Guys working in the yard wear safety glasses. <u>Half</u> the written stuff on <u>anything</u> you buy is a warning label. All of this comes to you courtesy of yuppie lawyers. Yuppies browse through marine stores like they do Bloomingdales buying stuff like designer packaged bilge cleaner (real boatmen know you just simply dump some dishwashing liquid into the bilge to do the job).

A boatyard/cafe ... it boggles the mind. What the hell's coming next? An engine rebuild shop/health spa? A boat supply store/deli? A carpentry shop/Mrs. Field's Cookie store? The end of an era is here folks. My advice is to pee in the woodpile while you can.

August 1989

Tender Behind
Part 1

This month I must pose a provocative question which many of you might take as being too personal to be discussed in a family publication such as this. Nevertheless, the question has to be asked because it is the premise for this entire article. My question is, DO YOU HAVE A TENDER BEHIND? It seems this condition was far more prevalent in the nineteen thirties, forties and fifties then it is now. Back then, people nearly always had a tender behind. Today, the condition is not common. I can see this opening paragraph inspiring two groups of readers. One group will get very indignant and fire off nasty letters to myself saying "Fexas is talking dirty again" or some such thing. The other group will send in their latest hemorrhoid jokes. Before any of this happens, please be advised that the question "Do you have a tender behind?" simply means <u>are you presently towing a dinghy behind your boat</u>. Okay?

A couple of months ago, my dad and I were sitting in my backyard doing what we've been doing for a collective hundred and thirty five years: <u>watching boats</u>. I guess we watch boats the way most guys watch women. Both pursuits are good for the eyes. Anyway, we're sitting there on the river watching all these boats go by and my dad made a comment something like "You know, you just don't see boats towing dinghys the way you used to." I hadn't really noticed! I had become accustomed to the "modern" way of doing things. He was, however, absolutely right! Dinghy stocks are down nowadays. Many boats we saw didn't even <u>have</u> a dinghy. <u>None</u> of the boats viewed were towing dinghys, and it was then I realized the art of towing dinghys -- in fact the art of dinghys themselves -- is largely becoming a lost art.

Hey, I'm a dinghy guy myself. I was brought up in dinghys. My dad's dinghy became my first boat when I was about four years old. Nowadays dinghys don't get much press or attention. They are viewed as necessary evils which spoil the lines of a boat and/or take up valuable partying space on deck.

But it wasn't always so.

In the twenties, thirties, forties and fifties, a dinghy served many important purposes. Primarily, it was usually the only way to get to and from your boat at her anchorage or mooring. It also served as a scouting craft running ahead of the mother ship in unknown waters searching for sandbars and obstacles. It was used to set a second anchor. It was a platform from which the hull could be washed. But it was, most importantly, <u>a</u> <u>life</u> <u>boat</u>. These "life boats" were normally towed behind their mother ship always at the ready. Today tenders are stored in some out of a way place on deck, usually launched by a clumsy davit. To the modern boatsman, they are nothing more than funny shaped deck boxes which collect all kinds of gear and junk. Yes, the lost art of a dinghy today is a sorry one.

Anchoring is also becoming a lost art. Fact is, anchoring (or more accurately, <u>not</u> <u>anchoring</u>) is the reason people don't tow dinghys anymore. These days, boating is usually conducted between 115 volt AC dockside receptacles. Boat owners get panicky if they can't plug in. Rarely do boats anchor out and, therefore, rarely do they need their tenders. (I've found most people don't anchor because they are afraid to. Afraid to look foolish amongst their obviously more experienced brethren anchored around them or afraid of drifting or afraid of being lonely at night without the close company of other boats around.) Let's face it -- we live our lives parallel parked. We dwell in houses lined up side by side on a street, we line up our cars in closely spaced slots. The herding instinct leads us to "park" our boats the same way. The fact is that's exactly the reason to anchor out -- to get away from the smelly crowds of people peering into your boat. To escape the noise and pollution. To enjoy the boat swinging freely, nose into the wind on her anchor line. To be a totally self-sufficient island at sea.

Another reason dinghys aren't towed these days is because people don't know how to tow them behind fast boats. Back in the old days, the length of your dinghy painter was a prestigious indication of the speed of your boat. The faster your boat, the longer the painter would be. These extended painters -- sometimes 30' or 40' long -- would sometimes be fitted with floats at six or eight foot intervals, to keep the line afloat when backing down. Towing a dinghy at high speed is truly a lost art. The trick is to let out enough line, see, so that the tender rides on the first roller just behind the rooster tail. It's position on the wave is critical for it's important to tow the dink on the face (downhill side) of this wave for least resistance. It takes a "calibrated arm" on the painter to feel the resistance and accurately position a dink at high speed. When done properly, however, the tension on the painter will be nil and the dink will ride along "for free."

Next month, we'll look at the history of yacht tenders. In the meantime, at the start of the weekend, pull that dusty, dingy, dinghy down off the deck and launch it. Then tow it to a secluded cove and anchor. Jump in and go to the beach or to town or to look at other boats. On the way back, run around your boat a few times and look how pretty and independent she looks on the hook. (Launch the dinghy <u>before</u> leaving for the cove because, if you wait till you're there, you'll get wrapped up in some important task like cocktails on the fantail and put it off.) Leave the dink in the water all weekend -- you'll find all kinds of uses for it. If your boating has been limited to mad dashes between power receptacles at marinas, you'll discover a whole new world -- thanks to your tender behind.

September 1989

Tender Behind Part 2

The art of dinghys! Back in the days when boats were wood and men knew how to anchor, dinghys were looked upon as an important piece of seagoing gear and usually were miniature replicas of their mother ships. Dirty, crummy, leaky mother ships would usually have dirty, crummy, leaky dinghys, while "Palm Beach" condition boats would have dinks in similar condition.

America has gone through a number of fads and trends when it comes to dinghys. Sadly, today we are in the whoopee cushion dinghy era -- a flexible, air filled donut boat made of cloth that's impossible to row.

That's not a real dinghy -- it's a caricature dinghy. I'll tell you what a real dinghy is. A real dinghy is typified by the famous Penn Yans of the 1930's. These beautiful, round bottomed creations were built like an old canoe of thin mahogany planking over closely spaced bent oak slat frames covered on the outside with canvas. This was <u>my</u> first dinghy which came with my dad's Wheeler. The hull was commonly painted to match the mother ship and the inside was usually bright varnish with the golden oak frames contrasting beautifully against the red mahogany skin. A pair of brightly varnished spruce oars would be carried aboard with leathers neatly tacked to them and copper oar tips fitted. One or two sets of bronze oar locks would be mounted on the rail and varnished spruce floor boards were fitted. Around the rail was tacked a canvas-over-sponge rubber bumper and, at the bow a triangular cork filled canvas bumper (I haven't seen one of these in 20 years) was fitted to protect the brightly varnished transoms of the day. Now that's a real dinghy! The lineage of the American dinghy starts before the turn of the century with lapstrake round bottomed rigs or transversely planked flat bottomed ugly things -- oftentimes homemade. These types of dinghys were used right up through the twenties until the previously mentioned Penn Yans came to the fore. After the Penn Yan era came the laminated plywood boats. Here, we had a frameless dinghy built of numerous thin diagonal planks glued under heat and pressure to form a one piece hull.

The inside and the outside were thus smooth and usually brightly varnished. Then, in the fifties, we started seeing plastics being used. One of the first was the famous transparent dinghy. These were completely transparent prams with a wooden rail at the sheer and wooden thwarts. When one rowed one of these rigs across the harbor, from a distance all one could see was the oars, the oarsman, the sheer rail and the seats mystically suspended above the water. Talk about Ghost Ships!

What did a guy with a couple of drinks in him think upon viewing this apparition suspended above the water? Next, we moved to the era of the full fiberglass dinghy, the best of which was typified by the Dyer Dhows which were (and are) a classic dinghy. Dyers are real tenders -- modern day Penn Yans -- and, when properly fitted out, are a joy to behold. These are <u>real</u> <u>dinghys</u>. Waterman's dinghys. Speaking of homemade dinghys, my grandfather used to build dinghys. He built a pack of them. These days, people don't build dinghys themselves. My grandfather could put a flat bottom dinghy together in a few days: spring a couple of planks for the sides, add a transom/thwarts and plank the bottom athwartships. Instant dinghy! In the days before World War I, the family lived in a tenement in downtown Manhattan -- not the best place to build a dinghy. But the urge to build boats is irrepressible and one was built on the tenement <u>roof</u>! Like all things that float, when completed, the dinghy appeared huge on the roof and even bigger after they lowered it down to the street. With such a grand dinghy, great plans were made. They bought a pair of long oars. Back then the family had no car but they did have a cruiser which was kept in North Beach (where La Guardia Airport is presently situated). How to get the dinghy from lower Manhattan to North Beach? Well, the dinghy appeared so confidence inspiring on the street that grandfather and a friend decided they'd take it down to the river and <u>row it</u> north up the east river, <u>through treacherous Hell Gate</u> and thereafter to North Beach. With the boat sitting on the cobblestones, it was a perfectly feasible idea. They took the dink to a local dock and launched it. Again, like all things that float, suddenly, in her element, she appeared <u>very</u> small. The oars were much too big. Furthermore she was quite narrow and <u>very</u> tender. A smart alec yard owner later informed my grandfather, "That thing is so tender, before you get aboard you'd better make sure <u>your</u> hair <u>is</u> <u>parted</u> <u>in</u> the middle!" Great line! After the initial sea trial, the plans for the grand voyage were scrubbed and the mother ship came down to fetch her new baby. The next year a Mark II wider version was built and granddad could, once again, part his hair on the <u>side</u>.

Other uses for a dinghy? How about a floating barbeque? I've seen guys set up barbeque grills in their dinghys (not marine barbecues mind you -- I'm talking about el cheapo $7.99 K-Mart specials with those funny crossed legs) to grill steaks safely away from the mother ship. (I can tell you, a flaming backyard barbecue set up in a dingy is a strange sight reminding one of some sort of Pagan ritual.) How about an <u>exercise</u> <u>machine</u>? I'm sure some of you have shelled out big bucks three thousand or more for a chrome plated rowing machine that sits on the damn floor. How about rowing a <u>real</u> boat? On real water! A dinghy gives you a built-in exercise machine for a completely new experience in exercise.

Today, unfortunately, we're into the aforementioned bladder boats -- ugly, amorphously shaped wimpy substitutes for dinghys filled with air. The reason for their popularity is simple to understand. A deflated bladder boat takes up no partying space on deck you can simply roll it up and stow it in the bilge where nobody has to look at it. Also, since the boat is essentially one huge bumper, a greenhorn operator can land the thing alongside the mothership without gouging her $50,000 diamond flake paint job. The age of the bumper boat has arrived. Back in the old days nearly every boat towed a dinghy. Hell, I can remember boats that weren't much bigger than <u>dinghys themselves</u> towing dinghys. A dinghy, like a puppy, was a faithful friend, always obediently tagging behind, always ready to serve. To this day, I don't feel right running without a tender behind. So come on folks, live dangerously. Be the first in your marina to get your dinghy wet. It will add a whole new dimension to boating.

October 1989

The Wimpification of Our Boatyards Part 2

Apparently I've struck nerve. When the August '89 article came out, on the degradation of our old boatyards, the response surprised me. In that piece, I compared the new, modern "Boating Centers" to the great old boatyards. Not only did I receive a good number of letters, but a more than a few phone calls, mostly from people that I knew, telling me the article was "right on." I've also gotten some calls and hate mail from yuppies (I <u>love</u> hate mail!) and have been accosted by yuppie acquaintances on the street concerning the piece. With this kind of response, I couldn't help but do a sequel....

First, I must apologize to the yup-type people who have sternly taken issue with me concerning my comparing yuppies with cockroaches in the original piece. It seems they were greatly offended. I'm sorry. I really am ... but if there's any living thing on earth (other than a yuppie) that earns its living with more greed and avarice than a cockroach I'd like to know what it is. There's more to the analogy. Cockroaches hang out in social groups just as yuppies do and they all look the same. Also, if you have the stomach for it, look at a cockroach closely in the face. Just like yuppies, they look like they're wearing big, expensive sunglasses! Most people don't like to have roaches or yuppies around them. Black Flag has developed particularly effective counter measures for roaches including sprays and their famous Roach Motel. Why can't they do the same for yuppies ("Yuppies check in but they don't check out")? If some kind of yuppie spray repellent could be developed I'm sure the inventor will find himself a very rich man. Then, when you find yourself at a cocktail party surrounded by yuppies telling you how important they are, you might give a little spray here and a little spray there and they'd be gone. I would suggest a spray with the essence of greenbacks. Spray a little in the corner of the room and the yuppies will fight over one another to get there.

People have asked "Won't saying all these terrible things about yups hurt your business?" Well, I've thought about that and after pondering long and hard, I really can't think of one yuppie client I've ever had. Yuppies, it seems, don't have yachts designed. One reason may be that it takes too long to design and build a custom yacht. They want theirs NOW. Additionally, they don't want anything that's very different from what their yuppie friends have (remember the yuppie uniform code). Enough about yuppies ... this is supposed to be an article about old boatyards.

Even though thirties, forties and fifties boatyards weren't a place you'd want to take your mother or girlfriend, but they were a great place for kids to learn about the world. They learned about work. They learned about responsibility. They learned other things that their mothers weren't too happy about (but, hey, that's all part of being worldly, isn't it?). I remember as a kid in the fifties feeling sorry for my little friends because they had nothing better to do Saturday or Sunday other than stick ball or punk smoking or playing hopscotch or riding their Schwinns. I couldn't wait for my dad to get home on Saturday (he worked half days Saturday until the boat was launched after which he'd take full weekends until the boat was hauled) so I could go to the boatyard with him. We'd spend all day there on Sunday too -- often missing weddings, funerals, birthday parties and the like ("Why did you pick a silly time like June to get married? Don't you know I'm working on the boat?"). On the way back from the yard Sunday evenings, my dad and I would plan future tasks and pat ourselves on the back for the great work we'd done that weekend.

The boatyard! A place of great excitement -- especially in the Spring. There was always something great going on down at the boatyard. For example, there were always some dorky guys working on their boats that everyone else in the yard made fun of. These were guys who had their boats blocked extra high so they could paint their bottoms in the standing position with <u>rollers on the end of long sticks</u>. They always used expensive bronze bottom paint (remember bronze bottom paint?). When completed, the bottoms had a beautiful metallic bronze, hard finish that soon turned a cruddy green after launching. The rest of the group in the boatyard (who used brushes and copper paint) questioned the manhood of these people, and viewed them with great suspicion. These same paint roller guys would spend about six weeks diligently puttying every seam below the waterline. Most of us in the know realized that soon after launching, the planks would soak up and swell tight anyhow so we didn't waste time on this foolishness and spent it in other more profitable areas such as the topsides or deck.

Like I said, there was always something great going on down at the boatyard. Most exciting of all from my viewpoint was simply to be able to study boats out of the water. I'd walk all around the boatyard looking at stems, struts, rudders, deadwoods, propellers -- anything that caught my interest and was at my little kid eye level. I also really enjoyed marine stores. Marine stores back then were not the marine stores we have today. These were <u>real</u> marine stores with <u>real</u> boat hardware usually hung from rusty nails hammered in the wall or strewn around on dusty shelves. Here you could find the real stuff: stuffing boxes and seacocks and bronze strap hinges and bowden wire. Go through a neat, well lit marine store today and what do you see: sunglasses, key chains, signs that say "The Captain is King," skull and crossbone flags, cocktail flags, tee shirts, Captain's hats with scrambled eggs on the visor, striping tape and boat wax. Any marine fittings they <u>do</u> sell are usually of the modern trash hardware variety: fittings made of plastic and zinc castings made with materials like Delrin, Acrylic and Zamak. What kind of stuff is this to put on a boat? And just what the hell is Zamak anyhow? Give me Tobin Bronze and Monel and 316 Stainless and Silicon Bronze and Copper and Everdur. Zinc castings ... this stuff turns to crud the instant it gets a whiff of salt air. Today too much so called marine hardware is made of compressed pig poop. If you're looking at a boat with plastic hinges or zinc hardware turn around and find a <u>real</u> boat.

You know the guys I was talking about who painted their bottoms with rollers? These same guys usually wore respirator masks and safety glasses and gloves and white coveralls and <u>snoods</u> for God's sake. Hell, part of the fun of scraping and painting a bottom was a month of digging copper paint out of your hair, nose, and ears and other assorted body crevasses. My father and I used to go the boatyard wearing the same old clothes every weekend -- splotches of copper paint or blobs of grease were badges of honor. We were threadbare in our knees and elbows and every weekend we looked like a couple of panhandlers or refugees. I remember my mother getting very upset when the neighbors used to look at us leaving for or arriving from the boatyard. Who were these bums anyway?

Real boatyards never had parking lots. You simply drove your car right up to your boat which made it easy for loading and unloading stuff or using the hood and roof of the car as a two level scaffold or painting the bootstripe in the glow of the car's headlights the night before launching.

My personal favorite old boatyard is in Northport Harbor, Long Island, New York. It's called Seymour's and it's virtually the way it was at the early part of the century when it was founded. The owner lives in a Victorian house up the hill on boatyard property. Here is a great collection of rickety sheds, floats, ramps, stiff leg cranes, docks and real marine railways (no travel lifts here). The yard's mini tugboat, "Active," must be 60 years old. The workshops and marine store are built out over the bay on wooden pilings. A walk through Seymour's is a walk into the past. If it were up to me, I'd make Seymour's a national landmark or museum. I'd also charge admission. There's no parking lot, no paving and you certainly won't find a cafe there.

Yuppies would hate the place.

November 1989

Our Prez is a Boat Guy
Part 1

Let's face it. Guys driving cigarette powerboats are usually the marine equivalent of Natzi helmeted, scruffy bearded, pot-bellied, black tee shirted, tattooed up the yin yang, Hell's Angels driving a menacing chrome and black Harley Chopper. When you see a guy in a cigarette, your eyes automatically wander for the requisite bikini clad bimbos on either arm of the hairy, pot-bellied, gold adorned driver. These boats usually have names like "Hot Mama" or "Zuit Suit" or "Thunderballs."

But there is at least one cigarette owner I know who's different. He's well past middle age, tall and taciturn. His companion is a handsome woman with grey hair. Their dress is usually preppy and the boat's name is, would you believe it, "FIDELITY." FIDELITY? What kind of name is this for a cigarette? Why not a name like "WOMANIZER" or "SWORDSMAN" or "SKIRT CHASER?" Why not indeed. This cigarette is owned by none other than George Herbert Walker Bush, President of the United States of America.

Yes, our president is a powerboat guy. Not an effete,

snobbish, sailboat type like some other presidents, but a <u>real</u> <u>boat</u> <u>guy</u> <u>who</u> <u>owns</u> <u>his</u> <u>own</u> <u>powerboat</u> -- one of us!

In my lifetime, no president has ever been a "powerboat guy." Yes, they've all had the use of the presidential yacht "SEQUOIA" and many used her quite frequently. Franklin Roosevelt, a member of the effete, used the "SEQUOIA" as a party fishing boat. Harry Truman, a haberdasher from Lamer, Missouri installed a piano and used the yacht for poker sessions. John F. Kennedy, another member of the effete, used the presidential yacht often. Kennedy with his PT 109 service came close to being a powerboat guy but was really (shutter) <u>a</u> <u>ragbagger</u> at heart. Lyndon B. Johnson was a cattle farmer who liked to show movies on the upper deck of "SEQUOIA." Richard ("I am not a crook") M. Nixon spent a lot of time aboard, but probably more for the purpose of hiding from his inquisitors than enjoying the sea. Gerald Ford used the presidential yacht quite frequently and probably would have used her more except there are so many places on a boat where one can bump your head or trip and fall .....

Then we come to "Jimmuh what's his name?" Carter I think it was. He seemed to be a nice enough man but probably was one of the most ineffectual presidents ever (I have a pet theory as to exactly why Jimmuh wasn't the greatest president. It was his <u>name</u>. How could anybody be "Presidential" with a name like "Jimmuh?" Had he used "James Carter," things probably would have been entirely different.) Anyway, Jimmuh was part of the "Nucear Navy" (four years in office, thousands of speeches and the man never did learn to pronounce "NucLear"). Jimmuh, a peanut farmer from Georgia, had little use for yachts. He was the one to end the grand tradition of presidential yachts and had the "SEQUOIA" sold during the "economic malaise" of 1977. The end of a tradition. The "SEQUOIA" had a checkered life between '77 and November '88 when, once again, she was returned to the U.S. Government.

Calling any one of these presidents a "powerboat guy" would be akin to calling a Staten Island ferry commuter a "yachtsman." President Bush, however, is a breath of fresh air to boatsman around the world.

I can just imagine a presidential press conference of the future (fade to west wing of the White House)...

President Bush is nattily attired in a blue suit, white shirt and red tie with diagonal stripes and a crisp white handkerchief in his pocket. Three microphones are clustered in front of the presidential podium. Gaudy gold curtains adorn the walls behind, looking somewhat like seconds from a Las Vegas cat house. The reporters are ready to hang on the President's every word, notepads at the ready. (I always wondered why they write everything down when they can simply look at the tapes afterwards and get it word for word.) I guess it's part of the reporter thing -- trench coats, notepads and all that stuff.) A hush falls over the crowd and the conference starts:

The President: "I'd like to start this conference by making a statement. First, by presidential decree, henceforth, all draw bridges over all U.S. waterways will normally be kept in the open position. They will be lowered every half hour for auto traffic. Additionally, our fellow Republicans in the House and Senate are introducing legislation for government subsidized boat loans. At the same time, legislation is being introduced allowing all Yacht Designers to be exempt from paying income tax retroactive to 1960 (Hey! It's my fantasy). And, finally a new National Holiday will be proposed: John Hacker's birthday. That is the end of my statement." The President has now donned his bifocals and acknowledges the reporters with a terse "Yah" as he points to them.

Terrence Hunt, Associated Press: "Mr. President, you've had a deep "V" boat since 1972. Since you haven't had a modified "V" or a round bottom or flat bottom craft in 16 years, doesn't this indicate favoritism on your part?"

The President: "I like to steer steady course through treacherous seas and uncharted waters. It's necessary to maintain an upright position in the face of adversity and be able to move swiftly when the going gets rough." (This, in fact, is an excerpt from one of the President's foreign affairs speeches which he resurrected for the occasion.)

Joanna Newman, USA Today: "Mr. President, you've had several meetings with Chairman Gorbachev, what is your view on the effect of Glasnost on the Russian boating industry?"

The President: "You know Joanna, before Glasnost the Russians had a pleasure boat industry, however, the KGB had a man stationed at every factory whose job it was to bash a hole in the bottom of each and every boat that came down the production line before it was delivered, so they could be assured that no one would escape Russia by water. Now, you know, with Glasnost things are much better. Holes are still bashed in each hull, however, a <u>scoop bailer</u> is now provided to each buyer."

Ken Walsh, U.S. News and World Report: "Mr. President, did Mike Dukakis have a boat?"

The President: "Yes, he did, but he had to get rid of it. It would only turn to <u>port</u>."

Walsh: "May I have a follow-up?"

The President: "I'm sorry but we're out of time. You'll have to save it for the next conference."

What a coincidence! <u>I'm out of space</u>. Tune in next month (in our exciting Fungal Growth issue) for the dramatic conclusion of the Presidential press conference.

December 1989

Our Prez is a Boat Guy Part 2

The President briskly strides into the room, takes his place behind the presidential podium and acknowledges Leslie Stahl from CBS News.

Stahl: "Mr. President, what's your view on the new line of luxury yachts from Lebanon called Lebship?"

The President: "I'm against it, Leslie, and I'll tell you why. I take great exception to their method of building boats from spent, cutup and flattened shell casings. It's dangerous. Sometimes there is still gunpowder in these casings and Lebships have been known to explode upon contact with a dock."

David Montgomery, Ft. Worth Star Telegram: "Mr. President, we understand the Russians will be participating in the upcoming America's Cup competition. What's your view on this?"

The President: "Well, as I understand it, their boat is very crude. It's being built in Siberia by an outfit called Siberia Craft with Lebship as their consultant. Their hull is built from old German shell casings and the sails are fabricated from babushkas. Furthermore, our Russian friends have stolen a set of drawings from one of America's Cup top designers. Fortunately for us, the plans were folded and, in building the boat, the Russians reproduced the exact image shown on the blueprint complete with four sharp athwartship creases in the hull. We feel with an effort like this our chances are good that we can beat the Russians in the America's Cup. Additionally, in the spirit of Glasnost, I've offered to send Dennis Conner to Siberia to oversee construction and then skipper their boat. The Russians have declined my offer, however."

Michael Gelb, Reuters News Service: "Mr. President, your boat is a dark color rather than white as most boats are. Isn't this simply a form of patronizing the minorities of the world?"

The President: "Certainly not! And to demonstrate my feelings about this, I plan to have one side of the boat painted white."

Julia Malone, Cox Newspaper: "Mr. President, we are in the midst of a drug war. Boats like yours are used to ferry contraband onto our shores. Shouldn't you be setting an example by having a different kind of boat ... like a sailboat for example?"

The President: "First, let me say that I have nothing against sailors. Some of my best friends are sailors and I believe we can all live together in peace and harmony on an equal basis without discrimination or tension. Heck, I've even invited sailors into my home. But the fact is that the President of the United States needs a boat like "FIDELITY" that can run from point A to point B on a schedule. Often, you know, I entertain important heads of State at my home in Kennebunkport. It just wouldn't do much for international relations if these guests had to be told "I'm sorry the President will be late. He's in irons out there on the bay somewhere and we really don't know when he'll be back."

Robert Ellison, Sheraton Broadcasting: "Mr. President, what do you plan to do about the dearth of boat slips for the increasing boat population?"

The President: "I have proposed a new Federal Agency for developing marinas in crowded downtown areas of our great seafaring cities. This agency is called The Agency for Marina Urban Development, or "MUD" and I expect great things to be slung from it."

Robert Ellison: "As a follow-up Mr. President, what are your thoughts about the over population of fiberglass boats on our waterways and your feelings about controlling the number of fiberglass boats out there? Some people, as you know, advocate destroying fiberglass boats while they are in the mold. How do you feel about this?"

The President: "You know, Bob, I'm a staunch advocate of <u>berth</u> <u>control</u>, however, I can't condone the destruction of boats already in the mold, because I believe that the life of a fiberglass boat starts in the mold as soon as the resin impregnates the fiberglass. The only conditions under which I would condone destroying the hull, while in the mold, would be in the case of uncured resin or severe warpage. Thank you Ladies and Gentlemen." (With a crisp "Thank you Mr. President" the press conference ends and the President leaves the room.) No President, excepting Roosevelt and Kennedy, could remotely be called a "yachtsman." And even Roosevelt and Kennedy were merely <u>day</u> <u>guests</u> aboard their presidential yachts with their every whim catered to. But here's a president who likes to wrap his fist around a set of Morse controls and wear foul weather gear. Here's a president who <u>owns</u> his own powerboat. This brings up some interesting questions: Now that George Bush is president, who maintains his boat? For security reasons it certainly can't be a guy named Wilfred or Vern or Zack down at the Kennebunkport boatyard. And where is "Fidelity" stored in the winter? Most surely not under a tarp on blocks in the parking lot. Does the U.S. Navy maintain and store the President's boat? George Bush is a man you could picture stripped down to the waist, trousers slipping down to near scandalous levels leaning over the engine compartment fooling with points or a carburetor. Can you see Roosevelt or Kennedy doing this? And this president <u>uses</u> this boat. It's great to see those guys with the Uzis in their briefcases trying to keep up with him with their boats. OUR PRESIDENT IS A BOAT GUY. He's one of <u>us</u>. Keep up the good work Mr. President.

P.S. I guess you could say I'm biased. I was for George Bush in '80 and voted for him last year. I suppose, to be fair, I must give members of opposing parties equal space so, therefore, bleeding heart liberal ragbaggers should address their rebuttals to me.

January 1990

The Californication of Florida
Part 1
You don't Really Want to Move to Florida, do You?

It's 8:15 a.m. I'm in my little red Corvette somewhere in Florida and I'm in a big traffic jam. Most of the cars around me are driven by DFNU's ("Dead From The Neck Ups"). The DFNU redneck in front of me occupying two lanes is driving a rusted out pickup truck with a "How's My Driving? Call 1-900-EAT-XXXX" bumper sticker. His DFNU Labrador retriever is relieving himself (Labrador Reliever?) in the pickup bed. What a great way to start the morning! The tractor trailer trying to cut in front of me is seriously threatening my beautiful $3,500 "catch me arrest me" Mille Miglia red paint job. DFNU's all! I wouldn't be upset if I was in a big city like Ft. Lauderdale or Orlando or Miami. But it so happens I'm in my hometown -- little Stuart, Florida driving the five miles from home to work and I'm upset. My seven minute drive to the office has turned into a fifteen minute hassle. (No big deal, I know, for straphangers used to two hour commutes, but my travel time has <u>doubled</u>.) It was at the stoplight in front of the Amoco Mini Mart that a revelation occurred. Suddenly I realized that to preserve what's left of paradise and an idyllic life-style, my mission in life (for the short term anyway) was to KEEP PEOPLE THE HELL OUT OF FLORIDA. There at the wheel, I started planning my next magazine column...

I'm from New York, see, so I should be used to this kind of thing. I <u>hate</u> traffic jams and, if I can help it, I don't wait on line for <u>anything</u>. I've been known, when traffic was heavy, to park the car and go to a bad Ninja movie. If there was a line for the movie, I'd go to a library. If there was no library handy, I'd go watch bugs - <u>anything</u> but wait on line. If a restaurant doesn't have a table immediately available, I'll eat at the Arches. You get the picture. One reason I moved to sleepy little Stuart (Population in 1980: 9,380 - Population in 1989: 16,400!) twelve years ago was to get away from all that rat race crap. Three years ago, Stuart didn't have traffic jams. Inexorably, however, the invasion from the north continues. New houses and condos are built, Walmarts are appearing on every corner, new shopping centers are erected and more cars are on <u>my</u> road. Upsetting is the fact that, deep down, I know that <u>I'm</u> one of the people who moved here from the north helping to produce these traffic jams. But, hey, it's all a matter of seniority, see. When you're a native, the "SYBIGM Syndrome" takes effect (SYBIGM stands for "Screw You Buddy, I Got Mine"). It's the Florida redneck creed. Therefore, before Stuart and other small Florida towns like it become <u>one</u> <u>massive</u> <u>K-Mart</u> <u>parking</u> <u>lot</u>, the likes of Orange County, California, and before I become a damned <u>California</u>

Raisin, I have a message for you Northerners thinking of moving South to experience an endless summer of boating.

DON'T MOVE TO FLORIDA! DON'T EVEN THINK ABOUT IT! FLORIDA IS A BAD PLACE TO LIVE. Let me tell you why.

You need to have a strong stomach to live in Florida. For example, anytime you move anything that's been in place more than five minutes, something darts, oozes, slithers, slimes, jumps, seeps, pounces, percolates or crawls from under it. This occurs anywhere whether it be in your driveway, garage, bedroom, or refrigerator! Let's talk bugs. Florida is a wonderful place to live... if YOU'RE A DAMNED ENTOMOLOGIST! There's a reason why half the yellow pages of any Florida town is devoted to exterminators companies. Florida is loaded with creepy crawlers. Like spiders. In Florida the most common spider is a huge, brown, ugly thing called Huntsman, about as big around as your fist. Huntsmen, are very interesting spiders -- one of the few of their species that don't make webs (which is nice cause it keeps the house or boat clean). What these guys do, see, is hide in dark recesses and attack their prey by jumping on them! My sweet wife was attacked stepping into the shower one night. Nevertheless, some people keep a couple of pet Huntsmen in their house or boat to kill the giant cockroaches. Excuse me, in Florida, we don't have cockroaches! Folks down here have neatly sidestepped the cockroach problem by simply renaming the insect -- Florida roaches are called palmetto bugs. Has a much nicer ring, don't you think? But the palmetto bug problem pales in comparison with our fire ant problem. Fire ants are little, innocuous looking red ants. If you step on their mound they'll attack you viciously -- they've been known to kill people. Florida is, in fact, one huge fire ant mound so no matter where you go, you will be attacked.

In late summer, Florida gets invaded by love bugs. These cute little black and red critters fly united (as the ad says). I'm serious. These bugs fly in tandem, hooked up together, carrying on in broad daylight (hence, the name love bugs). In late summer it <u>rains</u> love bugs and Floridians must get used to inhaling and exhaling the things, picking them out of their hair, ears, eyes, teeth, pockets and food. Drive your car and the entire frontal area of the vehicle soon becomes one big splat. How many millions of these little guys, flying in tender embrace give their lives up to radiators and windshields during the season? It must be in the multitrillions but what a way to go!

One should also know that <u>killer</u> <u>bees</u>, now in Central America, will be in Florida next year to join their carpenter bee brethren. We also have wasp and scorpion problems.

Traffic inches along. Who ever thought I'd write a column on <u>bugs</u>! But they are part of the Florida scene and must be considered when contemplating a move to Florida. What does all this have to do with boats, you might ask? Well, Florida is the boating capitol of the world. In fact, the Florida peninsula is the <u>world's</u> <u>biggest</u> <u>floating</u> <u>dock</u>. What happens in Florida directly affects boats and boating.

My clutch is starting to stink and I'm watching the temperature gauge go red. 454RTA motors don't like traffic. If something doesn't change soon, I'll have to get me a damned Yugo or Hyundai (with automatic transmission) for my commute. What a terrible thought! I continue thinking of reasons to keep people away from the Paradise Peninsula...

February 1990

The Californication of Florida Part 2

The traffic continues to inch along. The dumb, wide eyed DFNU (Dead From The Neck Up) broad in the Datsun behind me is blankly gazing into her rear view mirror and is applying <u>eye</u> <u>makeup</u>! With a quick glance at her face in my rear view mirror, I can see that the lights are on but there's no one at home! I pull off to the side of the road, let her by and get back in behind her. Bimbo mobile makeup parlors are one of the great driving hazards of the world. Meanwhile, I continue with my diabolical plan to keep people away from Florida...

Last month I discussed Florida bug life in detail. Now let's look at some other Florida wildlife. In New York in the 60's there was a late night T.V. movie called "Creature Features." Florida reminds me a lot of those terrible movies with their bizarre assortment of beasts and monsters. All Florida real estate is riddled with dark, mysterious holes. There are species of creatures living deep inside that <u>haven't even been discovered yet</u>! If you want to live in Florida, you'd better get used to seeing: snakes, rats, walking catfish, snakes, alligators, frogs, snakes, assorted reptile types, land crabs and snakes. Yes, when one goes walking in unlit areas in Florida, you learn to take a flashlight with you and whistle loudly. "Yankee Doodle" is good. So is "Oklahoma."

Ever see a land crab? They are mean, black, double ugly beasts measuring about a foot across. They live in holes in the ground and come out around August. These guys are fearless and will attack humans if cornered. They have huge claws and when they grab something they don't let go -- even if you kill the bugger. If you encounter one on the road with your car, they'll raise their claws in defense just before you run over them slashing your $400.00 Goodyear Gatorbacks.

There are a jillion lizards in Florida -- most of them living in your house or boat. Since many Florida houses are adorned with sliding glass windows (whose tracks don't seal very well) and boats usually allow easy access, lizards have free passage in and out (mostly in). Now, personally, I *like* lizards. These little guys change colors to match their surroundings and have beady little eyes that rotate so they can see behind them. When I was a kid, my mother bought me a lizard at the circus. He was a friendly little guy and I enjoyed his company until he got lost in the radiator after which I never saw him again. Now, I don't mind lizards in the house, but many people become upset when they get what I call a "Florida Surprise" -- a lizard (in a beautiful shade of endive green) in their *salad*!

Other than beasts and bugs, there's much more to the down side of Florida that must be mentioned:

- You're always under the threat of getting blown away by a killer hurricane anytime between June and October.
- Florida beaches are quickly eroding away on both coasts (in fact, in a few years, as the east and the west coast beaches erode towards one another, Florida will consist of nothing more than the <u>Florida</u> <u>Turnpike</u> running north to south!)
- The school systems have one of the highest dropout rates in the country.
- There are too many New Yorkers down here (I'm one of them).
- Drawbridges, always in the open position, hinder your progress no matter where you are driving.
- Sand spurs constantly find their way into your skivvies.
- Florida's flat landscape tends to give one a planer view of life.
- As the polar caps melt, Florida will be the first state to be underwater.

You also ought to know that electrical power in Florida goes out at least five times a day. I don't know why. Most houses are heavily laden with digital clocks: clocks in microwaves, stoves, clock radios, VCR's and T.V. sets. Don't forget the sprinkler system and pool pump. Every time the power goes down and comes back on, my house is transformed into a damned <u>pinball</u> <u>parlor</u> with lights flashing in every room. Then it takes about an hour to go through the house and reset all the clocks only to be hit by another power outage which repeats the whole process. Free Tip: If you want to come to Florida and make a bundle of money, consider starting a <u>digital</u> <u>clock</u> <u>resetting</u> <u>service</u>!

What's perceived as a wonderful climate in Florida attracts all kinds of low life. California and Florida have more slime balls per square acre than any other state in the Nation. Let's face it, if you're going to be a dirt bag, it's easier to be a dirt bag in Florida or California where the weather is decent. The preponderance of slime balls and dirt bags attract sharks to the area. I'm not talking about sharks with dorsal fins and tails, I'm talking about the kind of sharks wearing shiny three piece suits with law degrees (come to think of it, most Florida lawyers <u>do</u> have dorsal fins and tails). Florida simply has too many shyster lawyers all trying to create business. Florida, in fact, has <u>more lawyers than the entire country of Japan</u>! Think about that! (Question: Why are attorneys immune to shark attack? Answer: Professional courtesy.) Always trying to outdo the competition, these guys play the one-upmanship game with big ads in newspapers, radio and television. Ads for attorneys down here are, in fact, rapidly approaching the abysmal advertising standards set by used car lots.

Would you believe that presently in Florida there are law firms with <u>mobile law offices</u>? I said mobile law offices folks! These are converted motorhomes with big signs emblazoned on their sides saying something like: "Law Offices of Abramowitz, O'Keefe, Valez, Washington and Ho" (covers all of the bases doesn't it?). Under the name of the firm might be a phrase like: "No ambulance too fast" (I guess they might as well make ambulance chasing as easy as possible). These rolling parlors of justice will visit you at your home or the scene of an accident. Soon, I imagine, we'll be treated to something like this on our local news: "This is Biff Surf (all Florida reporters have names like that. Some actual examples: Jill Beach, Dwight Lauderdale and Al Sunshine). at the scene of a terrible multiple car collision on I-95. As you can see, police cars, firetrucks, ambulances, wreckers and mobile law offices have converged on the scene ..."

Although I've never been in one, I can just imagine what these barrister barges look like inside. Step in and you'll find the interior lined with cheap imitation wood paneling with the fake plastic "wood" peeling off at the corners. On the floor is a puke green dirty, fuzzy, shag carpet. There in the center of the space is a big, impressive wood grained Formica desk, behind which is a high backed imitation Naugahyde swivel chair with tears in the arms. Behind the chair tacked on the wall are a plethora of impressive looking diplomas in brown plastic K-Mart frames hanging at crazy angles. Only in Florida.

Actually Florida does have a few honest, ethical lawyers. I know <u>both</u> of them!

Approaching the Palm City Bridge, I'm accosted by cars trying to cut in from side streets. Since I believe that what you do in the early morning sets the tone for the rest of the day, I've decided that, if I'm going to be in a traffic jam, I will choose the cars I want to stare at for the next 15 minutes. Why ruin my morning looking at the fat ass of a rusty '77 Buick (with a "Florida Native" bumper sticker) when I could be admiring the soft aft contours of a Taurus? Why stare at the offending boxy back end of a Jeep when I can let a slippery Honda Civic in front of me? Traffic groans on and I continue my planning...

March 1990

The Californication of Florida Part 3

Still stuck in traffic trying to get to work. More reasons for people not moving to Florida pop into my mind with every push of the brake pedal. The yuppie twit in the Volvo ahead of me is preening himself in the rearview mirror. Geez! Now, he's picking his nose! The guy in the Trans Am beside me has his radio cranked up so high that my windows are rattling. I can't believe what I'm seeing in my rearview mirror. Behind me is a Chevette occupied by a young couple. He's driving while she's in the passenger seat with her arm out the window dangling a pair of <u>lace</u> <u>panties</u>! Go figure. If you are observant enough, you can see all kinds of things when stuck in traffic. Meanwhile, I'm still thinking...

But, hey, you say, I want to move to Florida so I can enjoy my boat <u>year</u> <u>round</u> in the beautiful Florida climate. Let me tell you, the tales of the Florida climate are a myth. A <u>myth</u> I say! Florida, you see, has two good months -- April and May. During June, July, August, September and October the climate is oppressively hot and humid. This is also hurricane season and the constant threat of being washed away makes everyone irritable. During this time, it rains <u>every day</u> and the humidity makes your belly button moldy. For the remaining five months, the weather alternates between warm and cool and gives everyone colds, hacking coughs and sore throats. When Ponce de Leon landed in Florida, you can be sure the weather was <u>partly cloudy</u>. In fact, in its recorded history, Florida has <u>never had a</u> totally <u>sunny day</u>. Every day is <u>partly</u> cloudy. That's why Florida gets all the reject T.V. weathermen. Down here, day in and day out, blankly stare into the camera and repeat "Today will be partly cloudy with a 30% chance of rain."

In fact, the weather here in Florida really upsets me. It seems everything I own is slowly turning to ca ca before my eyes. I mean <u>everything</u>. Cars left outside turn into a pile of rust in about two months due to the salt spiked air (good cars are kept in air conditioned garages). The summer sun (when it's out) is extremely strong and will dull a beautiful new metallic finish in about four hours. The inside of the car gets so hot, you can't touch anything metal and, in about a week, all the upholstery dries up, cracks and turns to powder. Boats suffer similarly. Wooden boats are virtually nonexistent down here because they are attacked by dry rot from above and worms from below. When the rot and the worms meet all that's left is a soggy pile of floating debris looking something like a <u>peat bog</u>! The average life for a wooden boat in Florida is about two months. Fiberglass and aluminum boats fare better, but the unrelenting sun eventually fades even the best gelcoat or polyurethane paint job. Warm salt water provides a very corrosive environment for underwater metal objects.

But it's not only cars and boats that suffer down here -- everything does: houses, lawn furniture, tools, clothes and shoes. Ever wonder why so many Floridians wear green clothes? These clothes, when purchased might have been red, blue, yellow or white but after being worn for about 20 minutes in the humidity, they all turn green! Makes me wonder. If the climate does all these bad things to all these inanimate objects and machines, can it be good for people? I know people move to Florida because they think it's a healthy environment but, after all, people and the above mentioned inanimate objects/machines are made up of similar atomic structure and I have some strong evidence that it adversely affects living creatures as well. It's a known medical fact that damp, hot climates produce a condition in humans known as "Cranious Softosis" (softening of the brain). Yes, high humidity and constant rapping from raindrops turns the brain into tapioca pudding. That this condition is prevalent is demonstrated by the meat headed things people do in Florida. Take my neighbor down the street. Here's a gent living in what must be a $250,000 house built on a wide, picturesque canal. The back of his house is all screened porch with a rolling lawn leading down to a beautiful, wide canal. Yet, this fellow spends his days sitting in his underwear on a five gallon can in his garage (wedged in between his car and the wall) looking out at the street! And is there any explanation for Florida politicians' actions other than Cranious Softosis? Examples: a while back they passed a law which, in effect, allowed everyone to carry guns. For a time, cities like Miami started looking like Dodge City with people openly brandishing pistols. Florida. The Gunshine State! The law was quickly retracted. Or how about our esteemed Governor who, in his infinite wisdom, proposed, strongly backed and pushed into law a tax on professional services rendered in Florida. After numerous businesses moved out or shut down and many, many complaints, he promptly reversed himself and strongly backed repealing the law! Talk about swaying with the breeze! It was eventually repealed, but in the six months it was in effect, there was utter chaos here. What other than meat headedness could explain why Florida tapioca legislators passed a Natzi taxing policy that, in effect, drives yachts out of Florida, costing the state multimillions of dollars. And what else but Cranious Softosis Tapiocas could explain the signs posted at tollbooths on the Florida Turnpike which, considerately, give these instructions to tollbooth robbers:

"WARNING: ROBBERY STAKEOUT AREA. WHEN CHALLENGED BY AN OFFICER DROP YOUR WEAPON, RAISE YOUR HANDS, DO NOT MOVE. VIOLATORS WILL BE DISARMED BY FORCE."

I don't make this garbage up folks! Here we see that the government, rather than trying to curb crime, has opted for accepting that the tollbooths will be robbed and, therefore, helpfully supply bandits with written instructions! Soon, I'm sure, we'll see similar signs in banks. While they're at it, how about instructions for selling dope at every street corner?

Rounding the corner onto state road 76, I'm finally in the

clear so long as I don't get nailed by the radar trap up the road. Because the Stuart traffic has given me so much time to think, I've been able to develop a lot of material for this piece. Next month, in the fourth and final installment, I will (finally) address the topic of Florida boating. Meanwhile, I've got to get to the office to see if I've gotten any calls from the Stuart Chamber of Commerce.

April 1990

The Californication of Florida Part 4

It is 6:15 p.m. on my way home. Traffic is backed up so far from the traffic light providing access to the Palm City Bridge that it's nearly obscured by the curvature of the earth! It's never been this bad and I'm really steamed. Luckily, I'm driving my SHO which, unlike Corvettes, doesn't mind stop and go traffic. Some dumb, pushy broad tries to cut in ahead of me. Being New York traffic trained, I instinctively pop the clutch and jump forward to close the gap (bad move, it turns out). She gives me a dirty look and pulls in behind me. We claw along. Suddenly, I feel a sharp bump at the rear of the car. Dumb pushy has rear ended me! I get out of the car ready to kill! Dumb pushy rolls out of her seat. She denies my queries concerning booze, illegal substances or her lineage. Her hair looks like something out of the "Bride of Frankenstein." Obnoxious rap music is blasting from her stereo. "My foot slipped off the clutch" she informs me, "I'm in a hurry because I have to get to Driving School!" While inspecting my bumper, I made the obligatory comment that driving school, indeed, was a good place for her. Saved from any damage by our wonderful rubber baby buggy bumpers, I return to the driver's seat and continue with a vengeance my plans to keep people the hell out of Florida ....

What about the fabled Florida boating scene? Believe me, folks, it's not all it's cracked up to be. Visions of palm lined, crystal clear waterways caressed by balmy zephyrs look pretty good in Northern Michigan in January, but I'll tell you how it <u>really</u> is. Florida suffers a similar fate as California so far as boating is concerned, that is, unless you want to travel relatively long distances, <u>there's no place to go in Florida</u>! Essentially, Florida waterways consist of: 1) the Intracoastal and 2) the Ocean. Florida has not been blessed with an abundance of bays and rivers. The Florida west coast is somewhat better than the east coast in this regard, however, there's no water on the west coast and, unless your boat draws nine inches or less, cruising there is troublesome. The Bahamas offer spectacular cruising, but you'll have to cross the open ocean to get to there. There are, of course, the Keys and the Okeechobee Waterway. The Keys are okay if you like druggies and dropouts. These days, if you want to cross Lake Okeechobee, you'd better have an <u>airboat</u> since the level of the lake has dropped to seagull wading levels. Most of Florida cruising, therefore, consists of cruises up and down the Intracoastal Waterway which can be great fun but extremely dangerous. Basically, people cruise the waterway (1) to get to waterfront restaurants (2) to admire the houses or (3) to show off their boats (an adult version of teenagers cruising the streets in their cars). Indeed, there are some spectacular houses along the Intracoastal, especially in the larger cities like Ft. Lauderdale and Boca. Unfortunately, most of these spectacular homes were designed along the principals of "Dufus Architecture." Dufus Architecture occurs when people have more money than taste. Unfortunately, many of these waterfront structures look like First National Banks or "Antebellum" mansions or the Palace of Versailles or the Whitehouse. Huge Grecian columns are prevalent as are large, ornate hanging chandeliers and cobblestone walks. Yes, a cruise up and down the Intracoastal in a place like Ft. Lauderdale can be quite amusing.

There is, however, great danger lurking in Florida's Intracoastal Waterways.

QUESTION: WHAT DO YOU GET WHEN YOU HANG GOLD CHAINS AROUND THE NECK OF AN ORANGUTAN? ANSWER: A <u>FLORIDA</u> <u>MUSCLE</u> <u>BOATER</u>! Here, where the balmy zephyrs blow over palm lined waterways (which might be 150' wide and packed with boats on a weekend), we find muscle boats running flat out. I'm not talking about the 25' outboard powered Scarabs running 40 m.p.h. I'm talking about 40' and 50' Ocean Racer clones powered by twin, triple or quadruple inboard engines capable of (and usually running at) speeds up to 90 miles per hour! You haven't lived until a bright red 50' Catamaran powered by four unmuffled Lamborghini V-12 engines blows by you at close quarters doing 80 knots! Your ears won't stop ringing for a week! Some of these rigs are driven by 12 year old kids! Sometimes their baby brothers are driving! Things are so bad down here that strict speed limits are inevitable (coming soon: hidden radar traps along the Intracoastal and marine versions of VASCAR (VASBOAT?)) and, I'm sure, it won't be long until mandatory licensing is law. For this, you can thank the gold chained simians driving muscle boats who rack up an impressive death toll on the waterways every year.

If you survive the blitz boaters, you'll have to contend with the bridges on the Intracoastal. It's funny, but when you're in a car, the damn things are <u>always</u> <u>open</u> stopping traffic. When you're in a boat, however, the bridges are <u>always</u> <u>closed</u> with the bridge tender snoring in front of a T.V. set tuned to "One Life To Live." Add to all this the scarcity of dockage, virtually no areas where one can drop the hook and you'll see that Florida boating is not as wonderful as you've been led to believe.

During these past four months, I have introduced you to the <u>real</u> <u>Florida</u>. A land of abundant bugs and mysterious creatures that live underground. A land rich in wildlife such as snakes, rats and land crabs. A land of a jillion lizards. An eroding land, threatened to be inundated every summer by killer hurricanes. A land of too many transplanted New Yorkers and of erratic electrical power. A land where slime balls and dirt bags congregate and the shark law industry thrives. A land of perpetual, partial cloudiness. Now really folks: DOES THIS SOUND LIKE A PLACE TO WHICH YOU'D WANT TO MOVE? They say that in the next ten years the world's population will grow at a huge rate resulting in a population of around 10 billion people in the year 2000. The way things are looking here, I'm certain most of these people will end up in South Florida! So stay in your big Northern cities or your snowy Western mountains or your great heartland. Florida is not the place for you. Now you must excuse me -- I've got to go squash a bug.

It's been 25 minutes and I'm not home yet! Normally this commute is about eight minutes. Here in Stuart, this only happens during the winter months when the area is inundated with "snowbirds" from all over the country (and the world). These "snowbirds" are predominantly made up of yuppers and retirees escaping from the dreariness of the northern winter. But there's something I don't understand. Here we have a group of people who are (presumably), smart enough to make enough money to be able to winter in Florida and chase Palmetto bugs around their comfortable southern homes. Why, then, do these (seemingly) intelligent people choose to venture out on our roadways between eight and nine in the morning and five and six in the afternoon to create these small town traffic jumbles? They don't need to be there like us working slobs. The only thing I can come up with is that it makes these idle wealthy feel <u>useful</u>: Creeping around in traffic gives them <u>something to do</u>! Yeah, that's it! In fact, I'll bet these people spend their mornings and evenings shuttling back and forth between their houses and town just like the old days when they served some purpose. Next to getting bitten by a land crab, that's probably the most excitement they'll have in Florida. As I finally make the turn approaching the Palm City Bridge, I'm happier knowing that I've done my part with these four articles to help preserve the

Paradise Peninsula.

May 1990

Two Hamburgers with Fries and a Chocolate Shake to Go
Part 1
The South Florida Fast Food Yacht Interior Phenomenon

I'M DAMN WELL SICK AND TIRED OF IT AND I'M NOT GOING TO TAKE IT ANYMORE! I'm tired of bumping into mirrored bulkheads. I'm tired of those little lights strung all over yacht interiors like F.A.O. Schwartz in December. I'm tired of little optical fibers intertwined in carpets that hurt your feet when you walk on them. I'm tired of worrying about heavy glass falling on me when a boat is in a seaway. I'm tired of having to wear sunglasses <u>inside</u> boats to cut down the glare. I'm tired of going aboard boats, looking around and having to <u>lie</u> about what I think of the interior. "Gee, it's uh ... different. Very unique ... Hey! Nice ashtrays." Let's not beat around the gilded bush. Many South Florida yacht interiors <u>stink</u>.

It all started in the early 80's, when a South Florida interior designer (who will remain nameless), but was known as "The Prince of Darkness," came up with some startlingly different yacht interiors. The trend started slowly but the look caught on and, by the mid-eighties was snowballing out of control and yacht interior design hasn't been the same since.

These "Prince of Darkness" interiors were usually very dark -- mostly black lacquer, highlighted by an abundance of etched glass, neon strip lighting, mirrors, and funny patterns in the carpet that looked something like those football plays John Madden scrawls out on the T.V. "chalkboard." Yes, the look may not have been in the best of taste but certainly was different and South Florida (never known as a bastion of great taste anyhow), embraced the trend and made it their own. Let's face it, folks, any place where people spend the time and money to remove the chrome emblems and hood ornaments from their Mercedes and replace them with <u>gold plated</u> emblems and hood ornaments because they think that's real class, cannot be said to have taste except what they perceive in their mouths. In the mid-eighties, in fact, an entire T.V. series named Miami Vice was built around this dark, brooding, and interior look. Although the trend manifested itself in the eighties, it's real origin, however, was in the <u>fifties</u> from places with names like "Orbit Hamburgers," or "Intergalactic Weiner House." These fast food dives with their abundance of high gloss surfaces, mirrors, neon lights, and chrome were the predecessors of the South Florida fast food yacht interior look and, consequently, anytime I step aboard one of these floating wiener houses, I have an irrepressible urge to yell "TWO HAMBURGERS WITH FRIES AND A CHOCOLATE SHAKE TO

GO!" Once firmly established in Florida, the look started spreading like a locust plague, North and West until we became mired in an age of Dufus design, arcade architecture, and Disney decor.

Damn it: Boat interiors should look like <u>boat interiors</u> -- not Fifth Avenue penthouses, not the Golden Arches, not the Taj Mahal, and not Tara from Gone in the Wind. Traditionally, yacht interiors were cool, calm, restful places for a reason. Mariners coming inside from a day in the sun, wind and rain needed a sanctuary to rest their eyes and weary bodies. Nowadays, coming from a day in the elements into one of these glitz palaces encourages one to turn around and go back outside into the sun, wind and rain where it's more restful!

Let's talk about mirrors. Some boats have so many mirrors they look like damned funhouses. I personally have been aboard boats where I went down a mirrored companionway only to be confronted with a foyer completely lined with faceted mirrors including the cabinsole and the overhead. Luckily, after a few hours, I was able to find the stairwell again and work my way out of that place! There's a story about a slightly tipsy gent aboard a large yacht who went to use the day head which was a small compartment on the maindeck. Here again, the four bulkheads, cabinsole and overhead were completely lined with mirrors. Understandably, he became confused and the poor guy ended up relieving himself on a <u>reflection of the water closet in the mirrors</u> thinking he was aiming for the water closet itself! In reality, it was on the other side of the compartment! Is it real or is it Memorex? Some boats have so many mirrors that a full-time mirror cleaning crew is necessary and Windex tanks must be permanently installed aboard. These full-time mirror cleaners are necessary to remove what I call the "Mark of the Confused." This "Mark of the Confused" can be found on any boat with extensive mirror treatment. The marks are <u>face</u> <u>prints</u> left on mirrors from people ramming into the damn things. Forehead print, nose print and chin print! Oh yes, and a trickle of blood from the broken nose.

Mirrors -- the bane of my existence. Not only are they impractical and dangerous, they are also wasteful. Glass mirrors are heavy and, if used in abundance, can significantly increase the weight of a vessel which will cut down speed and reduce fuel economy. Additionally, they are commonly <u>glued</u> onto rather flimsy, non-structural interior bulkheads and can come loose in a seaway. I remember spending a totally sleepless night in a large motor yacht's double bed over which was a big, glass mirror which was pasted to the deck liner. Let's face it, boat structure moves and works in a seaway and a 1200 pound etched glass divider (with the entire history of the Roman Empire graphically depicted in neon blue and pink) becoming unglued in your saloon while you're snoozing on your Connolly leather Italian sofa can ruin your whole nap.

Perhaps the ultimate in mirror treatments was specified by the owner of a large sportsfisherman for his stateroom. It was a flat, innocuous looking upholstered panel over a big double berth, divided in the center. At the touch of a button, the panels in the overhead swung down to produce what was, in effect, a mirrored tent with mirrors on the overhead and at an angle on each side. The side panels were electrically adjustable so the owner, no doubt, wouldn't miss any of the action ("Slow down a minute Trixie, I have to adjust the mirrors.") Like I said, is it real or it is Memorex?

Next month, I'll give you the inside story on colors, introduce the boating world to a yacht interior test and suggest some new directions that yacht interiors might take. In the meantime, if you're invited aboard a mirror laden yacht, be sure to wear a hockey goalies face mask. You might be mistaken for Freddie the Slasher, but your face will be safe and you can rest assured that you won't be leaving the "Mark of the Confused" on those lovely mirrors.

June 1990

Two Hamburgers with Fries and a Chocolate Shake to Go
Part 2

I've got a real Walter Cronkite for some of you folks: <u>Yachts are built to get people out on the water and enjoy the marine environment</u>! Why then do many people opt to isolate themselves in glitzy, no taste hermetically sealed splendorous cabins that reproduce their Central Park West homes. What the hell's the point? In part one I speculated that this brassy, flashy, no classy style actually originated in fast food dives of the 1950's.

Back at the turn of the century, it was common for large steam yachts to be fitted with heavy, baroque (if it ain't baroque don't fix it) appointments. Extravagant Louis the Fourteenth interiors were common. Today's fast food interior look might be called "Ronnie the First" interiors for it was during the Reagan years that poor taste ran rampant and the South Florida glitz look took off. These "Ronnie the First" interiors all basically look the same -- too many mirrors, too many glossy surfaces, too much etched glass, too much gold, too many Christmas lights strung around the edges of everything, too many designs in the carpet -- just too damn much of everything.

There seems to be an overwhelming urge for people to make the interiors of their boats "just like home." Boat interiors, however, need to be designed with the marine environment in mind. Unlike houses, that dirty machinery on yachts is only a piece of thin plywood away from the neoclassical onyx pedestal displaying the bronze bust of Julius Caesar. Service people need access to the machinery. Since most boats float on water, they are perpetually in a damp environment. I've put together a series of interior tests which can be performed to evaluate the practicality of any interior. If you are intending to buy a vessel with a fast food yacht interior, take note:

1) If you are confronted by a mirrored bulkhead and see more than one image of yourself in it (while sober) turn around and leave.

2) Bring a greasy, sweaty, sloppy, mechanic aboard with his grungy tool box and ask him to check the machinery. If the owner blanches as he drags his grease encrusted engineer boots across the priceless carpet originally woven for the Sistine chapel, look at another boat.

3) Have a friend come along who, while you are inspecting the boat, will dive overboard for a swim and come back aboard soaking wet. Have him stroll into the saloon and plop down on the sofa. If the owner goes ballistic, sputtering something about tapestry from the Palace of Versailles, the

boat has failed the test.

4) Have the boat opened up for a few days with the air conditioning off. After three or four days, close it up again. If it smells like a huge armpit (due to mold and fungi), it's time to look at more boats.

5) Go out on a sea trial. If, prior to the sea trial, the crew scurries around for a half hour laying chairs on their sides, removing and stowing art objects, putting lamps on the sole and generally making the interior of the boat look like it's been ransacked by robbers, politely beg off.

6) Place a glass of cheap, dark, red wine at the edge of a table. If the glass slips off the edge as the boat rolls due to a lack of fiddles and stains the Edward Fields, give it an "F."

Things are clearly getting out of hand. Carpets, usually about three inches thick, need to be <u>mowed</u> every week. They commonly have designs that look something like elephant turds inlaid into them. The latest fad is to interweave thousands of little fiber optic transmitters into the pile of the carpet. At the flip of a switch, little points of light appear throughout the carpet. ("Look Gertrude, someone's sprinkled <u>gold</u> <u>dust</u> in the carpet.") These points can be brightened or dimmed to suit. Maybe this is what George Bush meant when he talked about his "Thousand Points of Light."

Let's talk about colors. One owner told his interior designer that he would like his boat done in avocado and umber (translation: green and brown). The interior designer was aghast at such a passé color scheme and asserted that he (or she -- I'll never tell) wouldn't work in such gauche colors. The designer did, however, agree to take the owner's money to do an interior in <u>teal</u> and <u>ginger spice</u> (translation: green and brown). Why can't colors be called what they are instead of using foolish names? For your edification, I am pleased to bring you the following color dictionary so you and your interior designer can speak the same language:

        Mauve = Purple
        Silver = Gray
        Platinum = Gray
        Coral = Pink
        Fuchsia = Pink
        Heather= Pink
        Sorbet = Pink
        Avocado = Green
        Teal = Green
        Umber = Brown
        Ginger Spice = Brown
        Champagne = Light Brown
        Tawny Blush = Light Brown
        Doe Skin = Light Brown
        Safari = Light Brown
        Taupe = Light Brown

There is a lot of this kind of silliness going on which could fill an entire article, but you get the idea.

The South Florida Japanese pinball parlor look never caught on in Europe. For the most part, European interiors are tasteful and coolly understated, looking like (heaven forbid) <u>yacht interiors</u>. Even the flamboyant Italians haven't embraced the South Florida glitz look (probably because they didn't invent it).

After all this retched interior excess, it's time we go in another direction... to something refreshing and completely different... to break the mold. As usual, I have some suggestions: Let's see some new, large yachts have their cabinsoles covered in <u>linoleum</u> -- gray or maroon battleship linoleum would be nice, but marbleized linoleum is okay too -- so durable and easy to clean. Bulkheads, of course, should be varnished wood. And how about replacing the currently overdone poofter window treatments with something straightforward and simple -- like <u>venetian</u> <u>blinds</u> - big slatted, varnished, wooden ones. And let's replace those leather or suede headliners with something more practical -- like acoustic tile. You know, the white interlocking squares with little holes in them. And what about all those fancy, glitzy, imported light fixtures? Why not use <u>real</u> marine light fixtures: bare light bulbs screwed into chrome fixtures with those little twist switches on them and those little half shades that snap onto the bulbs with pictures of steering wheels or buoys on them. Upholstery should be Naugahyde, of course. Seriously folks, I would feel a lot more comfortable on a yacht done as described above than on some of the floating wiener houses I've been aboard lately.

When all is said and done, yacht interiors should make one feel <u>comfortable</u>. Too many interiors make me feel that I'm on a dammed Hollywood movie set. Happily, it seems the arcade interior trend may have peaked. We're starting to see some South Florida boats like the new 82' Burger "LAID BACK," fitted with tasteful, elegant but rather simple interiors. Let's hope this trend continues. In the meantime, I'll have ketchup and pickles on my hamburger. Oh yeah-- and hold the onions -- they give me gas.

July 1990

Storm Warnings
Part 1

The Sky is Falling!

S hort and sweet, my advice for pleasure boaters can be summed up by a verse penned by the 19th Century poet Robert Herrick: "Gather ye rosebuds while ye may ...." In the past I've done a number of articles and interviews concerning the future of power boating. Until only a year ago, these prognostications centered on technical advances: Hull shapes, power plants and construction materials. Well, listen up boaters, for things have changed rapidly and I'll tell you the chilling story of what boating will really be like in the future (unless we take a stand now). This is the <u>real</u> stuff and is not happy reading. No safe, whimpy predictions about increased speeds or zoomier styling or puff upholstery or new lightweight hulls made of resin impregnated goose feathers here. What could happen in the future would render all advancements in yachts since the dawn of man <u>insignificant</u>.

It pains me to say that future changes in powerboating will not come from within the industry, but from without (and I mean <u>without</u> because we will be doing <u>without</u> many things). What are these forces from without that will affect boating? Fruitcakes like Ghadafy? Invaders from space? Natural disasters? Well, it's none of these hazards. Actually, it's a group of <u>Chicken</u> <u>Littles</u>: whimpy legislators, do gooders, and bleeding heart environmentalists. Surprised? Don't be because these people are the greatest threat to boating and, in fact, life as we know it than anything else in the solar system.

Environmentalists pose the greatest threat, but Animal Rights Activists and the like will all contribute. Before the hate mail starts rolling in let me say that I am against destroying the earth and killing dolphins, etc., but there needs to be some <u>balance</u>. The problem with causes is that once supporters of these causes get what they want, they have nothing to do except go for more. As a result, their goals get ever more silly and insignificant. I applaud the small core of people truly concerned about the environment and animal rights. They should be listened to and respected, but this is a <u>very</u> <u>small</u> group of citizens. The rest are <u>phonies</u>. Let me tell you why. These phonies who attach themselves to the above groups aren't really concerned with the group's causes but with <u>social</u> <u>change</u>. Yes, folks, we're talking <u>social</u> <u>revolution</u>. To put it in easy to understand terms, let's take an everyday "environmental activist" (typically in need of a haircut) who may be driving a beat up '69 Volvo. He's promoting laws against big cars not because the cars pollute or waste fuel (in fact new cars pollute less and are more economical than '69 Volvos), but simply because <u>he</u> <u>doesn't</u> <u>have</u> <u>one</u> <u>himself</u>! It's the non-achievers against the achievers. The same goes for leaf eating vegetarians who wish they could eat meat and feminists who wish they were men. Please address your cards and letters to myself.

Before I get to the predictions, let me bring you up to date on some of the events, promoted by these non-achievers, that have already affected boatsmen everywhere. The circle is closing and it started
in ....

1971 - A law is passed requiring marine toilets on all pleasure boats to either contain their waste or treat it before discharging it overboard.

Comment: This is a perfect example of the pleasure boating public being bullied by environmentalists and legislators. While industries, cities and towns were dumping huge amounts of waste into the sea (and still are), Congress passed a law requiring pleasure boaters to contain or treat their waste. The fact that the contribution of waste by pleasure boaters is a mere plop in the bucket compared to other sources of contamination made no difference. As I remember, certain states invoked the law separately until a Federal law was passed covering all States. At the time, I was doing my boating in New York waters and was so upset when the New York legislature passed their version of the law, that I fired off the following letter (included in part) after observing an impolite flock of mallard ducks polluting New York waters:

"..... Mr. Politician, you have looked the other way when it comes to municipal and industrial polluters (they have lobbies) and picked on us boatmen, but here we have a politician's dream, a group even more defenseless than boatmen: ducks, seagulls, swans and other marine fowl. Think of it! Millions of them!! I certainly think legislation is warranted to curb this great threat to our environment.

A nice water fowl holding tank would be the animal carrying the device strapped astern and be hydrodynamically shaped. When the tank is full, the bird simply flies off and dumps it over land from, say, 5000 feet. For an ideal dumping area, may we suggest the state capital, Albany, New York.

P.S. After this legislation is passed, we suggest you investigate the matter of fish pollution.

And what about the big marine mammals like sperm whales? I submit that a single discharge from a sperm whale amounts to more sea pollution than the average boater dumps in an entire season! But let's face it, there's a big trend now towards making everything biodegradable and, when you think about it, nothing is more biodegradable than poop! Nature planned it that way.

Although this silly law was passed to contain or treat all discharge from marine heads, it didn't mandate pump out stations. So here we had boats running around smelling to high heaven with tanks full and no place to put it except back into the water (where it belongs). This law was and is a joke since nobody complies with it and is a perfect example of things getting out of hand. Do gooders, bleeding hearts and our legislators, greedy for votes, picked on people with no lobbies who, in fact, contribute an insignificant amount to the ocean's pollution.

1988 – Newly elected, confirmed powerboater, George Bush sends warm and cozy feelings throughout the pleasure boat industry which anticipates that a president, who is a boating enthusiast himself, would look out for their interests. That Spring, pleasure boaters discovered to their dismay that tin based bottom paints have been <u>outlawed</u> throughout the United States raising the hackles (and barnacles) of boat owners everywhere.

Comment: Despite the fact that pollution of the world's waters by TBT paints has <u>never</u> <u>been</u> <u>documented</u> and ignoring the simple fact that damn tin is <u>abundant naturally in seawater</u>, our wonderful environmentalists pushed legislation through anyhow. How long will it be before they go after copper paint? Not long indeed as you'll see below.

Next month, we'll look at my predictions for exactly how the pleasure boating public will be screwed by Chicken Little legislators, environmentalists and animal right's advocates. In the meantime, pick up them rosebuds as fast as you can folks.

August 1990

Storm Warnings Part 2

It's <u>Easy</u> Being Green

If we're nothing else, we Americans are trendsetters. Trends develop (often times on the West Coast) and spread through the country (and the world) like a virus. A trend can be as simple as pegged pants or as far reaching as a new way of life. Over the past 50 or 60 years, many trendy new ways of life have come and gone: prohibition, isolationism, the atomic family, the peace generation and the me generation to name a few. People ever hungry to be "in with the in crowd" latch on to entire ways of life as easily as kids pick up on coonskin hats or Ninja Turtles. Now we're in the nervous nineties and it is clear that the overriding "thing" for this decade will be the environment.

In part one, we talked about the phony underachiever anticapitalists who attach themselves to green groups (originally formed by dedicated environmentalists), not because they're concerned with the environment, but because they want to go after the achievers. In short, they are looking for social upheaval rather than environmental cleanliness. Besides, being into a "thing" makes these duds feel wanted. Their attitude is: "That guy has a boat and I don't, therefore let's make it difficult to own boats." I have nothing against green groups. We <u>need</u> green groups as a check against the big business polluters and land ravagers. I simply object to the phonies.

This "thing" of the nineties, however, could have far reaching effects over the next 50 years on boatmen who contribute a negligible amount to the world's pollution problem. Boatmen, in fact, have already been affected. In part one, I went back to 1971 when the environmentalists first attacked boatmen and pushed into law their foolish holding tank legislation. Then, in 1988, tin based bottom paints were banned and now...

1990 - Earth Day Spring Festivals are held throughout the world, with impressive numbers of attendees and guest appearances by people like Tom Cruise, Olivia Newton John, Jane Fonda and other celebrity opportunists. The die for the future is cast.

Comment: Why do I call the nice people who participate in these ventures "phonies?" The participants of the Earth Day festival held in New York City's Central Park left behind <u>250 tons of trash</u>! 250 TONS OF GARBAGE!!! About the same amount that could be expected after a heavy metal rock concert. Does this tell you something? While Tom Cruise was making speeches about the environment, his producers were wrapping up his latest film called "Days of Thunder" about stock car racing which wasted hundreds, if not thousands of gallons of gasoline during the filming and dumped copious amounts of unregulated exhaust from their straight pipes. While Olivia Newton John was working hard to be perceived as an activist, bulldozers were defacing the beach for her new Malibu home. Tell me these people aren't phonies. And speaking of phonies ... As Earth Day was approaching, on my drive to work I was behind some yuppie twit's wife in a new dark green (of course) Volvo wagon. The box back of the car was plastered with stickers proclaiming "Save the Earth," "Sierra Club," "Earth First" and "Greenpeace." Here, I thought, may be one of the few people truly dedicated to the environment. As I was passing, I glanced into the car and noticed an infant strapped in the car seat next to her. What's wrong with this picture? Nothing, except all the windows were closed and this phony broad was smoking up a storm! Makes a lot of sense doesn't it? Clean up the earth but make your kid breathe damned secondhand cigarette smoke in a closed car. Save the dolphins. Kill your kid. Wonderful.

1995 – The Senate and the House agree on what will be known as the Boating Bill of 1993 promulgated by the unwashed environmentalists. It seems innocuous enough at the outset: the bill requires that all discharges from marine vessels be contained including water drains, bilge pumps, waste and engine exhaust water. To the legislators who knew nothing about boats it appeared that, since most boats already carried holding tanks for toilet discharges, why not increase the size of this tank a little to contain all discharges. It never occurred to the Washington deadheads who passed the law that they had mandated boats to become, in effect, huge floating tanks growing ever heavier as they cruised until, eventually, they sunk themselves from the weight of their own discharges! Outgoing President George Bush with little to lose, vetoes the bill, but it is overridden and becomes law.

Comment: If this sounds farfetched, let it be known that the Swiss have already proposed severe emission level limits on all marine engines. Austria and Germany will soon follow suit. Marine engine ads in Europe are touting the "environmental friendliness" of their engines. Meanwhile, while environmental groups are worried about our marine engines negligible contribution to the greenhouse effect, a new U.S. Government study has just come out stating that the world's 1.3 billion cattle produce, due to their normal digestive process, 70 million metric tons of methane gas yearly accounting for nearly one fifth of the world's greenhouse gasses! And this is gas only -- the effects of cow patties was not addressed. Get those cows some Rolaids! Who will be the first country to mandate catalytic converters to be fitted under the tail of each cow and bull? And who will be the first to start a bovine liberation group to "curtail" (sorry) this cruel punishment to animals. It never ends.

2004 - President Tom Cruise sweeps to victory on a platform of barnacle rights. A huge mainstream of interest headed by BARF (Barnacle Rights Foundation) develops in the country. During his campaign, Cruise studded his speeches with penetrating, insightful phrases like "Barnacles have rights too". He bemoans the executing of barnacles on boat bottoms with scrapers and the poisoning of their little lungs with noxious copper paint. After an emotional "Barnacles Are People Too" speech by California Senator Donnie Osmond, the bill is passed by Congress. The legislation outlaws any form of torturing barnacles including scraping, poisoning or preventing their growth by hull vibrators. The little vibrating transducers attached to the inside of the hull were found to be cruel and unusual barnacle punishment. Boats left afloat soon become floating reefs encrusted with two feet of protected barnacles and marine growth with their owners helpless to do anything. Environmentalists are overjoyed since these floating marine gardens provide food and shelter for marine life and immediately start pushing to make each of these floating gardens part of the National Parks System. Speeds for boats left afloat drop by 85%. Dry stack storage yards for larger boats start springing up around the country. The prestigious North Cove Yacht Harbor at Wall Street is filled in and a megayacht dry stack storage building is erected.

Comment: It's only a matter of time before the environmental Nazis start going after copper paint despite the fact the runoff from fertilizers used in farms throughout the country constitute a far greater risk to the marine environment than slow dissolving bottom paints. Look for drastic increases in sales of boat lifts and the aforementioned dry stack storage for large boats.

Next month we'll look further into the future as legislators continue to smother boatmen with silly laws. In the meantime, I'm thinking of forming my own group: Cruisers

Against Pantywaist Opportunists (CRAPO). Stay tuned. The fight has just begun.

September 1990

Storm Warnings Part 3

The Emergence of Uncle Sam Yacht Design

*I*n parts one and two, I described how "green groups" have already affected the lives of boatsmen in this country, and proceeded looking into the future to see what effects these groups could have on boating in the next 50 years. I made the statement that what could happen in the next fifty years could render all achievements in yachts since the dawn of man insignificant. Last month, we looked at the year 2004 when United States President Tom Cruise was elected to office based on a platform of barnacle rights. During this time, people are forming new green and animal activist groups daily. My time machine is warmed up and we look at the year .....

2008 – Now that internal combustion cars have been outlawed and people must drive electric, three wheeled, padded cocoons governed at 20 mph, newly elected President Bo Jackson ("Bo knows politics") turns his attention to a bill that will lead the marine industry down the same federalized road that the automotive industry was forced to travel. This bill was initially proposed jointly by Senators Bryant Gumbel and Oprah Winfrey, working with governments around the world under the auspices of the Alliance for Ratification of a Marine Pleasure craft International Treaty, better known as ARMPIT and a special presidential commission (Presidential Action Commission for Marine and Navigational Standards) known as PACMANS. The "Comprehensive Boating Act of 2008," wide ranging in its scope, not only affects marine machinery but, for the first time, also addresses the actual design of pleasure craft. Some of the bill's more pertinent requirements are:

- All V-bottom hulls are banned. Only flat bottoms will be allowed. This law was based on an ecological study scribbled in crayon by students at the Smurf Day Care Center of Pasadena, California. Based on comprehensive sandbox tests, it revealed that V-bottom hulls, as opposed to flat bottom hulls, left ugly scars on the sand and mud when they ran aground or were pushed ashore. Furthermore, it was found that V-hulls were more prone to cause injury when running over aquadestrians and marine mammals.

- Bows of all boats must be square in plain view and plumb in profile. The presidential commission made the startling discovery that pointed bows pose great danger to bystanders around docks who might be inadvertently impaled. This was brought to light after a respected congressman was struck by a boat while crawling from the bar at his yacht club. Had it not been for the wads of hundred dollar bills stuffed inside his shirt, serious injury could have resulted. It was further found that, in side impact collisions, pointed bows tended to penetrate hull sides of the boats they hit. In conjunction with this, side guard beams, energy absorbent bumpers, collapsible steering columns, rollover safety structures and controlled crush bows and sterns also become law.

- Camber and slope on decks are banned due to the grievous danger they present to people slipping and falling. This resulted from Congressman Gary Coleman (a member of PACMANS) who was out for a morning stroll on a dewy deck of a friend's yacht when his <u>wing tips</u> slipped causing him to fall and injure his back.

- All forms of marine antennas are banned after PACMANS uncovers a book report by a high school student in Albania which intimated that marine antennas might emit dangerous electromagnetic pulses. This relegates radar, loran, sitcom and the like to the junk pile. Henceforth, navigation will be via charts, binoculars and compass only (although studies are proceeding to investigate the dangers of papercuts by charts, damage to the retina by binoculars and a compass's magnetic interference with the heart).

- Cleats on deck were pinpointed as great hazards after a 97 year old great grandmother with a club foot and arthritis testified at the PACMANS hearings that, in 2004, she tripped on a cleat after participating in an all night chugalug contest aboard a yacht. The law banishes all cleats and mandates that boats be secured by harnesses tied around their hulls.

- All forms of row boats are banned. Actually, the boats themselves are okay -- just the <u>oars</u> are outlawed. A flounder activist group, Flounder Activist Reform Tribunal

(FART) had a documented report revealing that, in 1978, a <u>single</u> <u>flounder</u> in Barnegat Bay sustained major scale injury incurred by a dangerously flailing oar.

- Anchors must be made of <u>soft</u> <u>rubber</u>. Heavy metal ones were known to damage coral reefs while anchoring and might injure fish on the way down.

- Exposed propellers are outlawed and propeller guards mandated reducing speed and efficiency of boats by 40% and causing them to burn a similar amount more fuel. This 40% reduction in performance added to the aforementioned 85% drop in speed due to severely fouled bottoms, totals a whopping 125% drop in speed which means that boats, when running at their cruising speed, would actually be <u>going backwards</u>!

Comment: After the safety and environmental Nazis are finished federalizing cars into mere shadows of their former existence, boats are the next logical target. In fact "off road vehicles" have already been targeted. That's right folks. With amazing logic, bureaucrats have classified vessels like "Trump Princess" and your 40' cruiser as "off road vehicles" and will treat them like floating cars. It started innocently enough with a head discharge law and progressed to bottom paint laws, after which they might invoke marine seatbelt laws. The creeping federalism will continue with cockpit safety padding laws, and, eventually air bags. This done, they will slowly work their way into federalizing the shape and structure of boats. Moving towards their goal of electric powered, floating, padded cocoons governed at 20 mph.

2009 - The Comprehensive Boating Act is made law and an

amendment is immediately proposed by California Congressman Charles Manson (elected on an anti-crime platform), to provide "law on water" for the wild waterways just like we have on our roads. This amendment includes such gems as strict boating speed limits on all waterways, fleets of radar equipped squad boats are disbursed on all U.S. Waterways to enforce the speed limits. Originally, aircraft were used to monitor waterways from high up, timing boats between white lines painted on the water, but this idea was discarded when it was found that manatees were eating the white lines. A system of billboards is erected throughout the waterways in order to give squad boats a place to hide. Money from the advertising space sold on these billboards would go to waterway beautification. Other features of the bill:

- Safety glass on all windows
- Safety padding of all cockpit surfaces
- Sealed beam head and tail light systems
- Seatbelts must be worn by all occupants
- Deep dish, collapsible steering wheels
- Padded sun visors
- Safety door latches
- Safety rearview mirrors
- Four way emergency flashing system
- Energy absorbing steering wheel with padded hub and collapsible steering column
- Side guard beams to absorb impact in crash situations
- Controlled crush front and back ends of boats
- Energy absorbing bumpers

- Anti-lock breaks
- Rollover safety structures under roof panels
- Five m.p.h. impact bumpers

2010 - In a startling announcement, President Bo quits the presidency to become a "color commentator" for ABC Sports (Bo knows television). Vice President Gloria Steinam assumes command. Naval Architect Tom Fexas retires to become a full-time writer, refusing to design flat decked, flat bottomed, square bowed, barnacle encrusted "monstrosities" that cruise backwards.

2011 - President Steinam's feminist advisers discover terrible sexism in the yachting community. A strong activist group, Women Advocating Neutral Gender Ships (WANGS) has developed. Ms. President strongly backs the Neutral Gender Marine Bill which would make it illegal to call boats "she." The law passes and all vessels must be referred to as "it." (The bill was so well received that, the following year, they make it illegal to call <u>women</u> <u>she</u>.) Further, she (sorry ... it) is horrified to discover that 98% of all boats are owned by men. Legislation is proposed for low interest boat loans to women.

Comment: Absolutely no comment.

Well, this is all very depressing. Next month I'll wrap up this sad story so I can proceed to other, more uplifting articles ..... like the one I'm preparing on marine sludge. In the meantime, get out on the water and enjoy your off road vehicles.

October 1990

Storm Warnings Part 4

Nest Feathering, Exhaust Pipe Sucking and Squad Boats

*E*veryone needs to justify their existence and feather their nests. It's a basic human trait. The problem with environmental green groups and animal rights activists is that most of them feel they have a pretty damn good thing going now. They are making progress on all fronts.

After one more whack at the auto industry (where they'll raise CAFE averages to around 45 mpg and further strangle emissions) the greens will, for all intents and purposes, be finished with automobiles. Auto exhausts will be so clean that people wishing to do away with themselves will have to use a method other than sucking on a tailpipe. Eventually, the forests will be preserved and the spotted owls will be flourishing and waterways will be overflowing with damn snail darter fish. The dolphins will be saved. Why doesn't anyone care about the poor tuna which are killed in far greater numbers than dolphin in the same nets? Is a dolphin's life more precious than a tuna's? Are tuna being discriminated against because they don't have cute smiling faces and TV shows? I don't think either species should suffer. Someone needs to start a tuna liberation movement. It could be called EFFECT (Environmentalists and Friends For Edification of Charlie Tuna). Pollution will be curtailed and the ozone holes will get smaller and acid rain will no longer dissolve our buildings. Yes, eventually, in the not too distant future all this will happen -- no question about it. Once all these wonderful things have been accomplished, however, the funny green people have a big problem. What else can they do to justify their existence? Many of the leaders of green groups are full timers and get paid well for it -- offices on Capitol Hill and the whole bit. Will these people simply close up shop and get real jobs? Doubtful. These groups, therefore, to justify their existence must set new targets. As major accomplishments are made, the targets become ever sillier. When these zealots are finished with the auto industry, they're bound to turn to the marine industry just because it's so easy and so visible. Even though the marine businesses contribution to pollution is absolutely miniscule worldwide compared to autos, municipalities, farming and general industry, these guys need another crusade to preserve their jobs. They've already begun attacking boatsmen well before they're finished with the auto industry. When they are finished with the auto industry, look out boatsmen ... er, excuse me, boats people.

Last month, we made projections through the year 2011 when President Gloria Steinem eliminated sexism in the yachting community.

The year is now ...

2012 - All previous legislation proved most damaging to powerboats and a huge resurgence in sailboats has taken place since the Boating Bill of 1993 was passed. A great aftermarket develops back fitting masts and sails to powerboats. Would you prefer a sloop rig or ketch rig for your Magnum? Noting those trends, the green groups rally against blow boats, crying for more legislation. Halyards slapping against aluminum masts are cited as major causes of marine noise pollution. Dangerous flailing booms caused 659 documented head injuries last year. Three hundred and fifty six people got their fingers (or other appendages) caught in deck winches. Deep keels are defacing underwater terrain. Tall masts are spoiling the landscape of our harbors and harming birds that inadvertently fly into them. But the most compelling reason for legislating against sailboats is because they are stealing -- yes <u>stealing</u> -- one of the earth's most precious natural resources -- <u>the</u> <u>wind</u>. Wind meters were considered but rejected as being impractical since no easy method of charging sailboaters for wind was found (How does one pay for wind? By the puff?). In the end, both houses of Congress unanimously vote to limit draft and mast height of all sailboats to a maximum of two feet and four feet respectively.

Comment: For years the blow boat guys have been pointing at us powerboaters as polluters, but I'm willing to bet that, if a panel of concerned scientists were gathered, they could develop a good case for <u>sailboats</u> contributing to global warming. Sailboats steal wind which would otherwise blow across the seas evaporating water. Evaporation, as we all know is a cooling process, ergo, sailboats contribute to global warming!

2016 - U.S. President Marla Maples signs a bill restricting pleasure boats at their source -- their places of manufacture. It seems the Water Level Increase Monitoring Panel -- otherwise known as WIMP, a committee set up by the Sierra Club, has discovered that the worldwide population of boats was responsible for the water level of all the earth's bodies of water rising by <u>one thousandth of a millimeter</u>. Gleeful at rediscovering Archimedes Principal, the panel decides that this is, indeed, a very menacing situation. As an outgrowth of this discovery, Senator Dennis Conner single handedly puts together and pushes through the "Boat Builder's Unified Restrictions and Practices" bill, otherwise known as the BBURP bill. Initially, the bill targets the fiberglass industry since it is the largest producer of vessels. Homing in on severely limiting styrene and acetone emissions, the bill effectively makes it impossible to build fiberglass boats in the U.S. Taiwanese and Brazilian fiberglass boats flood the market as American builders turn to wood and aluminum vessels. An amendment to the BBURP bill, however, puts an end to these endeavors with severe restrictions on wood dust and welding fumes. A great resurgence in ferro cement boats in the United States occurs.

Comment: Quit snickering. OSHA, previously regulated only 17 toxic chemicals in the American work place. In a surprising move taking only <u>six months</u> from proposal to passage, OSHA established new regulations on over <u>400</u> substances (including wood dust and welding fumes). California has already taken major steps to put fiberglass boat builders out of business.

2017 - Refusing to design flat decked, flat bottomed, square bowed barnacle encrusted, ferro cement yachts, designer Tom Fexas retires to Angra Dos Reis, Brazil to design unregulated boats for South America, continue writing nasty articles and become a full-time beach bum.

Comment: I can't wait!

2020 - United States King John John Kennedy strongly backs a national marine speed limit. Although individual states have had speed limits for years, enforcing them has been problematic. Squad boats had few places to hide along the waterways. Patrol aircraft were proposed to time boats between white lines painted on the water but that idea was scrapped because they couldn't find an environmentally friendly paint. In a stroke of genius, Congress comes up with a clever method of hiding squad boats along waterways. They devise a national system of <u>marine billboards</u> lining channels and waterways which not only provide a place for squad boats to hide, but also earn the government revenue from selling advertising space and promulgating their slogans like: "Keep Our Waterways Beautiful."

Comment: Marine cops are already using jet skis for patrol, and unmarked speedboats -- complete with bimbos are coming soon.

I know I promised this would be a four part article but I'm on a roll here. Next month in what <u>will</u> be the final installment of this series, we will look at some fatal flaws in the environmentalist's thinking. This is a highly charged subject. I've received more than a few calls and letters -- mostly from people who agree with what I said. Last week, however, I got a call from an ecologically minded friend. "I had to <u>hide</u> the August issue from my wife" (she's an ecology activist). "You've hit a <u>new</u> <u>low</u> with this article," he said. I thanked him profusely and hung up. Praise like that doesn't come easy.

November 1990

Storm Warnings
Part 5
The Human Race's "Reason for Being" Revealed at Last!

This really *is* the final chapter on this topic for a while but, unfortunately, the problem won't go away. Sadly, of all the crazy things I've predicted that could happen in the next 50 years (based on what's already transpired) <u>nothing</u> I've proposed in these past five months is impossible. Always remember, green is the "thing" for the nineties.

If there's any doubt in your mind about this, witness what's happening on television which mirrors, in the twisted view of producers, what's happening in real life. Believe it or not, folks, CBS has a new show this season called "E.A.R.T.H. Force." Although it's touted as serious drama, it's been reviewed as one of the funniest new shows of the season. It goes like this: E.A.R.T.H. Force is composed of a group that might be considered a green version of the Dirty Dozen. Here a group of over-qualified nerds composed of nuclear physicists, oceanographers, vegetarians, animal rights advocates, and just about every other eco-profession you can think of, play detective traveling the world righting terrible environmental wrongs. Believe me, folks, E.A.R.T.H. Force is G.A.R.B.A.G.E. (Catch it soon before it's cancelled.) Talk about <u>air</u> pollution!

In my opinion, the dictum environmentalists promulgate as fact -- that the earth is changing due to pollution and destruction by humans --may be overlooking a very important thing. Mother Nature in her infinite wisdom has devised an ingenious system of checks and balances for the earth. For example, let's look at spiders. Spiders were put here to kill creatures like grasshoppers and keep the grasshopper population in check. In turn, birds eat spiders, mammals eat birds, etc., etc. What these environmentalist duds are completely missing is the fact that <u>humans are part of Mother Nature's overall scheme also and must be included in the total picture</u>! And just what do people <u>do</u> in nature's scheme of things? Well, they consume, reshape the land, pollute and kill animals for food or sport. Let's face it, it's what we <u>do</u>! Ergo, it must be what we were put on earth for. (I know some people looking for the meaning of life will be quite upset to learn that, sadly, we were put here to buy Louis Vuitton luggage, build swimming pools, drive BMW's and eat meatball hero sandwiches -- but the conclusion is inescapable.) Although global warming has not yet been proven, let's assume that the funny green people are right and the earth's environment <u>is</u> being warmed by people pollution. Who the hell knows, maybe we were put here to <u>warm</u> the earth to prevent another ice age! In other words, if we weren't here, the earth today could, possibly, be one vast, frozen tundra! In that case, the ecologists then would be the ones screwing up the ecosystem. Who's to say? These jerks just love to blame quirks of nature on mankind. A couple of years ago when we had a terrible drought in the Midwest, green people doomsayers blaming global warming were solemnly predicting this was the end, the climate is changing, the earth will be a dustbowl in six months. Now, two years later, that same region is plagued by <u>floods</u>.

And let's never forget that <u>before people were around</u>, the earth took it upon itself to freeze up and kill <u>all existing life</u> during the ice age. Then, later on, dinosaurs disappeared from the earth due to <u>natural causes</u>. (If the environmentalists were around during this time I'm sure there would be numerous dinosaur rights groups with names like "Save our Brontosaurus" (SOB), blaming the dinosaur's demise on pollution.) LET'S FACE IT, NATURE IS NOT ALL BEAUTY, SWEETNESS AND LIGHT. NATURE CAN BE PRETTY DAMN VIOLENT AND ROTTEN SOMETIMES! Lightning sets fires which deface thousands of acres of forest and displaces or kills untold numbers of insects and animals. Volcanoes blow tops off mountains incinerating thousands of square miles, polluting the atmosphere and spilling hot waste into our seas. Earthquakes devastate the terrain and hurricanes and tornados flood and flatten forests killing thousands of trees and animals. Mammoth sinkholes swallow up Porsche dealerships (it happened in Florida).

So why don't we see these dopes out protesting Mt. Saint Helens or Hurricane Hugo? Well, it's like this, see. These opportunist groups have <u>no pull with The Big Guy</u>. If these people were <u>really</u> serious about ecology they'd be trying to do something about evolution and lightning and earthquakes and hurricanes and tornados and volcanoes by seriously taking up one religion or another and lobbying Him instead of the insignificant beings in Washington. In the overall scheme of things, the destruction and pollution caused by Mother Nature makes the impact of human pollution look very small indeed. No, you can't picket or pass laws against nature.

This series of columns has generated a lot of mail. One letter stands out written by Captain Paul Cox Jr. of Leesburg, New Jersey. Apparently, they are having a lot of trouble in his area with the Government trying to seize private waterfront property to put it under the auspices of the National Park Service. Captain Cox, referring to the green groups advocating this seizure says in part:

"I really believe it is a psychological flaw in their personality which gives them a need to be recognized and to constantly feed their egos... Why, I can identify them just in passing without them even opening their mouths. They carry a nasty smirk and just don't act normal outside their own pack of wolves... They are endangering a way of life which literally made our great nation strong... They are the most double standard people you'll ever meet. Anyone who advocates allowing any government to take control of public waterways and private land doesn't remember the late thirties and early forties in Germany. And we all know what was bred from that." The captain is a wise man.

This series of articles started with the phrase "Gather ye

rosebuds, while ye may ..." Take that phrase to heart because these funny green people will not allow us to live the way we're living for much longer. We must preserve our natural resources, they say. Yes, someday soon we will run out of petroleum, but look at it this way: What the hell difference does it make if I burn the last drop of high octane in my 454 Vette in 2005 or my grandson burns the last drop in his hybrid, three wheeled wheezing economizer cocoon in 2020? Whether now or then, technology will rise to the challenge and come up with substitutes. Hell, if we're going to run out of fuel, let's go out in style driving Ferrari F-40s, Aston Martins, Dodge Vipers and V-12 BMW's.

Yes, folks, my advice is to pick up all the rosebuds you can carry -- bring a wheel barrow! Go out now and buy that 400 horsepower Lamborghini Diablo or that 6000 horsepower turbine powered speedboat or that Lear jet and enjoy them while you can. At least you'll be able to tell your grandchildren that you once owned one of the world's great cars or boats or planes and they'll be worth big bucks after their ilk is legislated out of existence. Speaking of rosebuds, there's this black, 380 horsepower ZR1 Corvette that I need to have in my garage and, oh yeah, ... In my boat, I'm going to install the biggest mutha engines that'll fit through the hatches! And, as for my final prediction...

2028 - World Emperor Charlton Heston decrees that humanity is banned from earth. The planet becomes one great, spherical park which really is...

December 1990

Norway: Land of the Midnight Fun
Part 1

*I*f Norway were a person it would be a disciplined athlete, clean of mind and body running a 26 mile marathon. Although I've been to Norway a few times before, I never really spent much time in the place and therefore couldn't form any of my twisted impressions. After a week in Norway, however, I must say I'm hooked. Norway has got it all together and is a fun place to visit.

If I had to describe Norway in one word it would be "civilized." Totally civilized. Though I've never been a fan of socialism, it does, apparently, have its merits. Crime is virtually nonexistent even in big cities like Oslo. If anyone doubts this, he merely needs to compare signs that people post in their cars. In New York, for example, it's common to see a Mercedes or BMW parked at the curb with big signs stuck on the inside of the windows stating "NO RADIO." In New York, stealing car radios is a recognized profession (simply and quickly accomplished by smashing in one of the windows and dislodging the radio by means of a crowbar.) In Oslo, I saw a number of high buck Mercedes and Bimmers cruising the city with a sign proudly stuck across their back window saying "This Car Is Equipped With An Audiovox Super Hyper Ultra Sound System." Advertising their big Kroner sound systems -- can you imagine? In other countries at night or over the weekend, windows of jewelry stores are cleaned of their displays which are stuck in a safe. The windows are covered with roll down metal covers and barred. Then they post a guard. In Norway, jewelry reposes in unprotected windows all night and over Sunday (when all the stores are closed). CIVILIZED! Little kids cruise city streets unattended by adults. One can walk around cities safely at all times of the night. Bikes are left in racks in Oslo unlocked. CIVILIZED!

Norway is a country of great physical beauty both in its geography and its people. The coast is lined with thousands of deep water fjords with stark craggy hills leading to untouched forests. Norwegians are very much aware of their environment and ecology. Fjords are crystal clear. People don't spit (or leave other bodily droppings) on the clean streets.

As far as the physical beauty of the people goes, it's quite jarring to encounter beautiful people performing what some would consider menial tasks. In Norway, however, with their socialized system, no task is menial. People receive fair wages for all kinds of work from toll collecting to maid service. Tipping is not expected. You know on T.V.

sometimes they have these commercials where a guy jumps into a cab and yells to the cabbie "Take me to Madison and Fifth." We only see the cabbie's head from the back covered with one of those wool caps cabbies always wear. Slowly the cabbie turns around, removes the cap and ..... it's CHRISTIE BRINKLEY! Yes, <u>Christie Brinkley is driving the cab</u>! The reason these commercials work is because they are so jarring -- so removed from reality. (If you've ever taken a cab in New York, I'm sure you'll know what I mean.) Anyway, our party had just arrived at the airport and hailed the next two cabs in line (by the way, I'd say 60% of all taxi cabs in Norway are newish, 124 body style (300 series in the U.S.) Mercedes Benzs. Where Norwegian cabbies get the Kroner for new Mercedes taxis is a mystery to me. Government subsidies? Anyway, we grabbed these two cabs. The first one was driven by a typical Norwegian cabbie (which means he looks like something between a writer of mystery novels and your typical history professor). The second cab, however, was driven by <u>Miss Universe</u>! When was the last time you had a tall, blonde, statuesque cabbie? The fact is, Miss Universe can be found <u>all over</u> Norway doing <u>all kinds</u> of work. You'll see Miss Universe loading baggage at the airport or behind the fast food counter or at a toll booth. I guess the same could be said for Mr. Universe but I didn't pay that much attention. All I can say about the men is they are divided into two groups. The first group looks like the above mentioned cabbies -- average in height, darker hair, but distinguished looking (probably descended from slaves taken in Viking raids from countries like England). The second group, however, are pure Norwegian -- big, tall, blonde guys usually with longish hair and craggy features whose faces just scream for one of those Viking helmets with horns. Sit at dinner opposite one of these dudes and your mind does a fast fade. There before you, is a guy dressed in bear skins and a horned helmet gnawing on a ham hock! Remember the character, Ragnar, that Kirk Douglas played in "The Vikings"? Well, these guys make Kirk Douglas' Viking look like an imposter.

Norway is full of health freaks. Most are very athletic. Hiking, fishing, skiing, jogging, are all part of Norwegian life. You see very few fat or overweight people here -- even older people stay fit and trim. If you ask directions to get to any place from your hotel and you're told "it's only a short walk", you'd better take a taxi. Our "short walks" invariably turned into <u>long</u> <u>hikes</u>. To Norwegians, however, they <u>were</u> only "short walks." Norway's marine industry is rooted in history. The Norwegians were one of the first transoceanic explorers and maritime history is deeply rooted in the area, mainly because Norway is surrounded on three sides by the sea. The craggy coastlines are laced with beautiful fjords -- extremely deep inlets extending inland surrounded by rocky mountains. The fjords are pristine -- cool, clear water virtually uninhabited by boats. This is, indeed, cruising paradise. The Norwegians are well ahead of the rest of the world in high speed marine craft since water taxis are a primary means of transportation there. Having developed the monohull to its practical limit speed wise, they went to catamarans and, now, SES vessels. Water taxis or fast ferries are big business there.

The large SES water taxis are constructed of extremely lightweight, cored fiberglass usually 135' long by 50' wide. These vessels, carrying hundreds of passengers, cruise effortlessly at speeds around 40 knots. Effortlessly but wetly -- if you like to spend time on deck bring rain gear. The blowers necessary to lift these vessels to their cruising displacement create a wall of spray forward and the hull seems to run enveloped in a cocoon of spray (kind of feels like driving through a carwash!). This is a small price to pay for the speed and efficiency gained, however and spray suppression devices are being developed. The interior of these vessels look much like jumbo jets except they have twenty-five or thirty seats across. Norwegian water taxis are marketed around the world.

Many monohull water taxis are commonly powered by high speed controllable pitch propellers. C.P. propellers are extremely interesting and warrant a close look for fast motoryachts here in the United States. By controlling the pitch of the propellers, reverse gears are not required and the propeller can be tuned to the optimum pitch for a given engine power output (Normally, a propeller is sized and most efficient at only one speed -- top speed. At any speed less than top, efficiency is lost.) With C.P. props you get maximum efficiency at any rpm level. The engines are loaded by means of exhaust pyrometers which indicate optimum exhaust temperatures and engine load.

My space is up and I haven't told you about Norwegian bread or the great museums or the climate or SAS. Maybe I'll continue this next month. In the meantime, let us become more civilized. Park your Benz or Roller on a side street. Put a big sign in the window saying "High Buck Radio Installed." Of course the radio will be gone in a matter of minutes, but at least you can be content knowing that you did the <u>civilized thing</u>.

January 1991

Norway: Land of the Midnight Fun Part 2

Revelations, Helmets and Raw Jelly Fish

One of the great mysteries of Norway was revealed to me during a three hour automobile trip in New Jersey of all places. There were four Norwegians in the car and as the countryside flowed by, we discussed many things including boats, politics, the weather, breakfast, the meaning of American slang terms like "shifty," and more boats. Finally, the subject of women came up.

It's always been a big mystery to me why there are a preponderance of great looking women in Scandinavia. I remarked about this to my Norwegian friends and that's when the revelation came about. They had an interesting story. Between the years of 800 and 1050 AD when the Norsemen were in their rape and plunder period, the Vikings made journeys over most of the Northern hemisphere. From Scandinavia they sailed west over the North Sea to the British Isles, then over the Atlantic to Iceland, Greenland and North

America. Others sailed south down the coast of Europe and entered the Mediterranean while still others sailed East down the great rivers of Russia and the Black Sea. It's been recorded that other explorers brought back to their homeland such things as spices from the Far East, gold from Central America and potatoes from North America. The Norsemen, however, appeared to have been different. What they brought back with them were <u>women</u>... and not just <u>any</u> women. What the Norsemen did, see, is <u>cull</u> <u>the</u> <u>foxes</u> from all the countries they plundered and spirited them back home. With a gene pool like this, Scandinavian women couldn't help but turn out to be Miss Universe's material.

While I was mulling this over in my mind, the Norwegians offered that they thought women in the <u>United</u> <u>States</u> were incredibly attractive! That's when I realized that "The Dictum of Strange Stuff" had taken effect. Though I don't buy it myself, this dictum states that women from one country compared to women from another are not necessarily more beautiful, only <u>different</u> and something new and different is what attracts men most. Well, I guess I can understand this. Stuff your face with filet mignon for a couple of years and hot dogs look pretty damn good.

When I learned I'd be going to Norway, I decided that the principle mission of the trip should be to obtain an authentic Viking helmet complete with buffalo horns. A pass through downtown Oslo revealed no such chapeau except for cheap plastic beanies with plastic "pop in" buffalo horns. I already had one of those. I wanted the <u>real</u> <u>thing</u>. My wife Regina's mission in Norway was to buy some authentic Norwegian sweaters. Norwegian sweaters are typically heavy wool, weighing about 50 pounds, with intricate patterns (most commonly, renderings of reindeer). Our search through the stores revealed plenty of nice sweaters made in places like Italy, Germany, Japan, Taiwan, India and England, but no Norwegian sweaters! It reminded me of the time I was in Turkey and couldn't find a damned belly dancer! Shopping harder, we were told of a store that specialized in Norwegian made products. There, my wife found a couple of 50 pound sweaters (with gloves and caps to match). To my delight, up on a shelf stood a row of beautiful Viking helmets. These were made of bright, hammered pewter <u>riveted</u> together. When was the last time you saw a riveted hat? A pair of huge, curved, real buffalo horns were attached. It was indescribably beautiful. I slipped one on my head and looked in the mirror. I decided that, except for my dark hair, I could probably pass for a Viking. Yeah... I mean <u>Ya</u>, that's it! A little peroxide when I get home would do the trick! I pictured myself wearing my Viking helmet to important business meetings, wedding receptions and on sea trials (I like to get into the spirit of a country I'm visiting). Whipping out my AMX card, I asked the salesclerk to write it up. <u>The price was over four hundred bucks</u>! The cost of being a Viking these days is very high indeed. Crestfallen, I passed on the helmet. Maybe next trip.

No trip to Oslo is complete without visiting the great maritime museums located in the area. A quick ferry ride across the fjord takes you to a peninsula on which is located the Viking Ship Museum, the Kon-Tiki/Ra Museum and the

Artic/Antarctic Exploration Ship "Fram" Museum among others. The Viking Ship Museum was most interesting. Housed in a cross shaped building were three Viking vessels, two of which were fully restored. The three ships from Oseberg, Gokstad and Tune were all found in burial mounds in the Oslo fjord area. They were built during the ninth century A.D. and later used as burial ships for wealthy men and women. Then, as now, naval architects had differences of opinion. The Oseberg ship was long and lean and, believe it or not, <u>had a chine hull</u>. In fact, it was a <u>deep vee</u> hull! The lapstrake planking even formed a series of spray rails or lift strakes on the bottom. (Interestingly enough, back in the '60's, when the deep vee was "invented," it's developer applied for a patent, then took a number of boat companies to court for infringing on his patent. The case was lost because it was brought out that deep vee hulls existed since the time of <u>Noah's ark</u>! When I first heard that, I didn't buy it, but seeing this deep vee vessel built in 900 A.D. brought home the fact that very little new, as far as hull shapes, can ever be conceived.) The Gokstad ship was in great contrast to the Oseberg ship. She was round bilged and much beamier -- a truly lovely shape.

That these ships were used as tombs and buried in the <u>clay</u> was a big disappointment to me. According to Viking authority Kirk Douglas, bodies were placed on Viking Ships which were set sail at night, unmanned, down a dreary fjord. Norsemen on shore would set the vessel ablaze with <u>flaming arrows</u> which certainly is more showbiz than simply dumping the ship in the ground.

There's great food to be found in Norway. As expected, fish is very big there although we sampled delicious venison, beef, veal and poultry. Salmon is big. You can have salmon appetizers, salmon soup, salmon steaks, salmon salad, and, I'm sure, <u>salmon dessert</u> if you really want it. They have the greatest bread. Following the Norwegian's zest for the healthy life, Norway produces the healthiest grainy, nutty, chunky breads I've ever seen. Dark and heavy, the average loaf weighs about 30 pounds (which makes for excellent exercise when eating a sandwich). One of the finest meals in Norway can be had by buying bread at the supermarket along with some rare roast beef and mayo to make your own sandwich in your hotel.

There are, however, some Norwegian dishes that take some getting used to. Before we traveled to Norway, Regina and I had heard about a traditional Norwegian delicacy called "Lutefisk." Proud of our inside information, we prowled Oslo restaurants inspecting menus, but couldn't find it anywhere. As always, the unattainable becomes more desirable. The more restaurants we found that didn't have this dish, the more we wanted it. After a couple of days searching for the stuff, we found ourselves in a little town on the northwest coast of Norway. Our host was overjoyed to hear that we knew about Lutefisk and arranged for a Lutefisk dinner for Regina that night (not being as adventurous as my wife, I chickened out and ordered salmon steaks). Apparently, preparing Lutefisk is a big deal that takes all day. It's usually served on holidays. Lutefisk, see, is prepared from dried codfish which is marinated for hours in a lye solution. That's right, lye. The end result is a plate heaped with a clear jelly like substance that was once cod fish. The stuff could be mistaken for raw jellyfish. Lutefisk is usually served with big hunks of bacon and boiled potatoes. When Regina's dinner came, she did a masterful job of rearranging her plate, making sure she ate all the bacon and boiled potatoes. Actually, she did very well, not gagging once! Although it's touted as a great delicacy in Norway, not one of our four Norwegian hosts accepted when offered some. "Fisk" means fish in Norwegian. "Lute" must be Norwegian for "barf."

Norway has it all. It's a beautiful, clean country filled with beautiful, clean people. I must say that, unless the USA makes some big changes in the future, Norway is on the top of my list for retirement spots. I know Norway's not the easiest country to immigrate to, but, with my peroxide hair and the Norwegian helmet (that I'll eventually get), I'll be a shoe in.

February 1991

You've been a Very Bad Boy, George
Now Eat Your Broccoli and Go Up to Your Room

August/September 1990. Sadman Insane is raping and pillaging Kuwait. During this same time frame, George Bush and the likes of representatives Foley and Rostenkowsky are doing the same to American boatsmen. If you are looking for funny, you won't find much here this month. The Bozos in Washington have provided us with enough laughs during the preparation of their "deficit reduction package" to last us for <u>years</u>. You may have watched some of this on C-SPAN. It should have been carried on the <u>Comedy</u> <u>Channel</u>. In case you've just awakened from a coma (which, unfortunately, is a condition indigenous with many congressmen), George Bush and some dunderheads in Congress, in their infinite wisdom, have elected to, among other things, impose a ten percent tax on so called <u>luxury</u> items.

I hate to admit it, but I was wrong. In December '89 I wrote a two part article in this space titled "Our President is a Boat Guy." In it, I extolled the wonderfulness of having a president in office who is one of us -- a president who understood boats and boatsmen and would look out for his compadres. WRONG! George Bush and the Dundering Dunderheads in the Cockamamie Congress (hereinafter known as the "D.D.C.C.") have really done it to us this time.

I am extremely disappointed in George Bush, a man who privately owns his own powerboat and knows what boating is all about. When he was elected, I had great expectations for him to serve the best interests of pleasure boatsmen. In a couple of short years since his election, boatsmen have been subjected to: 1) tin based bottom paints being outlawed (I wonder how much fuel this law wastes due to fouled bottoms?), 2) the mandatory addition of another foolish plaque aboard our boats indicating how to care for garbage, 3) a user tax on all boats (which will not come back to boatmen but be dumped into the black hole of the deficit) and, the subject of this article, 4) the ten percent luxury tax on all boats costing over $100,000. You've been a very bad boy, George. Now eat your broccoli and go up to your room. Newt Gingrich is my new hero.

This is a bad tax. A deceptive tax. A discriminatory tax. A tax conceived by liars. Not that I'm opposed to raising taxes. The D.D.C.C.'s in Washington have allowed this country to get in such abysmal fiscal shape that a tax increase was absolutely necessary. As usual, our friends in Washington could not go about this in a straightforward way by simply fiddling with income tax rates to raise the necessary funds and/or imposing an across the board national sales tax of, say, two percent. No, they went about it in a devious, deceptive manner to try and cover their very ample asses. Congressmen decided they would have to raise the income tax, but then they would be in the hot seat from their middle class constituents -- maybe even lose their cushy jobs. That would be a disaster -- no more voting themselves fat raises, no more opportunities to stuff their pockets with cash, no more monkey business on yachts like "MONKEY BUSINESS." They needed to come up with a diversion -- a dog and pony show to make the middle class feel better. Thus, the D.D.C.C.'s came up with the ten percent luxury tax which, they <u>knew</u> would raise little, if any money but would sure make Joe Bluecollar feel good.

First, let's get one thing perfectly clear. THE TAX BASE OF THE UNITED STATES IS THE MIDDLE CLASS. You got that? This is a fundamental fact of tax life and the D.D.C.C.'s in Washington know this better than anybody. Less than one percent of the population of the United States makes over $100,000 a year. <u>Less</u> <u>than</u> <u>one</u> <u>percent</u>! If the government confiscated <u>all</u> the assets of these people, the funds garnered might carry the country for a <u>few</u> <u>weeks</u>. I'll say it again: The tax base for the United States government <u>is</u> the middle class. As you probably know by now, the luxury tax affects jewelry and furs over $10,000, autos over $30,000, private aircraft over $250,000 and, of course, our "luxury yachts" over $100,000. A little research reveals why this tax is blatantly discriminatory towards boatsmen. Let's look at jewelry. High rollers wishing to purchase baubles over $10,000 can buy same on one of their frequent jaunts out of the country and effectively beat the tax. Furs: My uncle Mike in the fur business tells me the heart of the fur market is in under $10,000 furs and doesn't expect to be hurt by the tax at all. Autos: This luxury tax was actually <u>welcomed</u> by the American auto industry since it really was an <u>import tax</u> on expensive foreign cars (there are very few American cars that cost over $30,000). Private aircraft: Who in his right mind would buy a private aircraft that would cost over $250,000? I'm willing to bet 90% of all planes costing over $100,000 are for "business purposes." So it's clear that the luxury tax doesn't hurt jewelry, furs, the American auto industry or the small aircraft industry. The boating industry, however, will be devastated. These days any "luxury yacht" over 28' will cost more than $100,000! Hell, even George Bush's little cigarette "FIDELITY," would cost over a hundred grand if purchased today. The D.D.C.C.'s realizing that they were safe from the jewelry, fur, auto and aircraft lobbies and that the boating industry didn't have much of a lobby, decided to bully the defenseless.

I'd like to congratulate Senator Bob Dole for a job well done. I'm serious. The tax on aircraft was originally proposed at a much lower threshold but, since many manufacturers of small aircraft were within his jurisdiction, he personally got it boosted to a level that wouldn't hurt them. Like I said, he did his job well. Conversely, Congressmen from boat building states like Florida and North Carolina certainly <u>didn't</u> do their job and should be held personally responsible for the great numbers of people (often in rural areas with little chance of re-employment) who have been or will be laid off from their jobs as a result of this tax.

Never forget that this is a blatantly discriminatory tax. The law allows one to buy: as many multi-million dollar houses as one wants (Hell, you can buy one house in every state if you want) and never pay a luxury tax or a five million dollar race horse without tax or a forty million dollar Van Gogh painting without tax or a five million dollar Calder sculpture without tax or a 1.5 million dollar Chippendale card table without tax or a hundred thousand dollar bottle of wine without tax. You can also join as many fancy golf, tennis or country clubs as you wish tax free. One might ask "What differentiates boats as a "luxury item" from the stuff mentioned above?" I'll tell you what differentiates boats. Boats and boating are a way of life -- a lifestyle. A boat is a home afloat. You live on a boat. Sculpture can hardly be called a way of life. Antique furniture isn't a way of life. Wine isn't a way of life (unless you're a bum in the bowery). You can't live in autos or planes. Unless you're Liberace, jewels and furs certainly are not a way of life.

The D.D.C.C.'s know only enough about boats to make them very, very dangerous. The closest most of these guys ever get to large bodies of water is in the bathtub (or, in some cases, in the tidal basin of the Washington monument -- you remember the Senator and the Stripper frolicking in the tidal basin don't you?). George Bush doesn't have that excuse -- he knows what boats are all about. Next month we will look into what boats really mean to the economy.

March 1991

What is a Yacht?
(And How to Beat the Luxury Tax)

*I*n part one of this piece I cried about the ten percent luxury tax that had been applied to "luxury yachts" over $100,000. My contention was it was unfair, discriminatory and a bad tax because it would hurt the economy rather than help it. Now, of course, the importance of all this pales in comparison to the war in the Persian Gulf, but after I-RACK becomes A-WRECK and attention is once again turned to the economy, this foolish tax will be at the forefront for repeal.

There at a dock sits a recently launched magnificent 100' motoryacht. To say she carries all the amenities of a home is understating the fact. Actually, she is a <u>mobile island</u> providing her own power, potable water, heat, air conditioning and waste disposal systems. Her cost is around four and one half million dollars complete.

While some will view our 100 footer as a floating gemstone or a symbol of decadence, I see it differently. I see a floating <u>work of art</u> comparable to the famous cathedrals in Europe. Both structures were built by a group of dedicated artisans. In fact, a large yacht is the last bastion of collective artistry in the United States (or the world).

It is my premise that the U.S. gets more economic "bang for the buck" when a large yacht is built in the States, than from any other private endeavor. The fact is that yachts are some of the most labor intensive private sector endeavors of modern mankind.

Our 100 footer will take approximately 100,000 man-hours to fabricate. That's <u>30 guys</u> with full-time employment for 83 weeks. In addition to the 30 guys actually building the boat, there may be another 10 overhead people supporting this project. What other five million dollar object, a mere 100 feet long, requires this kind of man loading?

Think about it! Thirty guys working for 83 weeks. Thirty families being supported. Twenty mortgage, car and MasterCard payments. Eighty three weeks of groceries, ballet classes, piano lessons and veterinary payments. And this is only the beginning. Before the first gooey piece of fiberglass is applied or the first plate cut or the first timber sawn, an architect will spend approximately 4,000 or 5,000 man-hours on the design which equates to two and one-half guys working full-time for a year. More families taken care of. Then there is the sound consultant and the interior designer who will employ another one or two people for a year on this project. And <u>that's</u> only the beginning of it. What about the materials that goes into this magnificent vessel? Teak trees are felled in Burma, dragged out of the forest and shipped to lumber mills to be milled into teak boards. Bauxite is mined in Jamaica and smelted into aluminum ingots to be shipped to the States.

And what about the equipment that goes into the yacht? Well, there are watertight doors from Washington, textiles from Pennsylvania, hoses from Missouri, passerelles from Germany, foam from Sweden, generators from Florida, portholes from Italy, trim tabs from Wisconsin stabilizers from Connecticut, main engines from Illinois, gear boxes from Japan and davits from England. Are you getting the picture? Each of these components and thousands more provide gainful employment for people around the country and around the world.

Then, once this magnificent vessel is in service, she will provide full-time employment for two or three crewmen, pay the insurance company fifty or sixty grand a year, and require maybe $400,000 a year to be spent for fuel/maintenance/upkeep and marina fees.

Remember, all this is for a <u>single</u> <u>vessel</u>. (Smaller production boats, also labor intensive, make similar contributions to the economy.) In the end, does this 100 footer help or hurt our economy? The answer is obvious. Why penalize endeavors that contribute to the economy? When a damn Van Gogh painting is purchased (luxury tax free) for <u>forty</u> <u>million</u> <u>dollars</u> and gets squirreled away in some collector's gallery, what does this add to the economy? If you want to talk "luxury," let's talk about some hundred year old paint smeared on an old canvas by a one eared guy for forty mil. <u>That's</u> decadence!

Eventually, I am certain that this foolish tax will be repealed since it's clear that it does absolutely nothing to decrease the deficit and, in fact, will increase it due to people out of work. In the meantime, prior to repeal, I have some suggestions for beating the luxury tax. These suggestions may be as silly as the luxury tax itself, but we must fight foolishness with foolishness. The beauty behind these suggestions is that, while it's relatively easy for the stiffs in blue suits in Washington to solemnly sit and pass judgement on tax tables, deductions, etc., it will be very difficult for these bozos to seriously deliberate about boats since they don't know a damn thing about boats. My suggestions should tie Congress and the courts up for five to ten years while they try to sort out the mess that will ensue.

The way I see it, this tax provides five huge loopholes for new boat buyers. Sales tax can legally be avoided by taking one of the following measures:

1. Build your new yacht and use it as a business for two years. Marinas like Pier 66, Bahia Mar and North Cove Marina on Wall Street can help here. My idea is to establish huge <u>floating</u> <u>markets</u>, similar to the ones in Hong Kong and Singapore. Then when owners of yachts like "SILVER SHALIS," "MERCEDES," and "TIME" decide to build new vessels, they could easily do it without paying luxury tax. The new "SILVER SHALIS" could become a floating deli. "MERCEDES" might become an auto repair shop. "TIME" might become a watch repair facility. These vessels would be rafted up side-by-side for two years. Afterwards, they would become tax free yachts and the owners could cruise happily ever after.

2. Turn your boat into a house. There's no luxury tax on houses. The trick here is to determine when a boat becomes a

house and vice-versa. When exactly does a boat become a house? When it's hauled out on a cradle on dry land? When it's aground in the mud? When engines are removed? If you buy a yacht and dock it in concrete behind your house, is it still a yacht or an adjunct to your house? Conversely, when does a house become a boat? If your house is washed from its foundations in a hurricane and floats down the river, will it be subjected to the ten percent luxury tax? Yes, Congress and the courts will need a lot of time to sort this one out. We can confuse them further by building yachts with tile roofs and chimneys or houses that are pointy on one end.

3. Place your boat in an offshore corporation. This is a good way to beat the tax, however, traveling to and from that offshore corporation to use the boat may be a pain. Of course, I have a solution. I propose that the states of Washington, California, Maine and Florida secede <u>from the Union</u> thereby allowing yachts within their domain to be registered under offshore corporations making travel to one's boat much easier. Let's face it, California, Washington, Florida and Maine really <u>are</u> different countries anyhow, so why not make it official?

4. Put your boat to military use. It would be relatively easy to prove your boat is a military craft. Simply use her to <u>invade</u> a foreign country -- one of the small islands in the Bahamas will do (an uninhabited island like Great Sail Cay would make things easier). Using your boat to help Washington, California, Maine and Florida secede would be good too.

5. Put minimal boats in service. This will take a bit of

ingenuity. The law states that equipment installed in a vessel six months after it has been put "in service" is not subject to the ten percent luxury tax. Why not build megayachts with Styrofoam hulls, papier-mâché interiors, cellophane windows and outboard motor power? They'd be launched and put "in service." Six months later, the boat would be dragged back into the yard and rebuilt as a real yacht with a fiberglass or aluminum hull and superstructure, wooden joiner work, glass windows and inboard engines.

Yes folks, our first Styrofoam 100' megayacht with papier-mâché interior and cellophane windows is already on the drawing boards. She's not very strong, but she sure is light! With materials and labor (we're using used outboard motors), her cost will be around $3,500. I am available for consultation.

April 1991

Rosary Beads and Sausages
Part 1

An Unforgettable Trip to Italy

The Alitalia 747 that departed JFK for Rome was packed. Due to poor planning and general cheapness on my part, my wife and I were stuck in the peanut gallery seats in the middle row at the tail of the plane which, from the lines of people, seems to have been stuffed with about 50 toilet compartments. As usual, the plane left late and we had that old, familiar travel feeling -- cramped, sweaty, sleepy and wondering what the hell we are doing sitting in two undersized chairs by the toilet compartments of a long aluminum tube hurdling through the atmosphere at 500 mph. I thought about our home in Florida and "old gray," our soft, enveloping, leather sofa in the living room.

Normally, night flights like this are bad enough but this one was special. It seems that except for Regina and myself, THE ENTIRE PLANE WAS PACKED WITH NUNS AND DAMNED OSCAR MEYER YUPPIE EXECUTIVES AND THEIR WIVES. Both were on group tours -- the nuns to pay a visit to the pope and Oscar Meyer people on their way to some sort of foolish European wiener festival. By 11:30 pm, the place was jumping. Regina and I felt like we were trying to sleep in the middle of a huge, loud, cocktail party. The problem was that everybody in the nun's group knew everybody else and all the damn wiener yuppie cockroaches knew all the other wiener yupps and their wives (for those of you who just tuned in, I compare yuppies to cockroaches because: 1) They both hang out in social groups; 2) They all look the same and; 3) With their ubiquitous sunglasses, yuppies <u>look</u> like cockroaches). Nobody except Regina and I was in their seats. The aisles were packed. There we sat huddled in our chairs surrounded by black habits and Gucci loafers. The yuppos were strolling around with drinks telling each other how important they were, how much money they made and what schools they sent their kids to.

The plane hurdled eastward into the night. The only good thing about our situation was that we got a chance to observe and speak to nuns. Now I never hung around much with nuns -- I've always considered nuns as otherworldly people. However, once you are sitting next to a line of nuns waiting to use the head, your opinion of them changes fast. I realized on this trip that nuns were just nice, regular people with an unusual profession who wait on line to use the head just like us mortals.

A few weeks before, I had received a letter from the assistant to the editor of Mondo Barca magazine. Her name was Donatella and as nice as she was on the phone, she was even nicer in person. The letter read in part "...We want to invite you to a meeting in Viareggio (Tuscany) ... During this meeting will be a conference about the phenomenon of megayachts... For this reason we've invited the most important international architects... The meeting is organized by TOSCONAUTICA, the association of the most prestigious Italian shipyards in Tuscany such as: Perini Navi, Tecnomarine, Versilcraft, Cantieri di Pisa, Cantiere San Lorenzo, Cantiere Codecasa, and so on... Present at the conference will be specialized press, newspaper and television network. Obviously you'll have complete hospitality from Tosconautica and you'll have an excellent occasion to meet mega yacht owners... I hope to hear from you soon."

The list of awardees was impressive: Jon Bannenberg, Pieter Beeldsnijder, Frits de Voogt, John Disdale, German Frers, Alan Gilbert, Gerhard Gilgenast, Ron Holland, Frank Mulder, Susan Puleo, Paola Smith, Bruce Farr, Pierluigi Spadolini, Paoulo Caliari and Luigi Sturchio. I have to tell you, I'm not much of an award ceremonies kind of guy (much less a "meet the press" kind of guy) and, normally, would have been content to stay home, rooted in "Old Gray" and watch "All in the Family" reruns, however: 1) The trip was paid for; 2) We love Italy; 3) I wanted to meet some of the living legends in the yacht design business; and 4) We'd never been to Viareggio. I wasn't really sure why they invited me but, hey, the trip was prepaid and I decided to jump at it before somebody realized their mistake.

The big plane touched down in Rome none too soon since the yuppie cockroaches were at it again in the morning, swarming around with their antennae up looking for scraps of food. From Rome we hopped a plane to Pisa where a car was waiting to take us for the half hour drive to Viareggio. The road between Pisa and Viareggio was interesting: It's a two laner that goes through deserted woods. Picture this: It's about 9:30 in the morning. It's chilly and foggy. The big Fiat proceeds in traffic through the forest filled with huge, closely spaced pine trees, rocks and bushes. There appears to be no civilization around for miles. Then, I spot her (remember, it's 9:30 <u>a.m.</u>). She's tall, wearing a tight, short, low cut evening dress (with legs that went all the way up) and a fur coat open in the front. She is wearing sunglasses and leaning against a pine tree along the side of the road, smoking a cigarette. Then I see another one and then another one and then yet <u>another</u> one! The woods are <u>teeming</u> with women in tight dresses and fur coats standing along the side of the road smoking cigarettes. I wondered "What the hell is going on?" I felt like I was in a bad Fellini movie. Then it hit me. These were <u>Italian</u> <u>hookers</u> working the morning shift. You expect to see hookers on the Via Veneto but the vision of them dotted about the woods was mind jarring.

Saturday night was the awards dinner but we had a conflict. Saturday night is one of our favorite times in Italy: it's the night "Colpo Grosso" is on T.V. Believe me, it was a tough choice deciding what to do but we figured we could attend the dinner, then rush back to catch the show. Although I don't understand a word of Italian, "Colpo Grosso" is my favorite Italian T.V. show. And just what is this T.V. show that is so captivating? Perhaps a program about the glories of ancient Rome. A show about Italian food? A show about Italian culture? Actually, it is a show that reflects a lot about Italian culture. It's a little difficult to explain, but I'll try. It's a game show which comes on about 10:30 pm Saturday night. The show is hosted by a lecherous, lounge lizard type and includes a cast of about 10 very beautiful Las Vegas show girl-type women clad in bikinis called Cin Cin (pronounced "Chin Chin") girls. There are two contestants, one male and one female. As best as I can gather, each contestant picks one of the scantily clad women and must decide, when the woman removes her top, if she's wearing pasties underneath. Two pasties, no points. No pasties, you (literally) get a couple of points (I guess if there's one pasty you get one point, but I'm not really sure). Then, somehow during the course of the game, the contestants (who are normal, young Italian men and women in-the-street types) end up on stage answering questions and losing an article of clothing for every wrong answer. Women contestants typically end up topless in G-strings. This all takes place on public airwaves (not cable) on a normally straight Italian television station. The show lasts over an hour and it is truly an unbelievable display. I understand the Vatican was really upset when the show first came on but now, five or six years later, it seems to have been accepted and the show has since spread to other countries like Germany and France. Class always succeeds. I understand they are trying to bring it to the States. Intellectual that I am, I hope it gets here soon.

Well, I'm out of space and haven't yet told you about

Viareggio, the gala dinner or the press conference. All that, and more, will happen next month in our annual Spring "Dry Rot Spore Issue." In the meantime, write your local T.V. stations to replace "Wheel of Fortune" with "Cin Cin" girls.

May 1991

Rosary Beads and Sausages Part 2

Who was doing what to who, turkey boats, and the <u>real</u> speed of such and such motoryachts, were some of the topics discussed at the informal press conference on our first day in Viareggio (yacht designers are like a bunch of old ladies when they get together).

That evening, Tosconautica and Mondo Barca magazine sponsored a gala dinner and awards ceremony at the Hotel Ariston di Lido di Camaiore. The hotel was, at one time, a magnificent villa on the beach. We sat at round tables and were treated to a <u>seven course</u> dinner starting with carpaccio (I asked for seconds), risotto, pasta, shrimp and seafood, filet mignon, fruit and dessert. All this was accompanied by vino -- lots of vino. The Italians do things right. After the dinner, the awards were presented. Beautiful engraved silver plaques in velvet cases were on a little stage filled with dignitaries presenting the awards. A microphone stood center stage amongst a jumble of loose wires. When his (or her) name was called, the typical awardee (including myself) did the following: Staggered front and center trying to look cool, tripped on the step to the stage, snared himself in the microphone cables, produced screeching feedback on the PA system while he (or she) mumbled a few incoherent words into the microphone and departed smiling, repeating the whole snaring, tripping process in reverse on the way back to the table. One of the few of us who carried this off well was Jon Bannenberg -- a man so smooth he could be called the Mel Tormé of the yachting world. Another man who handled himself well was the elegant Frits de Voogt from Holland. This man is responsible for more large motor yachts, I would guess, than anyone else in the history of yachting; yet, he is unassuming, approachable, and eager to share his knowledge.

The Mondo Barca magazine dinner made me think of another Italian dinner courtesy of another magazine during the Genoa Boat Show a few months before. The publisher and editor took a group of people in the marine business and a group of subscribers out to dinner in Camogli, the small seaside village outside of Genoa I've written about. Being less than a memorable evening, I don't remember the details, but I do remember that we had difficulty finding a restaurant (we were a large group and had no reservations) and the only place that would have us was kind of a rickety hovel cantilevered out over the sea with crooked wooden tables and stools and nondescript dusty "things" hanging from the overhead which, occasionally, dropped into your food. Dinner, as I recall, consisted of spaghetti pudding and fish soup. Neither was intended to be what it was but, overcooked as both courses were, that's how they turned out. Some of the guests quietly departed after the first course. Some went to the bathroom and never returned. Sorry to say, our hosts were none other than (then publisher) Jeff Hammond and editor Bonnie O'Boyle! At least the company was good. (How's that for biting the hand that feeds you?)

Speaking of my sweet editor, Bonnie, brings me back to an incident at the awards dinner. Although the ceremonies were sponsored by an Italian magazine, somehow Bonnie crashed the proceedings (although no other boating magazine representatives attended). As I recall, Bonnie was trying hard all day to get an exclusive story from a certain Italian boat manufacturer, but he wasn't going for it. This guy happened to be sitting next to me at the dinner. After the feast was over and we were all "feeling the glow of great Italian wines" (sounds much better than "half in the bag" doesn't it?), Bonnie purposefully strode to the table and wavered over this poor guy with a glass full of <u>grappa</u>. Now grappa is nothing more than a mixture of Italian lighter fluid and jet fuel with some dye in it. It tastes like the fires of hell and goes down about as smooth as 60 grit sandpaper. Anyway, Bonnie's standing over this guy and says something like "and this is for you, buster" then <u>chugalugs</u> the glass of grappa, slams it (inverted) on the table in front of the startled boat builder, then turns and walks away. I thought it was a great gesture of something or other, but I couldn't quite figure out what. The guy just kind of shook his head.

The following day was the press conference. Everyone got up and gave a little speech, then were asked questions by the media. I was lucky enough to be queried by a mousy, Italian female reporter -- obviously a "Green" supporter -- who tried to sandbag me. Everyone else got questions like: "What's the future of megayachts?" or "What are the current trends in yacht design?" or "What color should staterooms be?" My question was: "How do you justify the construction of megayachts at a time when the world is being choked by pollution, is running out of fuel and millions of people are starving around the globe?" Thanks a helluvalot lot Granola Breath!

Viareggio -- the emerald city of boatbuilding. If you ever get the chance to visit Viareggio, go for it. While the place can't be called "beautiful," if you like boats, it's the most beautiful city in the world -- a city where, it seems, most of the businesses are devoted to 1) building yachts or 2) supporting the building of yachts. Viareggio is a seaside city built along the Mediterranean. There are boatbuilders all over the place. Some of the biggies like Perini Navi, Benetti/Azimut, Tecnomarine and Codecasa are right in the downtown area. The main drag runs parallel to the seashore; a big, wide, divided, four lane road that runs for miles. Fronting the beach was row after row of fancy stores like Fendi, Gucci, Valentino, etc. interspersed with restaurants, movie theatres, and gelato parlors. Viareggio is, in fact, a big summer resort area, but the seashore was very strange -- there were no undeveloped beaches. All the beaches were divided into walled little compounds, each one occupying maybe a hundred feet of beachfront and each with a different name. We thought this was very odd until we asked the locals and learned that beaches here are privately owned so when people want to use the beach, they must do so via a beach club. Strolling is big there. Over the weekend, the stylish Italians put on their Sunday best and stroll the wide road along the Mediterranean (which is closed to traffic on weekends), going no particular place. This is quite common in Europe. Sadly, the practice of strolling has been abandoned in the United States. Here, on weekends, people prefer to don their "Sunday Worst" (barf stained Bart Simpson tank top, ripped Donald Duck baggy shorts and thongs), sit home, watch the boob tube, drink beer and burp.

In looking over this piece, I came up with an inspired idea. What the yachting industry needs is a Nautical National Enquirer - type scandal sheet. This piece alone would have provided some grabber headlines like: YACHT DESIGNERS GATHER FOR DRUNKEN FETE. AMERICAN YACHT MAGAZINE MOGULS TAKE CLIENTS TO DIVE FOR DINNER. INFLUENTIAL EDITOR GUZZLES GRAPPA LIKE WATER. I <u>do</u> feel bad about the embarrassing stories concerning Jeff and Bonnie but they are both sports ... I think. But if you read my next column in a publication like "Model Boat Quarterly" or "The Dinghy Gazette," you'll know why.

June 1991

The Brazilian Way
Part 1

The First of Many Parts
A Brief Introduction to Brazil

I am driving a winding two lane road --- BR131 which passes for a super highway in Brazil. The serpentine road leads up a mountainside. Half the vehicles on the road are huge Brazilian trucks -- there's no railroad system to speak of in Brazil so Brazil moves on trucks. I am approaching a blind curve at about 120 kilometers per hour when, suddenly, I am confronted by a WALL OF TRUCKS -- one in my lane and one in the oncoming lane closing at a high rate of speed. I flick the wheel to the right putting my car on the shoulder, avoiding a "head on" by millimeters. Now in most other civilized countries of the world, this hair raising experience would probably warrant pulling off the road, shutting off your car, giving prayers of thanks, washing out your pants, and then, possibly, throwing up. In Brazil, however, while this scenario was unfolding before your windshield, conversation with your companion never ceases. You might reach up and adjust the radio or crank the air conditioning up a notch just as if nothing is happening. The fact is, in Brazil NOTHING IS HAPPENING. After all, Brazil is not a rich country and not much is wasted there including road shoulders. Shoulders are there to be used and driving experiences like this are the norm.

What strikes one about Brazil above all else, is that it's a country of totally undisciplined people. It's more than that, really -- they are <u>outlaws</u> and <u>renegades</u>. Stealing cars at gunpoint from their drivers, smoking in elevators, cutting into airport lines, and anarchy on the highway is all part of "the Brazilian way" which is complete disregard for the law. The law of Brazil is no law -- it's Dodge City time throughout the country. Brazil was a military dictatorship for many years before going "Democratic" in 1984. Now, because of all the craziness going on, many intelligent Brazilians are thinking that it might be better to revert to military dictatorship. Brazil is the fifth largest country in the world (about the geographical size of the U.S.). Population is around 140,000,000. If you think of Brazil as just another South American third world Banana Republic, think again. First, Brazil separates itself from the rest of South American by its language. Brazilians speak Portuguese -- everyone else speaks Spanish. It's a country of sophisticated technology and huge untapped resources -- both natural and human. Brazil's major industries include: shipbuilding, auto, aeronautical, citrus, and electronics. It is one of the world's foremost arms producers. It has its own oil reserves and has the capability of being virtually energy self-sufficient fuel wise by converting their vast sugarcane resources to alcohol. Brazil is a physically beautiful country from the Amazon regions of the North to the mountainous regions to the South. Along the thousands of miles of coastline, there are untold beaches, inlets, rivers, bays, of almost indescribable physical beauty. In short, Brazil has all the ingredients to become a world power.

Sounds pretty damn good doesn't it? Brazil has it made, right? Well.... not quite. Brazilians like to tell a joke about the creation of earth. After God created the earth, he sent an angel down to reconnoiter the place and report back to Him. The angel returned with a report "I'm afraid you made a mistake in Brazil," the angel told Him. "You've created a country of great beauty, lush rain forests to the North, snowcapped mountains to the South and a magnificent coastline. The climate throughout the entire country is mild. There are no volcanoes, earthquakes or tornadoes and hurricanes are unknown. All the other countries you've created are subject to multiple natural disasters, but Brazil has none." "Yes," He told the angel, "you're right, but wait till you see the people I put there."

Sad but true, it was Brazil's bad luck to be discovered by Portuguese -- if the country had been discovered by the English or the Germans or the Dutch, things would have been entirely different (our Polish jokes in the States are replaced by Portuguese jokes in Brazil). With a totally screwed up government and economy, Brazil is its own worst enemy. Between their periodic wage and price freezes, Brazil's inflation can run up to 30% a month! At one time, prices were changed in stores twice a day! Dinners could cost millions of monetary units. A few years ago, they devalued their currency by a factor of a thousand. Then a couple of years later, they did it again. This would be like Washington telling us that a ten dollar bill was now worth -00001 cents! Worthless coins litter the streets. Pay real close attention now. At the first reevaluation, Brazil issued a new monetary unit, the cruzado, which replaced the cruzeiro. Then, when it was devalued again, the cruzado was replaced with "new cruzados." Are you following this? Finally, last year the new president decreed that the "new cruzado" would again be called "cruzeiro." Confused? It gets worse --- the original currency, and the three new currencies, which all look about the same, <u>circulate</u> <u>freely</u> <u>together</u> so that, when transacting business, one spends a whole lot of time studying the bills and deciding whether or not to divide by a thousand, a million, or nothing at all. It's the Brazilian way.

To give you an idea of how Brazil can turn victory into defeat, Brazil had a severe energy crunch when the Arabs turned the oil tap off in 1971. Today, they are in the admirable position of having the capability of being <u>self-sufficient</u> as far as fuel is concerned. What they did, see, was develop their vast sugarcane resources and built plants that produced alcohol from cane. (The aroma of the exhaust of an alcohol fueled car, by the way, is something special. I use "aroma" purposely rather than "smell" or "stench" as one might describe noxious carbon monoxide fumes. Alcohol exhaust has a sweet, mediciney, Witch Hazely smell which is kind of pleasant. This brings up a very interesting question:

Can breathing alcohol exhaust fumes make one high? Could this explain why Brazilians drive like they do?).

Anyway, Brazil solved their fuel problem and became energy independent, but there was a problem. Alcohol was considerably cheaper than gas so everybody was buying alcohol cars. A few years ago, 90% of all new cars sold were alcohol fueled but all the oil companies were owned by the government and it soon realized it was losing a hell of a lot of cruzados. The government then proceeded to jack up the price of alcohol until it is, now, about the same price as gasoline. Now, people opt for gasoline cars because they run better -- again depleting the oil reserves. It's the Brazilian way.

You don't stop for red lights or stop signs in Brazil. If you do, one of two things will probably happen to you: You'll either get rear ended by a surprised Brazilian not used to having cars stop in front of him at red lights, or you'll get robbed. While you're at it, you can also ignore the posted speed limits and double lines on the road. In Brazil, you see, stop lights, stop signs, speed limits, and passing zones are merely SUGGESTIONS.

It all sounds pretty dismal doesn't it? Well, it isn't. Despite all the problems, Brazil is a delightful country that swings to a perpetual samba beat. Her people are gregarious and carefree. Next month in magazine's exclusive "Dr. Ruth Sex at Sea" issue (where we will discover if it's true that owners of twin screw boats "get more" than owners of single screw boats), I will tell the exciting tale of exactly how I got involved with Brazil. Who knows, I might even mention boats!

July 1991

The Brazilian Way
Part 2

The Second of Many Parts
It All Started with a See Through Blouse

I am caught behind one of Brazil's many lumbering trucks on a two lane "super highway." The road is hilly and winding and passing is difficult. Behind me is a long line of cars and trucks containing impatient, crazed Brazilians running bumper to bumper at, perhaps, 40 miles per hour. My neck strains trying to find a place to pass. Suddenly there's a short stretch of open road ahead and I check my rear view mirror and immediately pull out to pass. But wait! I'd best check that mirror <u>again</u> because, while I may have pulled out at the earliest possible instant that I deemed it safe to pass, three or four Brazilians behind me acted <u>before</u> <u>that</u> and are already <u>passing</u> me!

Brazil is part of my life now and, as I look back, I can see that my interest in Brazil all started with that <u>see</u> <u>through</u> <u>blouse</u> in 1979. I got a call from a Brazilian gentleman (now a good friend) in New York, representing his employer who was interested in having an American designed, 85' motoryacht built in Brazil. As a semi-starving architect, I was happy to accommodate them. About two weeks later, the Brazilian from New York and another Brazilian (who spoke very little English and turned out to be the builder), visited my office which was then a part of a small boatyard in Stuart. Happily, at the time, three of my boats were under construction at this yard and, apparently, the boat builder was impressed (unbeknownst to me, they had visited 15 architects all around the U.S.). About two weeks later, these two guys reappeared with a lady and their boss. Little did I know at the time that this business transaction would, eventually, change my life. The lady was typical of how you might fantasize a female Brazilian. She was stacked, had an impeccable tan, a smoldering face, and legs that went "all the way up." And she was wearing this see through blouse. We sat around the table talking about the design and, eventually, terms for the contract. I tried to keep my mind on the business at hand, but as the Brazilian bombshell was sitting directly across from me and kind of rearranging herself every few minutes, it was difficult. These guys were sharp! They were trying to distract me, to unsettle me so I'd make a very good deal for them. But I was sharp too! Yeah, Ol' Fexas didn't just roll into town on a citrus pickup. Imagine! Using a cheap diversion, the oldest one in the book, to try to get the better of me!

I made a very bad deal that afternoon.

After the contract was signed, I started asking questions

about how the vessel would be built. The repartee went something like this:

TF: "What's the largest pleasure boat currently being built in Brazil?"

Brazilian Boatbuilder: "61 feeter."

TF: "Where is the boatyard located?"

Brazilian Boatbuilder: "We don't have yard yet, but we build one. No problem."

TF: What's your experience building boats and the experience of your crew?"

Brazilian Boatbuilder: "I never build boat before and neither did my people, but we select best people from boss's company who work in plastics before. No problem."

TF: "Did you know the failure rate for a project like this is very high?"

Brazilian Boatbuilder: "I don't can't believe it!"

TF: "What will we do about equipment like steering wheels, portholes, cabin windows, mufflers, cleats and chocks?"

Brazilian Boatbuilder: "We make, No problem."

TF: "If nobody has ever built a boat before, how do you expect to successfully build a high tech, lightweight, large powerboat -- something that's never been done in Brazil?"

Brazilian Boatbuilder: "We follow plans. NO PROBLEM."

It was absolutely scary. The only damn thing he could say in perfect English was "<u>No</u> problem." Now, those of you well versed in the wiles and ways of boatbuilders, know that if there is one phrase that strikes terror into the hearts of owners and architects it is "No problem." When a boatbuilder tells you "No problem," it's time to cut your losses, pick up stakes, call your lawyer, and clear out of town immediately. "No problem" when it comes to boatbuilding invariably translates in any language to "BIG PROBLEM." Truthfully, I felt the chance of pulling this one off was slim to none, however, in 1979, two of my major priorities were a roof over my head and groceries in the pantry. So, skeptical as I was, we proceeded with the job. The boatbuilder's name was Arno Paupitz, a Brazilian of German extraction (since then, by the way, he's become a best friend and his English has improved greatly) and, you know what? It <u>really</u> <u>was</u> <u>no</u> <u>problem</u>! The boat, a complicated 85' high tech motoryacht built of double sandwich Airex core, turned out to be a huge success. Yeah, it took a while -- about three years, however, not only did Arno build the boat in this period -- he built an <u>entire</u> <u>shipyard</u> out of a vacant swamp! No ramshackle yard either. First, a concrete pad extending into the river was poured. Then a marine railway was built. Next, a beautiful wooden post and beam building covered with translucent corrugated fiberglass siding was erected. There were neat facilities for tools, fiberglass, etc. There were even his and hers heads! The place was always spotless. Workmanship on the boat was outstanding. Everything going on and off the boat was weighed -- even sawdust! Arno -- meticulous German that he was, followed our plans and specs <u>exactly</u> and the boat floated on her lines, made her speed, and completed a round trip to Florida on her own bottom. Altogether a very successful and satisfying project which made me think more about doing business in Brazil.

Here's a guy whose passing everybody on the shoulder, then makes a left turn across two lanes of traffic. Nice move. There's a guy tailgating so close it's like the damn cars are mating. Killer potholes are all over the road and can easily throw you out of control. Now you're being passed by a huge semi on the shoulder onto which two kids on bikes have latched to be towed up the hill! Driving in New York City, Miami, or even Italy is absolutely tame by comparison. It's no fluke that great drivers like Senna, Piquet, and Fittipaldi came from Brazil. You're either a great driver or you are dead on Brazilian roads.

August 1991

Inside My Head
Part 1

This month we will take a break from the "socially responsible" pieces on subjects like ecology, taxes, government intervention in boating, and travelogues on different countries. IT'S TIME TO GO BACK TO THE TRASH THAT MADE "SPECTATOR" GREAT, AND THIS COLUMN IS ABOUT AS TRASHY AS IT CAN GET!

It happened during the Ft. Lauderdale Boat Show last year, and it scared the hell out of me. Usually, we have a number of our designs displayed at the show. Last year, we had five or six. This story was related to me by people working one particular boat.

Two guys in their mid-twenties came aboard and went over everything, looking in every nook and cranny. Things got out of hand, however, when they started <u>pulling apart woodwork</u> to see what was behind. They were pounced on by the two people working the boat. "What the hell are you doing?" they were asked. Caught red-handed, one of the miscreants sheepishly muttered the following frightening statement:

"We've been following Fexas' work for years. WE WANTED TO <u>GET</u> <u>INSIDE</u> <u>HIS</u> <u>HEAD</u> AND SEE HOW HE THINKS."

Well, I can tell you it truly is scary when people want to get "inside your head" expecting profound revelations when, all the time, you, yourself know that there is little of anything of value in there!

I guess it's bare my soul time. You want to know what's inside my head? Do you <u>really</u> want to know what's inside my head? Well, I would <u>like</u> to say that stuffed inside my cranium were verbatim verses from Shakespeare or great passages of classical music or the history of yacht design from the dawn of mankind or the true meaning of life or fluency in Chinese or Portuguese. The truth of the matter is, however, that what's inside my head mostly is ... well ... if you must know: <u>verses</u> <u>from</u> <u>fifties/sixties</u> <u>Rock</u> <u>'n</u> <u>Roll</u> songs! There, I've said it!

In the fifties and early sixties, my friend Steve and I were professional performers! Well, I guess you could say that since we had a local band and eventually had a record issued (on the long defunct "Charm" label) which we co-wrote, sang and provided musical background for. Yes, we were <u>big</u> <u>stars</u> -- on our block, anyway. The record was issued and immediately became the "pick hit of the week" at a <u>Buffalo</u> radio station (this was around 1962) and that was the absolute high point of my musical career. I went on to college to study "straight" stuff like marine engineering. Steve went "Miami U", studied radio and television and went into the music business. Around 1966 I saw him lip synching one of his songs on a New York T.V. show. Haven't seen or heard from him since.

Anyway, complete immersion in Rock 'N Roll from its inception in 1954 (when I was 13) until the pinnacle of my musical career when our record was issued, left all these strange song verses dancing around in my head like baitfish in a little tank and they just won't go away. I'm not talking about fifties songs that everyone knows like "The Great Pretender" or "In the Still of the Night." I'm talking about obscure songs like "Shopping for Clothes" and "Young Blood."

So, guys caught taking apart the joiner work on one of my boats, I will let you know <u>exactly</u> what's in my head during the time I'm dictating this -- stream of consciousness and all that good stuff. Here goes:

> As I was motivating'
> Back in town
> I saw a Cadillac sign
> Sayin' no money down
>
> So I eased on the brakes
> And I pulled in the drive
> Gunned my motor twice
> Then I walked inside
>
> Dealer came to me
> Said "Trade in your Ford"
> And I'll put you in a car
> That'll eat up the road

"No Money Down" - Chuck Berry
Great lyrics - a song <u>never heard</u> on "oldies" stations

One thing that really ticks me off are bozo yacht designers jumping on the bandwagon with no previous experience or qualifications. You've heard the expression attributed to Andy Warhol who said something to the effect that everybody in the world will be a superstar for 15 minutes. I'm afraid that sooner or later everybody in the world will, at one time or another, be calling themselves a Yacht Designer. They may pick potatoes in the Ukraine or paint houses in Minnesota or sort eggs in Scandinavia or stuff cotton in aspirin bottles in Delaware but, if they want to, they can advertise themselves as "yacht designers." This started getting bad two or three years ago and we're just now seeing the results of these faux yacht designers. There have been many high speed motoryachts that weren't. There are boats that don't sit on their lines properly and "ocean crossing" boats that can't be run outside of bays or sounds. Many of these people are being awarded big design jobs although they have never done any vessels of the size, speed or type required and don't have the people to do the job. There will be more on this in future articles but, in the meantime, if you're contemplating a custom yacht, <u>check the damn background</u> of the prospective designer.

  Well he brought his camel to a screeching halt
  In the rear of Fatima's tent

> Jumped off Clyde, snuck around the corner
> And in to the tent he went

"Ahab the Arab" - Ray Stevens
These are what you'd call "class" lyrics

Looking at a profile of one of our latest boats on the floor of my office (all drawing boards and tabletops are piled with stuff), it occurs to me that sometime, somewhere, there's got to be a limit on how zoomy a boat can be styled. Boats are gradually approaching teardrop or wedge configuration and, when they get there, I wonder where we go. It occurs to me that, where we go from there, is <u>backwards</u> ...to "retro boats." After marinas resemble ammo dumps full of boats looking like projectiles, vessels with some <u>shape</u> and <u>style</u> will be truly refreshing. A good example of this is the Huckins Sportsman 40' – a reincarnation of one of their boats from the fifties. Amongst all the zoomo, raked bowed, reverse sheered, round windowed, blacked out striped, reverse transomed, swept back arched vessels, this boat and others like her really stand out as nice pieces of work.

> Well I saved my pennies and I saved my dimes
> Giddyap, Giddyap 409
> For I knew there would be a time
> Giddyap, Giddyap 409
> When I would buy a brand new 409

"409" - Beach Boys

Makes me want to go out and buy a '62 Chevy

Hey, this is fun! Maybe we'll do some more next month. In the meantime, besiege your record store with requests for my record. My contemporaries like Mick Jagger and Paul McCartney prove it's never too late to be a rock star.

September 1991

Deeper Inside My Head Part 2

*L*ast month, I described two guys at a boat show pulling apart one of my boats because they wanted to "get inside my head" and see how I think. Last month I told you about my early years as a "rock star" and the obscure song verses swimming around in my skull. You were treated to a "stream of consciousness" piece documenting <u>exactly</u> what was "inside my head" at the time I was dictating it. This month the stream continues.....

> There's a redskin a'waitin' out there
> Fixin' to take my hair
> A coward I've been called
> 'Cuz I don't want to wind up dead or bald

"Mr. Custer" - Larry Verne
Probably the most sorrowful lyrics ever written

The specter of Big Brother on the water in South Florida is scary and, if unchecked, will result in the downfall of boating here. On a typical cruise in the waterways around my house (St. Lucie River and adjacent intracoastal areas) you'll find: 1) Wildlife Service Squad Boats, 2) U.S. Customs Squad Boats, 3) Florida Marine Patrol Squad Boats, 4) Coast Guard Squad Boats, and 5) Town Squad Boats all competing for the glory of writing the most nautical tickets. You'll find signs stating that the speed limit is 25 mph in the channel but idle speed from 600 feet to shore. How in the hell does one know when one is 599 feet offshore? How the hell does one know when one is going 26 miles an hour rather than 25? Marine speedometers don't work. Loran is unreliable. GPS is best but expensive and subject to error. The only way to clock your rate of speed on the water with certainty is by <u>radar</u>. You'd better believe that the Marine Smokies are clocking <u>you</u> with radar. What is a law abiding boatsman to do? Well, remember you heard it here first folks. I predict that within the next five years someone will come out with a <u>radar speedometer</u> for boats.

Cruising off the coast of Maine last week was a refreshing experience. During a four day trip from Camden to Northeast Harbor we encountered <u>not</u> <u>one</u> squad boat, nor did we ever see a speed limit sign. If the eco freaks and liberal democrats can't be stopped, the South Florida Intracoastal Waterway will turn into one great idle speed zone from Ft. Pierce down to Key West. Nobody wants to see manatees injured or killed but, the fact is that Florida's municipalities kill far more manatees in their locks and power plants than boatmen do. It is, again, a case of defenseless boatmen getting picked on because they have no real lobby power.

> What crazy stuff
> She looked so tough
> I had to follow her
> All the way home
> Then things got bad
> I met her Dad (he said)
> "You'd better leave my daughter alone"

"Young Blood" - Leiber and Stoller and Doc Pomus
Poetry, pure poetry.

It has long been my conviction that the sophistication of a given country can easily be determined by the T.P.I. The T.P.I. is a rather simple rating system I developed during my travels to various countries. On a scale of 1 to 10 (10 being tops), the U.S. is definitely a "10" on the T.P.I. Italy comes in a strong "8" -- a great improvement in the last few years (only a scant five years ago Italy might have rated a "2"). Germany is a "6," England a "7," and places like Taiwan a "2." What exactly is T.P.I.? Well, T.P.I. is the "Toilet Paper Index" going from "1" which is one step up from 40 grit sandpaper to "10" which is Charmin with <u>lotion</u> (for our pampered American butts).

> Then the music stopped
> When I looked the cafe was empty
> Then I heard José say
> "Mon" you know you're in trouble plenty

"Come A Little Bit Closer" - Tommy Boyce, Bobby Hart and Wes Farrell

It has always been my impression that Jay of "Jay and the Americans" sounded like he was singing while eating a <u>banana</u> and a big piece was stuck in his gullet! Quick! Someone give that singer the Heimlich maneuver!

    I just received a brochure from a builder in Canada. One of the boats featured is a Bill Garden designed motorsailer. Bill Garden is one of the very few yacht designers on the planet who is equally adroit at drawing sailboats and powerboats. My rare attempts at drawing sailboats (believe me, I was <u>very</u> hungry at the time) always resulted in rag wagons that looked something like a Midnight Lace with sails. Anyway, from what I've seen, with the exception of Garden, guys who draw powerboats should stick with powerboats and the same goes for puff boat designers. Unquestionably, some of the <u>double</u> <u>ugliest</u> powerboats ever drawn have come from the boards of zephyr boat guys who, otherwise, do very graceful, respectable, sailboats. Anyway, Bill Garden has one of the best "eyes" in the business. He's also a very <u>efficient</u> designer, packing more information on five or six drawing sheets than most others would include on twenty or thirty sheets. I would love to meet the man one day.

> She bent down and turned around and gave me a wink
> She said "I'm gonna make it up right here in the sink"
> It tastes like turpentine, it smells like India ink

> I held my nose, I closed my eyes, I took a drink

"Love Potion #9" - Leiber and Stoller

Speaking of meeting heroes, brings to mind the time I had lunch with Lindsay Lord in Falmouth, Maine one summer afternoon. In case you don't know, Lindsay Lord wrote, in the fifties, the bible on high speed seagoing hulls titled "Naval Architecture of Planing Hulls." The book is now out of print and I treasure my two copies (one autographed by the man himself!). We correspond now and again. That man is an absolute wealth of high speed yacht information. Much of the information in his book was developed during World War II when Mr. Lord was stationed in the Pacific working with PT boats. It was there that much of the practical information contained in his book came about.

Lindsay Lord.... what a great name for a yacht designer! Back in the twenties, there was a very popular powerboat designer whose name was "T. Lockwood Haggis" -- another outstanding name! Maybe I should go by "T. Elias Fexas." What do you think?

> But when I kissed a cop
> At 34th and Vine
> He broke my little bottle of
> Love Potion #9

"Love Potion #9" - Leiber and Stoller
Probably the only early rock song ever written about an

aphrodisiac.

How come all the people you see on T.V. that have won a million, five million, or ten million dollars in some foolish sweepstakes always look and talk like complete dorks? Just a thought.....

> When I woke up and my head started to clear
> I had a strange feeling I was cooking gear
> I smelled something cooking and I looked to see
> That's when I found out they was cookin' me

"Stranded In the Jungle" - James Johnson and Ernestine Smith
Probably the only early rock song ever written about cannibalism.

Hey, I'm having so much fun with this that there will be a third (and final) installment next month. Stay tuned, trendsetters.

October 1991

Much Deeper Inside My Head Part 3

For the last two months we've probed the (rather shallow) depths of my mind in response to some guys at the Ft. Lauderdale Boat Show last year who were taking apart one of my boats to get "inside my head." This month, the "stream of consciousness" continues.

> I saw her standin' on the corner
> A yellow ribbon in her hair
> I couldn't stop myself from shoutin'
> Look-a there, look-a there
> Look-a there, look-a there

"Young Blood" - Leiber and Stoller and Doc Pomus

There's is a lot of pomposity associated with megayachts these days. Many builders who build them are pompous, many designers who draw them are pompous and, many owners who own them are most pompous of all. Always keep in mind that these are not floating palaces -- they're just damn <u>fun</u> <u>boats</u>! Big damn fun boats, but damn fun boats nevertheless. Pompous owners of megayachts can be identified very easily simply by what they call their spectacular vessels. These owners sound terribly pretentious when they refer to their magnificent vessels as "yachts" as in: "Muriel dear, I'm going to pop in and order a Lamborghini Diablo. I'll meet you on the <u>yacht</u>." Greenhorns and pompous owners refer to large vessels as "yachts" but owners should know better. Webster's unabridged defines "yacht" as follows: yacht (yot), n. 1: a vessel used for private cruising, racing or other noncommercial purposes." Technically speaking then, anyone owning any kind of private vessel could refer to their craft as a "yacht." To my mind, it sounds every bit as silly referring to a 150 footer as a "yacht" as it does referring to a 16 foot Bayliner as such.

I'll never forget talking to Jacky Setton, the young owner of "Belle France", a spectacular 181 foot Feadship (formerly "Cacique"). When I asked him why he acquired "Belle France," I was ready for the typical lofty megayacht owner answer -- something like: "I acquired my megayacht because it befits my social standing and financial worth. She's a magnificent example of splendid Dutch construction that can only be appreciated by a select few. I was particularly impressed by her gold leafed bilges." Do you know what Mr. Setton's answer was? He said, "I got "Belle France" because SHE WAS A NICE BOAT." <u>A</u> <u>nice</u> <u>boat</u> -- <u>I</u> <u>love</u> <u>it</u>! Describing

"Belle France" as "a nice boat" is like describing Princess Di as a "nice broad." I applaud your understatement, Mr. Setton.

> One day while I was eating beans at Smokie Joe's Cafe
> Just sittin' diggin' all them scenes at Smokie Joe's Cafe
> A chick I'd never seen before
> Came walkin' on in through the door...

"Smokie Joe's Cafe" - Leiber and Stoller
One of my personal favorites. Leiber and Stoller were the Rogers and Hammerstein of the rock 'n roll world in the 50's/60's.

Does anybody remember varnish work? Varnish work was that brown shiny stuff found on most every boat prior to the '60's. Nowadays you don't see much varnish on boats -- especially in Florida where there are very few <u>wooden</u> boats left. Believe me, you have to be a <u>purist</u> to maintain a wooden boat in South Florida. The last two boats I owned were postwar Elcos with beautiful African mahogany deck houses. I spent a lot of time maintaining these "varnish farms" and, in fact, I miss varnishing to this day (there was something very satisfying about laying on a slick coat of varnish). When I had these boats (I lived in the northeast at the time), I remember every time it rained, I felt kind of sick deep down inside knowing that those dreaded dry rot spores were having their way with my beautiful bright work. Now I live in South Florida where the appearance of a wooden boat is a <u>big</u> <u>event</u>. Two beautiful old wooden boats reside behind neighbors houses in the area where I live and on my way to and from work, usually in one of South Florida's hourly thunderstorms (South Florida rule: <u>anytime</u> you have to do <u>anything</u> in South Florida it will be raining hard at that particular time) I pass both boats and get that old familiar "kind of sick" feeling knowing the havoc that rot spores can wreak in the thousands of seams and butts of a wooden boat. (I always imagined that dry rot spores under a microscope must look something like "the alien.")

> When I take her to the track she really shines
> Giddy up giddy up 409
> She always turns in the fastest times
> Giddy up giddy up 409
> My four speed, dual quad, Posi-Traction 409
> 409, 409, 409, 409

"409" - Beach Boys

A number of people approached me at different California boat shows, telling me how much they enjoyed the "Californication of Florida" pieces I did a while back and suggested that I might do an article about "The Floridafication of California." I told them I'd give it a shot. Here's that shot.

After visiting California two or three times a year for the past six years or so, I've noticed subtle but distinct changes on the left coast. A cross pollination between Florida and

California is taking place. For example, the quality of some of California's finer hotels is becoming on a par with Florida's finest (i.e. poor service, rude staff, mediocre food). National Rent-A-Car doesn't rent Corvettes in California anymore just like they don't in Florida. South Florida glitz is spreading to California as evidenced by the "gold standard" observed there. By unofficial count, Southern California has as many obscene cars (mostly Mercedes and Cadillacs) with garish gold plated accessories and trim as we do in South Florida.

> Hey little girl in the high school sweater
> Gee but I'd like to know you better
> Just a'swingin' your books and chewin' gum
> Lookin' just like a juicy plum

"Hey Little Girl" - Phil Spector and Richard Barrett
That was a hot song in the '50s.

Speaking of California, do you know that when you enter Catalina Island's Avalon by boat you're greeted by the local marine super trooper who boards your boat and proceeds to drop a dye pellet in each toilet. Anybody foolish enough to pump their head or holding tank into the harbor will produce a great dye spot on the water (which glows in the dark by the way) to the delight of the nautical gendarme who will pounce on you and probably put you in the Catalina pokie forever. I hear that, in the future, everybody aboard will be forced to take a dye pill to prevent peeing while swimming.

> The guy must of wanted to pass me up
> As he kept on tooting his horn
> I'll show him that a Cadillac
> Is not a car to scorn

"Beep Beep" – Donald Claps and Carlo Cicchetti

Robot drawings -- I hate em! Admittedly, our office has been dragged, kicking and screaming, into the wonderful age of computers, but I don't like it much. Hand done drawings have personality and style. Each sheet can be a work of art. Robot generated drawings are bland, lifeless, and have the personality of a Russian diplomat. A hand drawn arrangement plan can be a source of great inspiration for a potential client. He'll look at the galley and <u>smell</u> the aroma of a fresh snapper frying in olive oil. He'll look at the bunk and picture himself warm and snug reading a book while a gale is howling outside. That same person will look at a computer generated interior drawing and see only a galley and a berth. Computer drawings do have their place. Schematic drawings, engine installation drawings, systems drawings, hull lines and the like can all be done quicker and better on the computer, but we'll stick with <u>art</u> for most of the others.

> I took my little Jenny to a party last night
> At 10 o'clock it ended in a heckuva fight
> When someone hit my Jenny she went out like a light
> Poor Jenny

"Poor Jenny" - Boudleaux and Felice Bryant

Sailboats: You know how the pretentious rag stuffers are always bragging about their boats being more seaworthy and that they are better seamen and that "stink potters" don't know nuthin' about boats and the sea? I have one simple question for these guys: WHY THE HELL IS IT THAT WHEN THESE "MASTERS OF THE SEA" GET IN TROUBLE (AND THEY DO FREQUENTLY), THEY ARE ALWAYS RESCUED BY A POWER BOAT? Think about it! Did you ever hear of the Coast Guard sending out a damned breeze boat on a rescue mission? "Ahhh Roger, this is the Coast Guard. We copy your distress call. We are dispatching a rescue sloop to your area. She should be there in about 16 hours if the wind is right."

> Transfusion, transfusion
> My red corpsuckles are in mass confusion
> Never never never gonna speed again
> Put a gallon in me Allen

"Transfusion" - Jimmy Drake

And so the fantastic journey "inside my head" thankfully comes to an end. It's been fun the last three months talking about whatever came to mind but, serious, responsible journalism is what's called for in this time of "political correctness." Important topics that scream out to be addressed such as "101 uses for a fid" will be featured in future articles. Stay tuned.

November 1991

Five Favorite Designs
1984

Midnight Lace 44'

The 44 Lace was and is very special to me. She was commissioned by Scott Meissner -- now a good friend and business associate -- who placed no restrictions whatsoever on the design. Having seen only a preliminary profile and arrangement plus a paper model, he had the courage to go ahead with the project and design and build her as I thought best. Given this freedom, I set out to create the meanest, sexiest, most elegant and fastest boat possible based on sketches dating back to when I was 12 years old.

There is much the 30's vintage commuter boat on her. Being a great admirer of Elcos (especially post-war Elcos), there is also a touch of Elco in her styling, especially in the windshields. She was designed skinny because I wanted a boat that was fast and efficient with relatively low power. The slinky, S-sheer has always been a favorite of mine and we designed in a unique full-length topside step just above the waterline to act as a spray deflector, add stability and extra width to the accommodations. Many people said the round-bilged hull would not work very well at high speeds. One magazine editor to whom I showed the plans said she was a "funny boat that nobody would ever buy." With much intrepidation she was launched in October 1978, just in time for the Ft. Lauderdale Boat Show where she was to make her debut.

She floated on her lines, running level and clean, making a top speed of about 31 m.p.h. with a pair of 175 shaft horsepower diesels installed in her stern. She was a great success and required absolutely no modifications once launched. She created a great deal of attention and soon generated many more design commissions for me.

Cheoy Lee 66' Sportfisherman

After the success of the Cheoy Lee 48 Sportsfisherman, Cheoy Lee commissioned a really large, powerful sportfishing boat that would combine the best qualities of a tournament fisherman with the "wretched excess" of a full bore motor yacht. She is one of my favorite designs because she is so big and hunky-looking and has what I consider to be one of the finest high speed hulls that ever kissed the sea. Sometimes designs just fall together and sometimes one must really push to make them work. This was one of the designs that fell together and her hull is, to my way of thinking the ultimate in head sea, following, and beam sea performance. The key to success is a very sharp, long entry which was successfully blended one night in 1980 into a straight run aft.

Running the boat is a simple joy. She is light, responsive, and near impossible to impact into a sea. The softly rounded trunk, cabin, and flying bridge faces are a sharp contrast to the angular, squared-off after end of the vessel but, somehow, it all works well together.

The overriding impression of this vessel is one of power and mighty strength.

Palmer Johnson 82' Motor Yacht

Here was a chance to test my theory that a really large Midnight Lace-type bottom would be successful for a fast motor yacht. Working with Richard Bertram and Company, who marketed the design and Palmer Johnson, who masterfully constructed her, she was designed to compete head-on with motor yacht offerings in this size from all over the world. She is rather traditional design, yet different enough to instantly separate her from the pack. In silhouette from a distance she looks like a mean, marauding gun boat and yet, as she draws closer, she seems to transform herself into an elegant motor yacht. The Midnight Lace bottom functions so well in this size range that she is capable of 25% higher speeds than similar yachts with identical power. The hull step forward knocks the waves flat and contains them for the length of her hull. She runs with less wake than many 45-footers and is capable of accelerating from zero to maximum speed of approximately 21-1/2 knots in a scant twenty seconds!

This is, hopefully, the first of a long line of Richard Bertram and Company/Palmer Johnson motor yachts.

Fabiola – 85' Motor Yacht

Our first shot at a Mediterranean-type fast motor yacht! Although she provides the same flair and excitement of a Mediterranean yacht she is, in fact, the antithesis design-wise of these blown up race boat hulls with strange, sharp, angular superstructures. By employing our graceful S-sheer again and designing a superstructure with softly rounded contours, Fabiola has a very smooth, sensuous look to her. The pilothouse face is a segment of a tapered cone – very difficult to construct – but worth the time and money. The long, rounded, laid-back bridge face is a magnificent space waster but well worth it. She is built of super lightweight fiberglass and laminated timber. She made 21 knots with a pair of 650 SHP diesels.

Whenever I'm feeling lousy, I look to Fabiola for inspiration!

100' Motor Yacht

This vessel, although not yet constructed, rates as one of my favorite designs because it embodies the slinky, menacing appearance of the smaller Midnight Laces into full blown 100 foot motor yacht.

Although a bit too radical for today's taste, I'm looking forward to the day when designs such as this will be accepted and eagerly anticipate the day I find a client who will want to build her.

Engineering a Large Jet Powered Motor Yacht

Never having designed a large jet powered motor yacht before, we approached the project with extreme caution and thoroughness. Although other large jet drive installations had been done before, ours was to be the first utilizing MTU's new TB94 series 12 cylinder engines which produce approximately 600 HP more than the old series TB93 units. We started with a lot of reservations, each one of which had to be satisfied. We heard a lot of stories concerning the fact that large jet drive motor yachts don't steer at low speeds and hunted at higher speeds while on auto pilot. We knew of a number of other installations where rudders had to be added after the vessel was finished. After checking the stories, we determined that low speed wandering and high speed hunting on the auto pilot were probably more a function of the hull shape than jet drives. This was subsequently substantiated in TIME's sea trials. She was extremely responsive at low speeds and did not hunt at higher speeds on the auto pilot. We also heard stories concerning poor efficiency of the jet drives at low passage making speeds, the jist of the stories was that even operating on one engine/jet the efficiency of the jet drive was so poor at low speeds that a light, high speed yacht couldn't possibly carry enough fuel to go Transatlantic. Here, we had to rely on the jet manufacturer's data. As it turned out, Kamewa was spot on with their predictions and sea trials proved that we indeed had the range required. Another major concern of ours was the totally electronic control system for both the engines and the jet steering and reversing mechanism. In this office, we advocate mechanical backups for all electronic controls where possible. In this case, however, mechanical backups were not possible and, to be honest, we still have reservations about the electronic control system although, to date, it has given us virtually no problems. After these initial obstacles were addressed we proceeded with the hardcore engineering which presented many new challenges, namely: design and implementation of the very critical water inlet plenum to the jets, designing a transom around the jet drives which protruded nine feet from the actual transom, engineering the complicated hull structure around the jet drives and particularly at the transom, engineering the exhaust, engine room air and engine combustion air systems which were all critical to the operation of the vessel.

Would we do anything differently on the next one? Not really. In fact, we are now working on other large jet drive yachts and will implement a virtually identical engine/jet installation as on TIME.

About the Author

Tom Fexas was born in Queens, NY in 1941. His dad, Achilles "Chick" Fexas was an optometrist and had emigrated from Greece via Elis Island in the early 1900's. He had a busy practice and in his free time he worked in the improvement of contact lenses with his friend Murray Leinster. His Mom, Antonia "Toni" Fexas was a teacher, she was born in Manhattan and was from Greek descent also.

Tom always knew he wanted to design boats. He was about four when he got his first paint set and that was the first thing he painted – a boat. When he was growing up, he really wasn't much interested in anything but boats, in fact, his whole life revolved around the boating season in the Northeast. His father bought a nearly new 32' Wheeler in 1943 (only to have wrecked by the great hurricane of 1944). He bought another Wheeler in 1947 -- which was the boat Tom grew up during 20 summers -- followed by two Elcos.

Tom became a yacht designer extraordinaire with more than 1,000 boats to his design. His most famous design is the Midnight Lace -- "While there are many "classic cruisers" available on the market today, few have the heritage of the Midnight Lace, although the first Midnight Lace was completed in 1978, the Lace heritage goes back much further than that -- back to the pre-World War II commuter boats and World War II PT boats creating a distinctive vessel that will never be mistaken for anything else.," in his own words.

He also had a sharp sense of humor, an observing eye for everyday life and wrote for several nautical magazines for more than 20 years.

To be continued...

Made in the USA
Monee, IL
08 April 2024

56571902R00177